Smoke in Their Eyes

Smoke in Their Eyes

Lessons in Movement Leadership

from the Tobacco Wars

Michael Pertschuk

Vanderbilt University Press

Nashville

Library of Congress Cataloging-in-Publication Data

Pertschuk, Michael, 1933-
    Smoke in their eyes : lessons in movement leadership from
the tobacco wars / Michael Pertschuk.
        p. ;   cm.
    Includes bibliographical references and index.
    ISBN 0-8265-1390-5 (cloth : alk. paper)
    ISBN 0-8265-1393-X (pbk. : alk. paper)
    1. Antismoking movement—United States. 2. Tobacco
industry—Government policy—United States.
[DNLM: 1. Lobbying—United States. 2. Tobacco Industry—
legislation & jurisprudence—United States. 3. Consumer
Advocacy—United States. 4. Leadership—United States.
5. Public Policy—United States. 6. Smoking—prevention &
control—United States. HD 9137.U5 P469s 2001]
    I. Title.
HV5763 .P47 2001
362.29'67'0973—dc21   2001003506

To Karla Sneegas and all the other less-sung, warm-spirited, bridge-building movement leaders who continue to make the tobacco control movement alive with promise.

Contents

Foreword

David Cohen

Sound and sober contemporary political history by historians and journalists is not rare, but lively and evenhanded storytelling of political struggles by those who have lived them is. And historical analyses of landmark political challenges that actually yield practical lessons for those who might face such challenges in the future are even less common.

You are about to read a book by my colleague and friend of nearly forty years, Mike Pertschuk, that captures the essence of a landmark event in the history of American civic movements. For three decades leading up to the spring of 1997, the tobacco industry had fiercely resisted all serious efforts to enact regulatory and other public health policies appropriate to the vast human damage cigarettes were proven to cause.

Suddenly, that spring, the companies offered concessions of a breadth and magnitude that no tobacco control advocate had ever considered remotely possible. As a result, Congress came within a hair's breadth of enacting comprehensive tobacco control legislation that would have transformed the tobacco industry from an unregulated, unrestrained marketer of the world's best-selling addictive lethal product into a tightly regulated marketer of a controlled substance. But it did not happen. Why not?

No one could have been better prepared and situated to find the answer than Mike Pertschuk, no one better able to extract the broad lessons for the leadership of civic movements. He brings converging sets of skills and experience to this story.

Mike came to Washington in 1962 to work as a legislative assistant to a strong consumer advocate, Senator Maureen Neuberger of Oregon. He was soon energetically working with her to press President Kennedy to form a national commission—as the British had done—to provide an authoritative judgment on the proven health risks of smoking. At the time I met Mike, I was lobbying for Americans for Democratic Action (ADA), supporting Senator Neuberger's consumer protection advocacy. Neuberger's efforts provided at least part of the pressure that led President Kennedy to authorize the convening of the first Surgeon General's Advisory Committee on Smoking and Health, which declared in 1964 that smoking was a proven cause of lung cancer and other disease. On Senator Neuberger's behalf, Mike then worked with allies within the Federal Trade Commission to prod the commission to issue its landmark rule forcing cigarette manufacturers to carry strong and explicit warning labels on their packages and in all their advertising.

He soon moved to the Senate Commerce Committee to staff a new Consumer Protection Subcommittee under the leadership of Chairman Warren G. Magnuson of Oregon. There, he formed a strong alliance with emerging consumer advocates Ralph Nader and Joan Claybrook and staffed a succession of consumer protection laws that have stood the test of time, from automobile safety legislation to the flame proofing of children's sleepwear.

Mike Pertschuk's reputation as a thorn in the side of the tobacco industry followed him to Senator Magnuson's Commerce Committee. In his first year on the committee, he was barred from working on tobacco matters—tainted by his being labeled "biased" against tobacco by the tobacco-state Democrats on the committee. In 1965, by the time he was allowed to staff Congress's first cigarette label warning bill, he found himself stymied by the pervasive power and presence of the industry. He laments that he ended up facilitating an industry-crafted bill that greatly weakened the label warnings that the FTC would have required, and that barred the FTC and any other federal or state authority from strengthening the warnings or mandating them in advertising. What happened is the bane of the powerful special interests, a positive unintended consequence. Mike Pertschuk learned from the lessons the tobacco interests taught him: verify and squeeze but never trust.

By 1969, he had become staff director of the Commerce Committee. Having won the full confidence of Senator Magnuson and other senators, including Republicans, he was better able to challenge Big Tobacco's political power. Under the skilled leadership of Chairman Magnuson, he developed the 1969 legislation banning the broadcast advertising of cigarettes.

In *Ashes to Ashes,* his Pulitzer Prize–winning history of the tobacco wars prior to the events of this book, historian Richard Kluger well captures the qualities that made Mike an effective, as well as dedicated, inside consumer advocate within the Senate. Labeling him "the tobacco industry's most dangerous opponent on Capitol Hill," Kluger observed: "Blessed with acutely tuned political antennae, adroitness at exchanging confidences, and an unstudied puckishness that softened his high purposefulness, Pertschuk served Magnuson so well that he was delegated great authority in drafting legislation and thus became one of the most powerful appointees on Capitol Hill."

In 1977, President Jimmy Carter appointed Mike chairman of the Federal Trade Commission, on the advice of Ralph Nader, as well as me in my capacity as president of Common Cause. Many others, including legislators, weighed in as Mike's backers. At the FTC, with the skilled support of a young lawyer, Matt Myers, whom he had recruited from the American Civil Liberties Union, he undertook an aggressive investigation that reported to Congress on tobacco industry marketing abuses. So powerful was the report that it brought down the wrath of the tobacco senators from his old committee, who reacted by attempting to shut the FTC down!

When Mike left the Federal Trade Commission in 1985, he joined with me to create the Advocacy Institute, stepping back from frontline advocacy to a counseling and mentoring role in advocacy leadership for the tobacco control movement, and for many other contemporary movements seeking social justice. In this capacity, from the mid-1980s to the mid-1990s, he provided strategic counseling and earned the trust and friendship of virtually all those tobacco control leaders who would be confronted with the challenges of 1997 and 1998.

As if this were not enough, Mike undertook yet a third career, which led, perhaps inexorably, to the writing of this book: that of student, analyst, and writer on movement leadership. In 1984 and 1985, he was awarded a fellowship at the Woodrow Wilson Center at the Smithsonian to write *Giant Killers,* a series of stories of successful citizen campaigns for progressive causes in the midst of the Reagan presidency, ranging from the saving of a wild river to the halting of funding for a new generation of nuclear missiles, united by the critical role of uncommon movement leadership.

Giant Killers was followed, in 1988, by *The People Rising,* with Wendy Schaetzel, the analytic account of the extraordinary grassroots campaign that denied President Ronald Reagan and the resurgent Right their goal of placing Robert Bork on the Supreme Court to decimate the great advances made in equal justice and democratic governance started in President Franklin Roosevelt's administration.

What makes me especially proud to contribute the foreword to *Smoke in Their Eyes* is that Mike's rich practical lessons provide the difficult judgments that activists and movement participants, and journalists too, are prone to duck. Mike doesn't duck. He willingly spends his political capital, risking the alienation of the powerful and the vengeful, to enable us to understand what we must know, and how we ought to interact with each other when we tackle the power of the tobacco industry—power that holds no redeeming social value. That is the essence of leadership.

Mike's story is deeply affecting, leavened with humor, undergirded with passion, and laden with the wisdom and insight born of nearly forty years as an advocate and student of advocacy.

Smoke in Their Eyes

Introduction

Movements born of adversity have a hard time with success. And movement leaders, hardened to decades of lost battles, do not easily adapt to the prospects of victory. This is not exactly a new story. It happens to the best of movements, and it happened to the tobacco control movement in 1997 and 1998. To many Americans outside the tobacco control movement, the year 1997 seemed to hold the promise of a triumphant ending to the thirty-year war against the tobacco companies.

On June 20, 1997, Mississippi attorney general Mike Moore stood before a bank of microphones and news cameras, flanked by a phalanx of allied state attorneys general, and proclaimed proudly that an agreement had been reached among the state attorneys general, representatives of the public health community, and the tobacco industry. The agreement set forth the terms of comprehensive tobacco control legislation, a "global settlement," which all parties would harmoniously entreat Congress to enact. This legislation would, Moore averred, transform the tobacco industry from one of the least to one of the most tightly regulated industries in America: "We are here today to announce what we think is—we know, we believe is—the most historic public health agreement in history. We wanted this industry to have to change the way it did business, and we have done that. This is really the beginning of the end for the way the tobacco industry has treated the American public."

The attorney general of Florida, Bob Butterworth, exuberantly wrapped Moore's claim to history in a metaphor: "The Marlboro Man is riding off into the sunset on Joe Camel."

Within a year, Senator John McCain of Arizona, chairman of the Senate Commerce Committee, invoked history again on April 1, 1998, after shepherding a bipartisan 19–1 vote of his committee's members in favor of a tobacco control bill that not only built upon but also markedly strengthened the public health provisions of the June 20, 1997, settlement. Senator McCain looked upon his work and pronounced that, in it, "Congress has a rare and historic opportunity to put an end to what the American Medical Association calls a 'pediatric epidemic.' " And, in that most rare of conditions for that most partisan of Congresses, Senator John Kerry of Massachusetts, on behalf of the committee's Democrats, fully agreed with the Republican McCain: "This is not just the opportunity . . . for a historic debate; it is an extraordinary opportunity for historic action by the U.S. Senate."

President Bill Clinton praised McCain and the bill and joined the chorus of amateur historians: "Over the next five weeks, this Congress has an historic opportunity to pass bipartisan comprehensive legislation to protect our children from the dangers of tobacco. It is time for the kind of comprehensive approach to the problem that Senator McCain's legislation takes."

The *Washington Post* quoted an anonymous tobacco lobbyist who predicted: "If the vote were held today, it would be 80–20 for McCain." This might have been the occasion to celebrate an exemplary civic movement—one whose leaders, having persevered through adversity, leapt surefooted to victory, when the moment for leaping had come.

But victory did not come. Six weeks after the McCain bill surged out of the Senate Commerce Committee, the Senate failed by three votes to reach the sixty needed to end debate and bring the bill itself to a vote. Like the rigid parrot in the absurdist Monty Python skit, Mike Moore's global settlement and the McCain bill were "Dead! Dead! Dead!" And the Congress has not since come close even to considering the bill's like.

What happened? And why?

When any effort to rein in the tobacco industry fails, most attentive citizens readily assume that the malevolent economic and political power of the tobacco industry has been mobilized to defeat it. And so it was here.

As former U.S. surgeon general Dr. C. Everett Koop saw it, in a talk to the National Press Club following the sinking of the McCain bill:

This is a scandal of some in Congress trading public health for PAC money and believing the slick ads of the tobacco industry . . . this is a scandal of politics for sale, and to my dismay, some Republicans going to the highest bidder.

The industry hired one lobbyist for every two members of Congress. The major manufacturers spent over $30 million in lobbying fees last year alone, a number that does not include the millions in campaign contributions or the billions spent on advertising, "grass roots," and front organizations. That, I suppose, is business as usual in defending the right to sell cancer to unknowing and immature minors.

Dr. Koop was dead right: if the tobacco lobby had not possessed and wielded the political power and economic resources to kill the McCain bill, it would surely have been enacted.

Yet, industry guile and boundless resources are only half the story.

Something had driven tobacco company executives to the bargaining table in 1997. Why did they seek "peace" with public health advocates after three decades of unrelenting resistance to even the most modest of public health demands? To gain that peace, the tobacco industry had been willing not only to accept but also actively to support legislation that, in its public health provisions, was not radically different from the provisions of the McCain bill.

What role did Dr. Koop and other public health leaders play in the negotiations leading to the global settlement, the ensuing legislative process in which the McCain bill was forged, the transformation of the tobacco companies from support of the settlement to scorched-earth opposition, and the ultimate failure of the bill to pass? With fifty-seven votes to end debate, lacking only three to bring it to a final vote—seven more than needed for final passage—the bill would have surely passed the Senate.

For its manifest successes by the late 1990s, the tobacco control movement had become the envy of citizen advocates in civic movements ranging from gun control to universal health care. What lessons for the leadership of these and other such movements might lie in the behavior of tobacco control leaders in this near triumph and ultimate defeat?

These are the questions that possessed me as events unfolded, and they are the questions that, in part, led me to undertake this book.

In the 1960s, 1970s, and early 1980s, I had been an active advocate for tobacco control and other public health and consumer protection regulation, first as counsel to the progressive Democratic leadership of the Senate Commerce Committee, then as a Democratic commissioner and chairman of the Federal Trade Commission.

Starting in 1984, when I left the commission and, together with David Cohen, former president of Common Cause, formed the Advocacy Institute, I became less a frontline combatant and more a chronicler of the tobacco control and other citizen movements, seeking to gain and pass on to newly emerging movement leaders the insights and lessons of effective citizen advocacy and movement leadership that could be drawn from past successes—and failures. After leaving the front lines, I first set out to study and write about the leadership of a handful of recent citizen group issue campaigns that seemed to have achieved unlikely success in the face of intrepid resistance from a popular Reagan administration closely bonded with formidable corporate interests.

The book that emerged from these studies, *Giant Killers* (W. W. Norton, New York, 1986), was my first effort to probe and celebrate the essence of what my colleague David Cohen has come to call "issue leadership." Among the *Giant Killer* studies was the lobbying campaign that led to enactment of the 1984 Cigarette Labeling Bill, the first tobacco control law enacted by Congress that the tobacco lobby had not either written or supported in its own strategic interest. This successful effort was led by Matt Myers, then executive director of the Coalition on Smoking OR Health, whose earlier work on the FTC's investigation of tobacco industry advertising and public relations deceptions had laid the groundwork for the modest victory in achieving stronger labeling requirements. In one sense, this book is simply a continuation of the storytelling and analyses in *Giant Killers* and my other writings on movement leadership roles and strategies in issue campaigns—applied to a remarkably rich tableau of leaders writ large upon a national canvas. But that is only part of my reason for writing this book.

The initial impetus to write this book came not from the dispassionate conclusion that it could be a lodestone of insightful leadership lessons, but from a deeply felt need to examine, and to set the record straight on, the leadership roles of Matt Myers, Dr. Koop, and others. For, as these events unfolded, they generated anger and hostility within the movement, among friends and colleagues who had fought in relative harmony against the common enemy of Big Tobacco until the moment in April 1997 that news of secret settlement talks leaked to the *Wall Street Journal*. From then on, those who supported the settlement—especially Matt Myers, initially the sole public health advocate at the bargaining table—were subjected to bitter personal abuse.

Men and women Matt had long fought alongside now charged that he had betrayed them. They scorned him as a dupe for tobacco lawyers far smarter than he thought he was. They grumbled that his unchecked ego had driven him to this secret flawed covenant with the devil. Keen strategists among them raged that he then committed the cardinal sin of the incompetent lobbyist—compromising while momentum for sweeping change was still building, before the legislative fight even started. In a torrent of suspicion, lone activists linked by e-mail discussion lists spread rumors that his organization, which bore the fighting name of the National Center for Tobacco-Free Kids, stood to gain millions for itself from the settlement and had hence metamorphosed into a shameful front for the tobacco lobby.

This portrait did not fit what I had observed of Matt Myers over almost two decades. It did not fit what I knew of the events leading up to the settlement and their aftermath—though, observing from the sidelines, I had to admit that there was much I did not know. I felt that fairness—to Matt and to the other tobacco control leaders as well—required a careful reconstruction of these events and the decisions that shaped them. I have tried to produce just that. But the larger goal of this book, as it has evolved, is to plumb the depths of this story for the rich and provocative lessons in movement leadership roles, strategies, and styles it readily yields: how a movement propelled toward a moment of historic opportunity by a cadre of passionate, resourceful, and gifted leaders fell victim, in part, to their conflicting visions of the Good. The tensions and contradictions they experienced may well inhere in the very strengths of such leadership.

There are, indeed, challenging leadership questions here. When, if ever, is the time to compromise with what is rightly viewed as a truly evil adversary? Indeed, how is it possible that *any* concessions the tobacco companies—or other predatory corporate interests—demand could simultaneously be in the public interest? How can leaders judge when a rising tide of support has peaked, and a moment of opportunity has arrived that must be seized—or lost? How can activists who are energized by mounting successes step back to evaluate coolly what the future is likely to bring?

Who speaks for a movement? Who has the legitimacy to negotiate for a movement? How is it possible to overcome the inevitable distrust and tensions between passionate grassroots activists and the more pragmatic movement leaders who operate at a national level? What if the vision of a leader as to what must be done is not shared by anything approaching a consensus of his peers? How can leaders reconcile the often competing needs of action and consensus? When does true leadership consist of the reasoned defiance of a flawed consensus among peers? And when is such defiance so destructive of the trust and cohesion vital to the future of a movement that it should be abjured regardless of the tangible benefits it may promise? Can secret negotiations without either undisputedly legitimate negotiators or an informed consensus ever be justified?

Behind these questions lurks a very human one: when is confidence in one's judgment—a strong ego—a badge of leadership, and when is it a curse? What can be done when leaders whose qualities served the needs of a movement well at its inception cannot adjust to the needs of the movement in its maturity?

As a chronicler of skilled movement leadership, I've often written of the strategic need for an "outside-inside," "good cop–bad cop" approach to hard negotiations. But when is public and private dissonance between negotiators and die-hard absolutists functional, when dysfunctional, and when destructive? The story of this settlement should serve to illuminate these and other hard questions, if not to settle them. I pray that the hard questions, and the generic leadership lessons that I attempt to derive from this story, will serve as a cautionary warning both to future tobacco control leaders and to the leaders of other civic movements for social change who have the skills and good fortune to come within sight of victory for their cause.

The book is divided into four parts.

- Part 1, "Leading toward Settlement," recounts the events, and the evolution in the strategic thinking of Matt Myers and others, that led to the decision to participate in the settlement negotiations and to accept the divisive conditions of secrecy.
- Part 2, "The Settlement," seeks to capture the reactions of other movement leaders to the leaked news of the settlement negotiations, the impact of those reactions, the various strategies adopted by movement leaders either to strengthen or scuttle the looming settlement, the fits and starts of the negotiations themselves, and the emergence of the June 20, 1997, settlement.
- Part 3, "The Rise and Fall of the McCain Bill," traces the festering internal schism among movement leaders, its impact on White House and congressional response to the settlement, the emergence of the McCain bill, and the collapse of momentum toward comprehensive legislation.
- Finally, Part 4, "Lessons from the Settlement and Its Aftermath," looks both backward and forward and seeks to gauge what was

gained and what was irretrievably lost in the defeat of the June 20, 1997, settlement and the McCain bill. It continues with a series of cautionary lessons that, for me, rise out of the narrative: "Thirteen Ways to Lead a Movement Backward," "The Wrong Leaders for the Right Moment," a revisiting of the criticisms of Matt Myers's leadership, and a somewhat fanciful reconstruction of what might have been a successful collaborative leadership strategy.

Because this book's focus is on the role of the public health leadership, you will need to seek elsewhere to find detailed accounts of the maneuvering within and among the tobacco companies (Richard Kluger's *Ashes to Ashes* is the most comprehensive); a full account of the attorneys general litigation and settlement (two books stand out: *The People vs. Big Tobacco* by Carrick Mollenkamp and others, and *Cornered* by Peter Pringle); and a detailed account of the key players within the Clinton administration, and their respective roles in the waxing and waning of the administration's support for strong legislation (*A Question of Intent* by David Kessler). I've tried to include enough context to aid the reader who comes to these events with only a vague memory that *something* of significance relating to tobacco control happened in the late 1990s, and to illuminate the reactions and initiatives of the leaders who are at the core of this book.

Even in narrating the roles and actions of tobacco control leaders and advocates, I have been highly selective, focusing both on those who played the most critical roles in affecting the outcome and on others whom I chose, somewhat arbitrarily, as representative of key constituencies. Some friends and colleagues who appear in this narrative will not be happy with me for the way in which they are portrayed. Many, many more will be at least as unhappy for my failure to pay heed to the important roles they played or believe they played. As I went through at least three complete drafts, my editors and readers enjoined me, again and again, to keep to a digestible cast of characters.

If it is any consolation, one of the minor characters who disappeared from the second draft was me. I had been present at some dramatic meetings; served as an intermediary from time to time, trying to bridge differences; even had a few public words to say of which I was somewhat enamored. But I could not honestly claim to have made much of a difference, so I disappeared, along with the others, gone.

Now, a few words more about method and objectivity.

The Robert Wood Johnson Foundation for many years has supported the tobacco control activities of the Advocacy Institute and made the writing of this book possible with a grant. The American Cancer Society has also supported the work of the institute, and I have consulted and continue to consult with them and with the National Center for Tobacco-Free Kids, now headed by Matt Myers. Each of these institutions and their leaders emerge from this chronicle with a generally more favorable judgment than others who have not supported our work. I am satisfied that this flows from a convergence of our strategic visions for tobacco control, not from any need to ingratiate myself with benefactors.

Still, to help counterbalance these personal feelings and apparent conflicts of interest—and their patent lack of the uninvolved journalist's or scholar's distance and objectivity—I've adopted several protective techniques. First, I've drawn heavily on the contemporaneous utterances and writings of the key actors, including the rich trove of spontaneous e-mail exchanges happily preserved. I've interviewed at length most of the key leaders on whom this book focuses and allowed them to have their say directly on the issues I explore. You will have their words to examine and judge, as well as mine. Second, when I'm aware that my views may be clouded by friendship or dislike, passion or raw instinct, I've said so.

Finally, I have also asked my friend, historian of labor and other civic movements Jeremy Brecher—not emotionally entangled in the minutiae and leadership personalities of the tobacco control movement as I am—to review the narrative, help me tell this story in a way that can be helpful beyond the parochialism of the tobacco control tribe, and deliver in his own words an afterword, where he highlights the lessons he finds herein for the aspiring leadership of other movements.

For you, the reader, there's plainly a benefit/cost trade-off here. On the one hand, I've lived with these issues and this movement for almost forty years and should know something about it. That closeness may also account for the willingness of many of those I've interviewed to speak openly. Those are benefits, but the costs must be reckoned in the inevitable distortions of judgment flowing from that very closeness to the issues and people involved. You've been warned.

One final introductory note. You will not find in this book data supporting the severity of tobacco use as a public health threat. I assume that the readers of this book will not be among the members of what a leading cancer epidemiologist forty years ago called "the Flat Earth Society"—those who are yet to be persuaded. But, just in case, let me quote the conclusion—rather startling even to me—of an April 13, 2000 essay in the *New York Review of Books* by the Nobel Prize laureate in chemistry M. F. Perutz, titled "The Threat of Biological Weapons:"

> There is no reason for complacency about the dangers . . . of acquiring and propagating bacteria and viruses for biological weapons. But the dangers should be seen in the perspective of other threats to human life. In 1995, the last year for which official statistics are available, the number of people killed by tobacco in the United States was 502,000, of whom 214,000 were aged between thirty-five and sixty-nine. On average, each of these could have been expected to live twenty-three years longer. In view of these alarming numbers, it seems to me that the still-prospering tobacco industry poses a proven threat to health and life that is many thousand times greater than the potential threat of bio-terrorism.

Part I

Leading toward Settlement

Thinking the Unthinkable

I was startled. I was intrigued. I needed to talk to Matt Myers. I'd opened my *New York Times Magazine* that Sunday, April 7, 1996, to find that Dick Kluger had written a cover story headlined, "A Peace Plan for the Cigarette Wars."

Kluger's voice carried great authority. His mammoth, definitive chronicle of America's hundred-year cigarette wars, *Ashes to Ashes*, was about to be published. It was destined for the Pulitzer. In it, he had unmasked Philip Morris's mendacity and given fair due to us hounds who had nipped at Big Tobacco's heels. He was, to be sure, a historian, not a tobacco control advocate. But he was no apologist for Big Tobacco. We had come to trust him. But the *Times* article, adapted from the concluding chapter of his book, was our first glimpse of his reasoned judgment of the most promising strategy *now* for the tobacco companies—and for us, the tobacco control advocates.

Kluger proposed that the tobacco companies "relax their rigidly combative posture and abandon their precarious existence under the volcano long enough to entertain a Congressionally brokered accommodation with the protectors of the public health." And he proceeded to lay out the broad outlines of "a sweeping legislative compromise" embracing the following features:

- Congress would issue a blanket grant of immunity to the tobacco companies against all pending and future product-liability claims on the grounds that the highly hazardous nature of smoking has long been common knowledge and adequately warned against.
- The FDA would be given regulatory oversight of the manufacture and packaging of cigarettes, including the power to set maximum levels for their hazardous ingredients.
- Health-warning labels would be enlarged to occupy the entire back

of all cigarette packs and would carry far more informative language.

- The proposed OSHA regulation restricting smoking at most workplaces to well-ventilated annexes and the FDA program to make cigarette marketing far less alluring to young people would be promptly implemented.
- The federal cigarette tax would be doubled to forty-eight cents to pay for enforcing these new regulations, and an additional two-cents-a-pack levy would pay for an antismoking advertising campaign and other public education programs like free quit clinics, to be run by the Office on Smoking and Health.

What was so startling about this peace proposal? And why was I intrigued? Because in more than thirty-five years of working for stronger controls on tobacco marketing, I had never once entertained the possibility that the tobacco companies would accept at the bargaining table such fundamental controls as Kluger now suggested they would be prudent to embrace.

To be sure, many in the tobacco control movement viewed Big Tobacco as on the run, especially those among the emerging cadre of citizen leaders who had led in the mid-1980s a series of successful campaigns at the community level. Perhaps foremost of these was Stanton P. Glantz, an eloquent scientist and founder of Californians for Nonsmokers' Rights (now Americans for Nonsmokers' Rights, [ANR]), who transformed the statistics of tobacco's toll on nonsmokers into a potent weapon of political rhetoric on behalf of smoke-free public places. At his side was Julia Carol, the codirector of ANR, as effective in organizing and weaving a powerful national network of grassroots advocates into a political force as Glantz was in motivating them. They, and the community-based activists they led, had begun to transform the indoor-smoking environment town by town through the enactment of local clean-indoor-air ordinances in city and county councils, where the reach of the tobacco lobby was most attenuated.

Meanwhile, at the national level a new surgeon general emerged, Dr. C. Everett Koop, to the bitter consternation of his patron, North Carolina's Senator Jesse Helms, who had advanced his candidacy on the basis of Koop's rigorous antiabortion campaigning. Dr. Koop transformed the relatively powerless post of surgeon general into a national bully pulpit to proclaim that tobacco use was at least as addictive as heroin or cocaine, and that "secondhand," "involuntary," or "environmental tobacco smoke" was a proven environmental killer as lethal as radon, lead, and other pollutants.

While Congress as a body did little, public health leaders in Congress, especially Congressman Henry Waxman, as chair of the House Subcommittee on Health and Environment, and Senator Ted Kennedy, as chair of the Senate Health, Education, and Labor Committee, skillfully utilized the platform of attention-getting tobacco control bills and congressional hearings to focus on tobacco industry wrongdoing and the need for appropriate legal restraints on this rogue industry. Thus, Waxman memorably summoned the heads of the tobacco companies and placed them under oath as they intoned their defiant denials that cigarettes were addictive—a performance that, perhaps more than any other event, brought home to the American people the ethical swamp in which these captains of industry perpetually dwelled.

And the media, especially television, freed by the 1970 broadcast ban on cigarette advertising from the constraints of placating tobacco advertisers, became more and more aggressive in undertaking illuminating investigative reporting—reporting that undergirded the message of Koop, Waxman, Kennedy, and others that the Philip Morris Companies and the R. J. Reynolds Tobacco Company belonged in the same rogues' gallery as the Medellin and Cali Colombian drug cartels.

Then, in the early 1990s, came three transformative events that catapulted tobacco control to the forefront of national attention and placed the tobacco companies—and their investors—at great risk:

- The election of Bill Clinton, among whose first acts on his first day was the banning of tobacco use in the White House. As his term progressed, Clinton, prodded by Vice President Al Gore and First Lady Hillary Clinton, became progressively more aggressive in supporting, then in pursuing, comprehensive tobacco control targeted at reducing youth smoking.
- The unprecedented assertion in February 1994 by Dr. David Kessler, commissioner of the Food and Drug Administration, of FDA regulatory authority over nicotine as "a drug" and cigarettes as "drug delivery devices" under *existing* law, despite none of Kessler's predecessors ever having claimed such authority. And Kessler, the pediatrician-lawyer, brilliantly framed tobacco use as "a pediatric disease," effectively evoking the moral imperative and the popular political support for government protection of children from predators: "Of course we all want freedom

for our children. But not the freedom to make irreversible decisions in childhood that result in devastating health consequences for the future. Addiction is freedom denied. We owe it to our children to help them enter adulthood free from addiction. Our children are entitled to a lifetime of choices, not a lifelong addiction."

- The audacious initiation in May 1994 by Mississippi attorney general Mike Moore, a young Democrat and an aggressive reformer, of the nation's first massive government lawsuit against the tobacco companies, claiming they owed Mississippi billions of dollars in excess Medicaid costs caused by smoking. Moore's suit had been followed quickly by Minnesota's, under the leadership of State attorney general Hubert "Skip" Humphrey III and a handful of other pioneers.

The great genius of these cases, unlike the failed personal injury cases brought for three decades by dying smokers or the families of dead ones, was that the juries would no longer have to overcome their instinctive belief that, no matter how duplicitous the tobacco companies were, the smokers really knew the score and made the bed they ended up in. In Moore's case, made possible by the legal acumen and financial resources of Mississippi's near legendary plaintiff's lawyer, Richard Scruggs, and in the seven cases filed by other state attorneys general by the date of Kluger's article, the victims were not weak-willed smokers but sturdy taxpayers with strong backs who had borne the costs of caring for the smokers—taxpayers like the very jurors who would be called upon to decide the cases.

But I hadn't thought much about where these cases might lead, other than to bring well-deserved harassment to the companies, dynamic publicity about industry wrongdoing (which would help move tobacco control laws forward), and perhaps—at the end of the rainbow—substantial, if not crippling, damages to the industry.

What I hadn't seen, and what Kluger suddenly illuminated for me, was how these cases, which I had thought were necessarily limited to monetary damages, could be leveraged to bring about what was for me (and Kluger) the single most important public policy goal for the tobacco control movement—broad, unfettered federal regulatory authority, mandated by Congress, over all tobacco manufacturing, marketing, and advertising. I would also learn that Moore and at least some of his colleagues were determined to seek "equitable" relief, asking the courts to mandate changes in the fundamental behavior of the companies.

The price Kluger told us we would have to pay—swallowing a grant of immunity to the companies for their past and future sins—troubled me. It would be galling to let these companies, arguably the most destructively corrupt corporate enterprises in history, escape accountability to their victims. But, since thirty years of litigation against the companies had yet to result in a single cent paid to any victim, since the novel legal theories of the state attorneys general were yet untested before courts or juries, and since Kluger's proposal would have encompassed every public health remedy that any of us had conceived of, his proposal did, indeed, intrigue me.

That this possibility had never before occurred to me was not exactly surprising. Those of us who had chosen to fight the tobacco industry as an avocation had spent much of the past thirty years with one polestar on our political horizon: the tobacco industry was as politically impregnable as it was greedy and corrupt. To be sure, obscure murmurings had begun to emerge from the new-generation head of R. J. Reynolds—a corporate lawyer, not a deep-bred tobacco man—that perhaps the time had come to explore an end to the tobacco wars. But those whispers hardly signified that the industry was prepared to make the kind of concessions Kluger was suggesting, despite the looming threats.

The industry had cut deals with Congress before, but always on its own terms, skillfully and cynically playing its dominant economic and political hand. In the 1960s, following the authoritative 1964 report of the Surgeon General's Advisory Committee on Smoking and Health, which forthrightly condemned tobacco use as a major cause of death and disease, some public clamor arose for responsive government action. Under the tutelage of a former deputy majority leader of the Senate, Earl Clements, who had become the chief tobacco lobbyist, the industry adopted the essential strategy that it would follow for the next thirty years: give an inch to gain a decade. The industry would accept, with a show of pain, largely cosmetic concessions with no fundamental restraints on its freedom to recruit each new generation of kids and adolescents.

The tobacco companies accepted a mealy-mouthed cautionary warning label in the mid-1960s. By the 1970s, the industry acceded to the ban on television and radio ads—thereby freeing themselves from the nettlesome antismoking "fairness" ads that an uncharacteristically bold

Federal Communications Commission had mandated in the ratio of one for every three cigarette commercials. By the mid-1980s, the industry, under pressure from a newly forceful public health lobby led by Matt Myers, yielded to somewhat more forthright warning labels; at the same time, the tobacco companies managed to keep off their products the dreaded label "addictive."

After each law was passed, the companies simply redoubled their artful exploitation of all the remaining unregulated forms of advertising and promotion. For our pains in achieving the ban on broadcast advertising, we were rewarded with the world's most powerful brand images—the Marlboro Man, vaulting from television to ubiquitous billboards, and Joe Camel, affably engaging the rebellious hormones of eleven-, twelve-, and thirteen-year-olds.

By 1996, we had gained in Congress only what the industry had chosen to give up, no more. We had made inches of progress, but for decades the White House had failed to seek, and the Congress to enact, any laws that held the promise of significantly shrinking tobacco's toll of disease and death.

And how could it have been otherwise? No other industry had the protection in Congress and the White House that tobacco commanded. Jimmy Carter became a forceful advocate for tobacco control—*after* he left the White House. But campaigning for the presidency in the spring of 1976 in North Carolina, the most bellicose statement he could utter on killer tobacco was, "We're going to do all we can to make tobacco *even more safe than it is now!*"

In Congress, the fifty or so tobacco district House members were known to their colleagues as "the Tobacco Boys," willing to trade votes for New York urban renewal or Western cattle-grazing rights in return for solidarity against any serious effort to curtail tobacco marketing. And the ranks of the industry's hired mouthpieces, its lobbyists, by the 1990s included two former Senate majority leaders—the bipartisan team of Howard Baker and George Mitchell—and hundreds of slightly lesser lights with the keys to virtually every congressional door, among them the closest friends of the strongest public health advocates, like Ken Feinberg, Ted Kennedy's fund-raiser and confidante. And the tobacco companies rained campaign money down upon Congress. So, as one wit put it, their power came not just from the tobacco leaf, which grew in only a dozen states, but from the green *lettuce* harvested in virtually every congressional district.

And now, in the mid-1990s, they had a Republican-led Congress that hated what they hated: government regulation of business, especially the Food and Drug Administration, whose commissioner, David Kessler, had the temerity to regulate. For this vice, he was labeled by House Speaker Newt Gingrich "a bully and a brute."And squarely in charge of any tobacco legislation in the House was its Commerce Committee chair, Tom Bliley, from Richmond, Virginia, Philip Morris's own hometown congressman.

Indeed, in that spring of 1996, what we most expected from the tobacco lobby and this Congress was not an inch of progress, but a giant step backward. What was in the offing was a Philip Morris–engineered Trojan horse of a "Youth Protection Law" with yet more token provisions to warn children to "Just say no!" to tobacco use. In its back pages, in its fine print, we would see the genius of tobacco's lawyers, shutting the door to any future effort by Kessler or his FDA successors to regulate this drug.

So, despite the looming threats, until I read Kluger in the *Times Magazine* that day, it never occurred to me that this industry would ever see the need to "make peace"—if the price were serious regulatory measures that held the potential for radically reducing tobacco use in this country and an effective national program to disenchant teenagers with the glamour of smoking.

If that idea were not mind-warping enough, in order to make this happen, the industry's lobbying army would need to be deployed, not to make the usual negative mischief, but to convince their good friends in Congress to swallow their hatred of regulation, and especially the FDA, and grant it vast police powers.

Still, here came Kluger, with the perspective of a historian and the detachment of a friendly observer, not an advocate, suggesting that these fundamentals of tobacco politics had shifted—at least for this particular moment in the political history of the tobacco wars.

> The cigarette makers, besides being the subject of five Federal grand jury investigations around the country, are enmeshed in lawsuits of unprecedented scope and peril. . . . Bill Clinton, moreover, is the first President to take an unequivocal stand on this issue. . . . Even in an era when deregulation is all the cry, many in Congress have begun to grasp that smoking may be an issue beyond partisan politics and that cigarettes are a product that will never be tamed without government intervention.

Kluger concluded, "The tobacco industry, then, may finally sense that time is running out on its bunkered status. So much so, that it

might well be willing, for the first time, to accept comprehensive regulation which would significantly diminish at least its domestic U.S.
market, and lead to the sparing of hundreds of thousands, even millions of premature deaths from tobacco."

I didn't quite trust my instincts on this. I needed to learn what Matt
Myers thought.

Why Matt Myers?

Why was Matt Myers the logical person to turn to for a prudent assessment of the Kluger proposition? Because no one working on tobacco control in Washington knew more about what was going on, had worked longer or harder at thwarting the tobacco lobby, or had displayed such sober judgment. For more than fifteen years, Matt had served as the chief strategist and lobbyist for the Coalition on Smoking OR Health, the tobacco control arm of the major voluntary health associations—the American Cancer Society, the American Heart Association, and the American Lung Association. It was Matt who had lobbied through Congress the 1984 cigarette-labeling bill creating four straightforward, rotating health warnings.

In the context of the mammoth challenges the tobacco companies faced by the late 1990s, this hardly seems a significant advance, but it was the very first time the previously omnipotent tobacco lobby, which battled to stop the bill, was outmaneuvered and out-lobbied in Congress. Before that, no tobacco control legislation passed that didn't serve the industry's strategic needs and bear its lobbyists' stamp of approval. It was only a small step for mankind, but as the tobacco wars went, it was a giant leap forward.

In *Ashes to Ashes,* Dick Kluger recounts Matt Myers's contributions often, and always with respect. He does not offer a colorful portrait of Matt, as he does of so many other activists whose less sober traits will also grace this book, but he draws out, again and again, Matt's solid attributes as "a product of the Sixties protest generation whose idealism had been tempered by years on the road as a troubleshooting litigator for the American Civil Liberties Union." He refers to Matt's "mental toughness," his "working seven-day weeks," his "square shooting;" he calls Matt a "knowing tactician" and a "skilled lobbyist."

In 1994 and 1995, The Robert Wood Johnson Foundation, especially its senior program officer for substance abuse control, Nancy Kaufman, took a hard look at the strength of institutional support for tobacco control advocacy in Washington and found it wanting. The foundation proceeded to commit $20 million over the next five years (matched by $10 million from the American Cancer Society and smaller grants from the American Heart Association and the American Medical Association) to the creation of a new advocacy organization focused solely on tobacco control—what would become the National Center for Tobacco-Free Kids (the Center), and its namesake coalition, the Campaign for Tobacco-Free Kids (the Campaign). To build and lead the Center, they recruited Bill Novelli, a pioneering advertising-agency founder and an innovator and practitioner of strategic communications, with strong management skills. Novelli, in turn, recruited Matt Myers as the Center's chief legislative strategist and lobbyist. So Matt and the Center were now, indeed, at the center of tobacco control strategy in Washington.

In the last few years, I had drifted away from day-to-day engagement. I found myself out of the loop on Matt's strategic thinking. We hadn't had a serious conversation about where he—or the movement—was heading for a long time. So first thing on the Monday morning after Kluger's jarring piece had appeared in the *New York Times*, I called him. Did he view Kluger's peace plan as a naïve fantasy, or a harbinger of things to come? I was to be startled for the second time in two days.

Matt had undergone, over time, a radical change in his vision of the future for tobacco control—going back more than two years, back to the February 1994 letter that David Kessler had written to the American Lung Association indicating his preliminary investigative determination that cigarettes were being deliberately manufactured and marketed to deliver calibrated doses of the addictive drug nicotine and hence fell within the broad existing powers of the FDA to regulate all aspects of the manufacture and marketing of such "drug delivery devices." Among the remarkable aspects of that letter was the fact that no previous Food and Drug commissioner had ever put so much as a tentative toe in the waters of tobacco regulation. Kessler was extremely careful to avoid any suggestion that FDA was prepared to take radical action to prohibit—or denicotinize—cigarettes. He spoke only of a regulatory regime that would bring an end to the industry's overt marketing efforts targeted at the very young. But looming in the wings, unstated, was the knowledge that if the courts upheld Kessler's assertion of power—the tobacco industry was sure to appeal all the way to the Supreme Court—and Congress kept its hands off, that power could be used in the future to fundamentally reshape the manufacturing and marketing of tobacco products in this country.

What promise did such FDA regulation hold for Matt? With this power, he visualized that FDA could promote a scientifically grounded technological race to remove the carcinogens and other toxic fumes and possibly some or all of the nicotine from tobacco products. Within ten years, cigarettes might be virtually nicotine free, virtually safe, or both. Kids who took up smoking to ape their peers would soon tire of it and easily quit. Those smokers who smoke, as the tobacco marketers insist, "for the taste of fine tobacco," not a nicotine fix, could continue to smoke but live longer. Others would have a choice of FDA-regulated nicotine delivery devices (patches and inhalers) that could be designed and marketed by the tobacco companies—who were already developing better nicotine mousetraps in fierce, open competition with the drug companies. In time, addicted smokers hooked on highly toxic cigarettes would become a doubly endangered species. And, in America at least, Big Tobacco would shrink in size, profitability, and political power.

Matt later reflected:

> We had made real progress since 1964, but by the mid-1990s, the tobacco control movement had been dancing around the periphery of accomplishing anything meaningful for years. As if health warnings that are an inch bigger are going to change the world.
>
> Yes, good things had happened in the states. You can't look at the last thirty years and not say we hadn't made very significant and meaningful progress. It doesn't diminish that achievement to recognize its limits. We had seen a decade of intense antismoking activity in states like California, but the smoking rates—even in California—bottomed out at roughly 20 percent of the population, with teenage smoking actually beginning to increase. Unless we were willing to accept a society with 15–20 percent of the population smoking, we had to think about doing something dramatically different.
>
> Then David Kessler made it clear he had to be taken seriously. Suddenly you had an agency that had the potential to try things that no one had ever tried with this industry, to bring about a fundamental change in the product itself.
>
> That affected my thinking in a lot of ways about a lot of different things. I realized I was responding differently to the prospect of this battle—the battle to secure David's initiative. Internally, I cared more deeply. This was a battle about more than winning and doing something good. When

you watched the FDA moving, what was incredibly exciting was the prospect of what could actually be achieved.

For Matt, this vision of FDA's ultimate regulatory scheme demanded
the defense of broad FDA authority over tobacco products themselves,
far more than FDA authority to regulate cigarette sales to minors and
advertising. His increasing focus on the primacy of that goal had convinced him that the public health community needed to mobilize, as it
had never effectively done before, to defend Kessler and the FDA. But
it also started him thinking about what concessions might ultimately
be necessary to win congressional support for FDA authority. A prag-
matist, he had little expectation that this Congress—or any future Congress—would simply do the right thing. But perhaps there might be
some kind of grand compromise such as Kluger envisioned.

As much as Matt relished the prospect of a cascade of successful
lawsuits from state attorneys general following Mike Moore's lead, a
threat that could drive the companies into bankruptcy, it was clear to
him that "the abolition of the tobacco industry through litigation wasn't
a realistic goal *from a public health standpoint.*" He saw it as a fantasy.
He was aware that the investment community took the new wave of
state attorneys general and private class action lawsuits very seriously,
indeed. Wall Street was especially spooked at the threat of bankruptcy,
which might come if three or four of these cases were tried to their
conclusion and resulted in not only compensatory awards to the plaintiffs but huge punitive-damage awards in the tens of billions of dollars.
The experienced trial lawyer in Matt considered this a possibility, but
not something to be counted on. No jury or combination of juries in
related cases had ever punished any industry with the severity it would
take to bankrupt the deep-pocketed Philip Morris.

The legal masterminds of the state cases, Dick Scruggs and his trial
lawyer colleagues, had learned from their polling and focus group studies of potential jurors that most such ordinary citizens remained dis-
appointingly indifferent and little disposed to punish the tobacco companies, however much their corrupt acts had been publicized and
condemned. A change in these attitudes might yet occur but could
hardly be depended on. Scruggs had confidence in his legal strategy
but was also keenly aware of the risks and limits of litigation. Matt
also doubted that bankruptcy—even if it occurred—would lead to fundamental or systemic public health reform in tobacco manufacturing
and marketing. While he believed that the cases brought by the state

attorneys general posed an unprecedented threat to the tobacco industry, he also believed that the courts were both unlikely and ill-equipped
to order the kinds of systematic public health changes that were needed.

But Wall Street so trembled before the specter of bankruptcy that
the stock prices of Philip Morris and R. J. Reynolds tumbled to a level
that reflected only the value of the companies' food businesses, de-
pressing the holdings of investment bankers and others by billions of
dollars. And Wall Street had been doubly traumatized by the decision
of the chief investor in the Liggett Tobacco Company to accept what
appeared on the surface to be a draconian settlement with Mississippi
and the other states and claimants. Once the proud purveyor of leading
cigarette brands (Chesterfield, Lucky Strike), Liggett had shrunk to a
miniscule market niche. Its major shareholder, Bennett LeBow, a Wall
Street takeover operative rather than a tobacco man, was engaged in
an elaborate scheme to take over industry giant R. J. Reynolds, which
involved swallowing virtually any concessions the attorneys general
demanded to dissipate their litigious threat to tobacco's future economic
viability. That didn't work, but the media spectacle of one of the "Big
Five" tobacco companies confessing sin and avowing henceforth to
tell the truth about tobacco opened a vast crack in the industry's solid,
three-decade wall of resistance.

Matt had played a delicate role in helping the state attorneys general and their lawyers build support for the public health aspects of the
agreement with Liggett. But he was under no illusions that this settlement signaled the collapse of the *real* cigarette companies—Philip
Morris, R. J. Reynolds, and Brown & Williamson, who together controlled more than 90 percent of the U.S. market. Even before Kluger's
article, Matt had begun wondering whether the time was close at hand
when the combined threat of the state lawsuits and FDA regulatory
action might drive the companies to seek to settle the cases, and to be
willing to make significant public health concessions to increase their
stock value.

Matt did not envision peace negotiations between public health advocates, attorneys general, and the tobacco industry. Instead, he had
begun to anticipate that the industry lobby would turn to its allies in
Congress. The lobby could also count on the White House's sensitivity to the pleas of politically vulnerable tobacco-state Democrats to
seek a congressional initiative. Such an initiative could give ground on
the modest and limited restrictions on sales to teenagers and advertising restrictions in the rules Kessler had proposed, and even write into

law the tearing down of the provocative Marlboro Man billboards and the retirement of Joe Camel, the health advocates' prize symbol of youth seduction. In return, Matt feared, the industry would ask Congress for blanket immunity from all civil and criminal liability and the elimination of any FDA claim of authority to regulate nicotine and other constituents of tobacco products and their advertising and marketing practices. This scenario would be a virtual Trojan horse, bold in its rhetoric of protecting children, but grossly inadequate in the fine-print regulatory authority—the classic industry strategy for three decades.

Matt and others who spoke for the public health community would then be called upon not only to just say no, but also to come back with a realistic counter-proposal. If public health advocates were going to have any impact on the outcome, they would have to make the kinds of hard choices they had never had to make before. Matt's take was: "You've got an unsympathetic, even hostile Congress. If Congress comes out of the block with a proposal that has surface appeal but actually does little, and public health's answer is just, 'No, we will accept no compromise,' no one's going to take that as credible. We're going to have to know what it is we really want—and what we're willing to give up to get it."

Nonetheless, Matt was deeply upset at Kluger's article. What troubled him was not Kluger's general vision of an ultimate grand compromise, but his argument that the public health advocates, as well as the tobacco companies, needed to compromise. Here, Matt thought, Kluger had ceded far too much ground to the companies. Methodically—and, Matt believed, mischievously—Kluger had set about undermining the key moral, scientific, and legal foundations of tobacco control advocacy. He had argued that the legal basis for the attorneys general lawsuits was unsound, and moreover, that smokers were not misled by the companies' PR spin but fully aware of the dangers of smoking. While Matt himself harbored private concerns about the viability of the cases, he felt strongly that Kluger had overstated their weakness.

It was, then, as an advocate that Matt reacted, and as an advocate he feared that Kluger's scorn for the legal footing of the lawsuits would be seized upon by the tobacco lobby to persuade the White House and public health–oriented members of Congress to accept weak legislation once again.

In the days following publication of Kluger's article, the tobacco companies remained publicly unresponsive to any talk of compromise.

But there was a kind of back-channel message to Kluger. Philip Morris, predictably, denounced *Ashes to Ashes* as the habitual distortions of a committed enemy of the industry. But Philip Morris's general counsel and leading strategist, Murray Bring, remained civil and sought to approach Kluger, even suggesting lunch. Lunch never quite took place, but in the last of several calls from Bring vainly seeking a mutually available date, Kluger asked Bring his reaction to his "peace plan."

"We read what you wrote," Kluger recalls Bring responding. "And we're paying attention."

Sinking the Unthinkable

In the months that followed the April 1996 publication of Dick Kluger's immodest proposal, and the hint delivered shortly thereafter to the *Financial Times of London* by R. J. Reynolds's new CEO, Steven Goldstone, that he might well be open to a negotiated resolution of all tobacco issues ("Why wouldn't the industry look at it?"), Matt Myers was a worried man.

He had been keeping close track of the attorneys general cases. He was also privy to the realistic analysis of former Maine attorney general, Jim Tierney, who had become a key counselor to the group of attorneys general who had brought or were contemplating bringing lawsuits against the tobacco companies. In a letter to me, Tierney reflects on the situation faced by the attorneys general at that time:

> These cases were a very high risk proposition for state attorneys general. For that reason, they sought allies. A few trial lawyers were enthusiastic, but most were not and attorney general after attorney general reported that they could not find lawyers in their state willing to take on this expensive fight. Some in the health community, such as Northeastern Univ. Law Prof. Dick Daynard, liked the idea of litigation, but they were few in number, disorganized and did not understand the immensity of the litigation. Most stayed away from lawsuits preferring local initiatives and referendums.
>
> In 1994, Mississippi Atty. Gen. Mike Moore, Minnesota Atty. Gen. Hubert H. Humphrey, III, and Florida Atty. Gen. Bob Butterworth took the plunge and threw up the "Hail Mary" anti-tobacco lawsuits. Each man took a huge risk and staked their careers on these cases.
>
> By late summer of 1995, three of the four filing states were in deep trouble. In Florida, the authorizing legislation had been repealed and Gov. Lawton Chiles' veto was expected to be overridden. In Mississippi and West Virginia, the Governors had joined forces with their legislatures and the tobacco industry. In cases prepared by the tobacco industry, they were suing to kill the litigation saying the attorneys general had acted without

legal authority. Only Minnesota seemed to have a clear shot of at least eventually getting to a courtroom.

Matt held both Mike Moore and Dick Scruggs, the trial lawyer who provided the legal resources to sustain the Mississippi case, in high regard:

> I thought incredibly highly of them and what they had done. They brought the cases that gave the FDA critical documents; they got [Clinton's pollster] Dick Morris to run a poll that helped to move Clinton forward on FDA; and they had vigorously sought to learn what public health changes were needed to make a real difference—and to fight for them. I did not underestimate the good that they had done. Their lawsuits revolutionized the debate and their skill and resources transformed the playing field.

What worried Matt was not that Moore and Scruggs cared less than he about the public health—or more about settling for a huge payoff. "I did not doubt their toughness, commitment, or ability," recalls Matt. "Rather, we disagreed about how far the industry and the White House could be pushed."

Matt knew that Scruggs, as an experienced litigator, understood only too well the weaknesses of the cases, the significance of their setback, and the risks of losing all. So he feared that Moore and Scruggs would be receptive to a compromise that fell short of what was necessary to achieve significant public health goals. Scruggs himself acknowledged that his generic strategy for grand-scale litigation, such as the tobacco suits, was "to get the stakes so high that neither side can afford to lose. When you raise the stakes through consolidations or bringing large numbers of claims together, you have given them an incentive to settle. . . . And usually a good settlement is far superior to trench warfare, trial-by-trial litigation."

As for the state attorneys general, Matt worried that, as politicians—however exemplary—they would be hesitant to gamble all at trial if they thought there was a viable alternative. He also worried that though Moore and Scruggs both genuinely cared about making public health gains, their lack of experience with the industry's genius for concocting high-sounding health concessions out of regulatory cotton candy could result in yet one more lost opportunity for serious regulation. And he worried that this would all happen without any opportunity for him or others who knew this industry's wiles to sit at the table and alert them.

Matt was right to worry. By July 1996, Scruggs and Moore, full of good intentions, were about to launch a settlement initiative: "The money mattered," acknowledged Scruggs, in an interview with PBS's *Frontine,* but

> it didn't matter as much as the public health. It is not often in life that you have a chance to make a mark on humanity. And we all got caught up in the opportunity that this presented to us. The money was an important public health tool. It was important to reimburse the states for their health care expenditures and to create a pool of money to fund the enforcement actions of the FDA. Other than that, it was the regulatory mechanisms that we were trying to put into place. The restrictions on marketing of this product to children. To try to reverse the trend in the proliferation of tobacco.

Scruggs developed a plan for making this happen. Trent Lott, the Senate majority leader, was his brother-in-law. Lott had also been a good friend to the tobacco lobby, and they in turn had rewarded him with generous campaign contributions. With Moore's support, Scruggs told *Frontline* he had called Lott: "I said, 'Trent, you haven't been involved in any of this. You are probably considered to be tobacco friendly by the tobacco industry. You are someone they would probably trust. You are someone that I would trust. Would you consider trying to set up a meeting to see if anything can be worked out on a national basis?' "

Lott said he'd think about it, made some inquiries with colleagues close to the industry, and came back with guidance for Scruggs. Lott told his brother-in-law to talk to John Sears, a Republican lobbyist who had served in the Nixon White House, and Tommy Anderson, a lobbyist who had spent seventeen years as Lott's chief of staff. For the next two months, they would serve as secret emissaries to the industry's key leader, R. J. Reynolds' Goldstone.

Two years earlier, as Moore and Scruggs were preparing to file their lawsuits, they had sought out David Kessler and promised to work quietly to provide political support for his FDA initiatives. Kessler, in turn, had introduced them to Mitch Zeller, his politically astute deputy. From that day on, Moore and Scruggs had kept in touch with Zeller, constantly seeking ways in which they could be helpful to Kessler's efforts to gain, first White House, then congressional, support for his tobacco control initiatives. In late July 1996, Scruggs asked Zeller to join him for lunch. Scruggs reported on the opening of the secret negotiations and told Zeller that the industry was prepared to offer as much as $90 billion in settlement of all the cases. But Scruggs insisted that the money was only part of what he and Moore were after. As Scruggs later told reporter Peter Pringle, "We wanted to include everything Kessler wanted in the FDA ruling on tobacco." As Zeller recalls that meeting:

> I have to admit that when I had my first conversation about these negotiations with Scruggs, I don't know if my jaw dropped, but surprise certainly registered on my face. I was wide-eyed at the number of zeroes [$90,000,000,000]. I'd had no idea how serious these negotiations were. Of course, I had a high level of distrust and cynicism for the industry, but this sounded new and different. My first reaction was amazement that the industry was so scared that they would be willing *even to talk* about $90 billion. Aside from whether that was the *right* figure or not, the very fact that the dialogue had begun was to me a sign of the strength and the power of what we were all doing.
>
> Scruggs and Moore had their connection with FDA. They obviously had a connection with the White House. But they really had no connection with the public health community, and I said to Scruggs, "The one person they should involve, above all others, if he would be willing, is Matt Myers."
>
> I thought that because of Matt's credibility and reputation for honest dealings, above all his knowledge and his intelligence, that he would be the right person for Scruggs to talk to, whether or not it led to anything.
>
> I asked Matt to breakfast. I told Matt that Moore and Scruggs wanted to talk directly to him. I said, "You know it's entirely up to you, but if there's going to be a dialogue with the public health community, I think they should start with you."
>
> His reaction was, "I'll be happy to sit down with anybody who wants to talk about these kinds of things." If Matt was a poker player, he would be a very good poker player, because I don't remember his jaw dropping at any point during the conversation. I remember him saying very seriously and very soberly that he'd be happy to sit down and talk with them— and get to know them.

Then, in the beginning of August, the predictable occurred. R. J. Reynolds (RJR) and Philip Morris, through their intermediaries, proposed a concrete offer. Scruggs called Zeller and Matt, urgently seeking a meeting. He told them both he'd been meeting with representatives of the tobacco industry, and that what they were prepared to agree to was simply "extraordinary." He was ready, at a moment's notice, to fly his own jet into National Airport in D.C. and meet them in a conference room in the private aviation terminal. Matt reluctantly postponed the start of a family vacation in Spain. ("Louise and Micah and Daniel were none too happy.") Scruggs's hopes were high, but the meeting proved disastrous. The industry had double-crossed him. The proposal they gave him and that he showed Matt and Zeller was nothing like what Scruggs said they had discussed. Matt and Zeller took one hard look at the summary of the proposed settlement prepared by the industry negotiators and pronounced it a disaster.

"That proposal was off the charts," recalls Myers. "It was outrageous; it was terrible; it was totally unacceptable—and it wasn't what Dick had described. Dick agreed that it was not what had been orally described to him and was really bad. We were all angry. The difference was that Mitch and I saw it as a typical act of bad faith—a classic 'bait and switch' con. Dick saw it, instead, as a tactical error and still believed he could get them to deliver on their promises of broad public health concessions."

Scruggs pleaded with Matt and Mitch to maintain secrecy about the negotiations for a few days—except for briefing David Kessler and Bill Novelli—while he went back to the negotiators.

Jim Tierney, counselor to the attorneys general, wrote to me wryly:

> Scruggs would have loved to avoid dealing with Matt, but his prime constituents, the state attorneys general, forced him to return to Matt as the voice of the health community. Washington State AG Christine Gregoire repeatedly referred to the health community as our "stakeholders," and Massachusetts's Scott Harshbarger vowed that he would not go anywhere without the health community.
>
> So Scruggs drafted his own outline of the terms of agreement the negotiators had orally agreed to, tracked down Matt on vacation with his family in Spain, and faxed the outline to him. According to Matt it was closer to what he had originally described and would have been considered remarkable by many. It was a good-faith effort by Dick, but still got way too little, and gave up way too much. We had a very honest discussion about it. Dick had not yet shared it with the industry, and I doubted that they would seriously entertain it if he did so.

Just as Matt returned home from Spain, news that Scruggs had been talking with industry representatives leaked to the *Wall Street Journal*, including the terms proposed in the Scruggs draft.

Matt quickly drafted a letter to be signed by the heads of the three major voluntary health groups—cancer, lung, and heart—and sent it to Mike Moore just as Congress was returning from its August 1996 recess, heading into its last days before adjourning for the November elections. They insisted that "the public health community be included and have input into the negotiations with the tobacco industry before an agreement is reached."

The same day, Matt sent out a call to action along an electronic network of tobacco control activists throughout the country:

> There has been a great deal of coverage over a so-called compromise allegedly being brokered by Trent Lott. The reports say the compromise would enact into law the FDA Rule, but strip FDA of jurisdiction and wipe out all product liability suits.
>
> Our position is: We will oppose any legislative compromise that
>
> 1. Weakens the FDA rule
> 2. Strips FDA or a comparable agency of the jurisdiction we have fought to get the government to assert
> 3. Frees the industry for past and future wrongdoing
> 4. Fails to require the industry to make available all of its internal documents concerning nicotine, addiction, and health
> 5. Lacks an effective enforcement mechanism, or
> 6. Preempts stronger state and local action
>
> Now that Congress is returning, we urge everyone to contact their member to urge support for FDA and opposition to any weakening proposals, even if they are promoted with all the glitz and gloss we can expect.
>
> Please let us know of any rumors or information you obtain on this subject.
>
> REMEMBER—CONGRESS IS IN SESSION FOR ONLY A MONTH—YOU NEED TO ACT NOW!!!

Matt wrote his own more detailed, concrete letter of opposition to Scruggs, but not without reaffirming his appreciation and respect for Scruggs's initiative: "You and Mike Moore deserve enormous credit for your roles in developing and sustaining this extraordinary level of public attention. I truly believe that in doing so, you have already made a major contribution to the public's health."

But he went on to point out, in addition to the specific policy shortcomings of the proposed settlement, that a premature settlement would dissipate the "momentum you have created."

Tobacco's newfound stature as a page one story, and indeed a major issue in the presidential campaign, owes in no small part to the profusion of state and individual lawsuits against the industry. The importance of this attention cannot be overemphasized. It has succeeded in exposing the cynical tactics of the tobacco industry and thereby demonizing the industry in the eyes of ordinary citizens. Maintenance of a high level of attention is essential to sustain the growing public disgust with both smoking and the industry that creates and promotes the product; ultimately, this serves directly to marginalize and thereby to reduce smoking. With the possible exception of a very large tax (or wholesale price) increase, there may be nothing more important than keeping up the public "noise" level. A settlement could kill it.

He concluded on a harsh note: "The public health interest ought to be paramount. The approach embodied in the proposed settlement gives the appearance that it is not even of secondary interest."

Looking back later, Matt commented: "My goals were, one, to make certain that there was no misunderstanding of our position—by Dick, especially, yet without undermining our working relationship, and two, to quickly frame the issue. After Kluger's piece, I was worried that the leaked terms might be seen publicly as a good deal. I wanted quickly to set forth its weaknesses so that we in the public community could set the public health terms of the debate and were seen to have laid out a standard to guide the media, the White House, and others."

Other attorneys general who were also troubled by Scruggs's initiative sought Matt's guidance and mutual support, including him in AG conference calls and meetings—and giving him a good opportunity to develop working relationships with those most committed to public health objectives. The reporters on the tobacco beat also turned to Matt for guidance on the proposed settlement, and he took advantage of the opportunity to blast the deal. "Why should the tobacco industry be immune, given the harm they've caused?" he challenged in the *Wall Street Journal.*

And he lobbied the White House: "I was concerned about the White House's reactions to Dick's discussions. I knew that Dick was well connected through Dick Morris and learned that he had been speaking regularly with close Clinton advisor Bruce Lindsay. I was very concerned that we could lose control of the process and that a settlement could move so fast we would be unable to stop it unless we acted promptly and in a way that would command respect."

Instead, Matt developed a White House strategy and went to work. He alerted members of Vice President Gore's staff whom he had earlier found supportive on tobacco issues. He urged Mitch Zeller to have Kessler follow up with the vice president himself, with whom Kessler had developed a good relationship.

Scruggs's vision of Clinton and Lott hand-in-hand on the White House portico, heralding the global settlement of the tobacco wars, faded as the Congress adjourned. This did not portend a harmonious future relationship between Myers and Scruggs. Although they liked and respected each other, Scruggs found Matt an immovable roadblock in the path of his grand—or grandiose—vision.

Indeed, later that fall, after Scruggs told Matt of continuing exploratory conversations with Bruce Lindsay, Matt called Lindsay so he could directly express his continuing concerns with Scruggs's settlement initiatives. Lindsay responded immediately and invited Matt to meet with him confidentially.

> I said to Lindsay, "This is a disaster waiting to happen. You need to be skeptical. I know you like to be a problem solver but there are real, real problems with the terms of this proposal. Be careful."
>
> At the same time, I told Lindsay that we in the public health community would be willing to work with him and the White House to develop an acceptable proposal if this was serious. I wanted him to believe that we wouldn't say no just to say no, and because he said the president wanted to get something done if it could be done right.

As the year ended, Scruggs told Matt that he had, in effect, received marching orders from Lindsay: Deal with Matt. Make sure he's satisfied with whatever you put on the table. We won't go near any settlement that Matt—speaking for the public health community—opposed.

The Search for Common Ground Begins

By late fall 1996, the Scruggs-Moore settlement initiative was dead, or at least stunned. But Matt Myers knew that the economic and political winds blowing toward settlement were still strong. The industry was still under pressure from Wall Street to get rid of the nettlesome cases—and its pariah status. In August 1996, just as the Scruggs-Moore deal was falling apart, a jury in Florida awarded Grady Carter, a lone lung cancer victim, $750,000 in damages, only the second time in history that a tobacco injury case had reached a jury. The award was against the Brown & Williamson Tobacco Corporation, but the reverberations were industrywide. Philip Morris's stock lost $12 billion in value in less than an hour.

The industry's new leaders, led by R. J. Reynolds's Goldstone, had signaled openness to settlement, if not yet willingness to make fundamental concessions. The White House, led by Bruce Lindsay, harbored the seductive vision of a negotiated settlement, brokered by the president and celebrated by all sides. And Moore and Scruggs were increasingly fearful of losing the Mississippi case, which had now been set for trial in the summer of 1997.

Though Senate Majority Leader Trent Lott and other Republican congressional leaders detested David Kessler, the FDA, and the regulation that crimped their business constituency, they were anxious to shed the growing taint of Republican indenture to the tobacco lobby—and to its campaign contributions. In 1996 Lott's predecessor, Republican presidential candidate Bob Dole, had refused to support FDA regulation of tobacco. He parroted the industry line that tobacco was no worse than any other consumer product. "We know it's [tobacco] not good for kids, but a lot of things aren't good. Some would say milk's not good."

This Republican unease was measurably heightened by Bill Novelli's decision to allocate a significant portion of the National Center for

Tobacco-Free Kids's $5 million annual budget to a series of aggressive advocacy ads in the papers Congress reads: the *Washington Post*, the *New York Times*, and Capitol Hill's "local" newspapers, *Roll Call* and *The Hill*. The ads attacked Big Tobacco's massive campaign contributions to members of Congress. Though the ads were scrupulously nonpartisan, since tobacco money was flowing disproportionately to Republicans, the impact was partisan. Lott and other Republican leaders began to view a Moore settlement initiative, supported or at least not opposed by the industry, as a painless way to foreclose the Democrats' opportunity to exploit Republican ties to Big Tobacco in the next congressional elections.

The leadership of the tobacco control movement had shown itself capable of uniting behind an ever expanding, all-encompassing shopping list of tobacco control policies, from broad, unfettered FDA authority over tobacco to full civil and criminal accountability for all the industry's past, ongoing, and future wrongs. The leadership had also united without stress in opposition to the Scruggs-Moore settlement, because it fell far short on virtually every item on that list. However, the leadership had not yet had to respond to any serious proposal that met some of the public health advocates' most important objectives but fell short of the ideal. Yet new, improved settlement proposals were sure to emerge. Matt, for one, knew that "Hell, no!" would not remain a sufficient answer.

Priorities would have to be set; hard choices would have to be made. The new Congress, still in firm Republican hands, would convene in January 1997, and a newly reelected and emboldened President Clinton would be looking for legislative achievements—and willing to compromise. Matt and Bill Novelli began to think through, for themselves initially, just what their top priorities would be—and what concessions to the industry might be tolerable in order to achieve their public health priorities.

The discussions Matt had pursued informally the summer before with both national and local tobacco control advocates, while he was organizing their common opposition to the Scruggs-Moore settlement proposals, convinced him that few others in the movement were yet thinking hard—or prepared to think hard—about potential trade-offs.

We were a public health community—really a bunch of individuals—who never had to cope with hard, hard choices and competing values. We had all been able to operate at the level of broad rhetoric, because we had never before come close to achieving *any* of our most ambitious objectives.

We could all recite the laundry list of desired policies, but it was very hard to get people to go below the surface rhetoric. I asked the people who were enthusiastic about FDA regulation, "Tell me what it is you think FDA ought to be doing? What is the authority you think they must have? What is it you want FDA to accomplish?" They had no answers. It was incredible how little people had thought that through.

The annual meeting of the American Public Health Association (APHA) was scheduled for mid-November 1996 in New York. It would draw militant as well as moderate advocates, regional and local advocates as well as national organization leaders and Washington-based health lobbyists. Matt, with law professor and tobacco control advocate Richard Daynard, jointly convened a broadly diverse group of tobacco control advocates at the APHA meeting to try to identify common public health legislative priorities, and to explore what concessions on litigation—if any—most might be willing to consider in order to achieve those priorities.

Daynard had strong credentials as co-convenor of such a meeting. A law professor at Northeastern University Law School, he had steadfastly promoted the deployment of litigation strategies as a tool to rein in the tobacco companies throughout the 1970s and 1980s, when most tobacco litigation had proved a dry well. In December 1995, working with Maine's former attorney general, Jim Tierney, Daynard had succeeded in drawing together, for a three-day conference, representatives of forty state attorneys general; the American Medical Association and their bitter medical malpractice adversaries, the trial lawyers; the American Cancer Society; Kessler's FDA in the person of Mitch Zeller; and Matt Myers.

Daynard had also been a volunteer community advocate and leader of a Massachusetts grassroots nonsmokers' rights advocacy group. He was well known, trusted, and liked by most community-based advocates. He would certainly not be seen by them as a weak-kneed defender of the tort system.

Until that conference, only four attorneys general had actually filed suit. But public health leaders came to see the potential in the litigation, and the attorneys general were reassured that they would have a supportive public health constituency if they filed their cases. The Daynard conference unleashed the parade of state attorneys general to their state courts. Matt wanted this dialogue to take place before the new Congress convened in January 1997, before any new legislative proposals were on the table. And he wanted to open such a dialogue free from the pressure and turmoil that would inevitably accompany the emergence of another concrete proposal.

The invitation list reflected the breadth of the tobacco control movement. The large national health voluntary associations, the American Cancer Society, the American Lung Association, and the American Heart Association (the "health voluntaries"), were represented by both paid staff and committed volunteers, as were the American Academy of Pediatrics and the American Medical Association. The director of the Massachusetts state tobacco control program, one of the best funded and most aggressive, was there. The Public Citizen Litigation Group, founded by Ralph Nader, which had actively supported tobacco control litigation, was represented, and so was The Robert Wood Johnson Foundation—the only major U.S. foundation actively funding tobacco control advocacy. Each participant would help shape the strategic response of the movement as a whole to any new proposals.

There were two invitees, in particular, whose willingness to entertain thoughts of compromise was most problematic, whose response most concerned Matt, and whose views would carry great weight with the most zealous of advocates around the country: Stan Glantz and Julia Carol.

5

Why Stan Glantz and Julia Carol?

In contrast to the representatives of the American Medical Association, the Cancer Society, and the other large voluntary health associations, Stanton P. Glantz, a teaching professor at the University of California Medical School in San Francisco and the author of the leading text on medical statistics, represented no formally organized constituency, commanded no army of volunteers. Julia Carol led a very small guerilla force, an organization that Stan had founded and left called Americans for Nonsmokers' Rights, whose few thousand dues-paying members were largely centered in California. Yet their willingness—or unwillingness—to accept Matt Myers's challenge to consider setting priorities and potential trade-offs in approaching new national settlement initiatives would shape, as well as reflect, the response of the national tobacco control movement as a whole.

In the early 1980s Stan Glantz burst forth as the prime mover in a small grassroots volunteer organization in San Francisco, Californians for Nonsmokers' Rights. He caught the national attention, especially among tobacco control advocates, in the fall of 1983 by masterminding the landmark defeat of San Francisco's ballot initiative Proposition P, the tobacco industry's formidable effort to repeal San Francisco's vanguard nonsmoking ordinance. To stamp out the threatened plague of local action inspired by San Francisco, the tobacco industry spent more than ten times as much money as tobacco control advocates did, hired artful public relations strategists attuned to San Francisco's libertarian culture, plastered local TV and billboards with rhetorical themes tuned to pluck San Franciscans' responsive chords. But Glantz, leading and driving his handful of colleagues every waking minute, outmaneuvered them.

Recounting Glantz's early leadership of Californians for Nonsmokers' Rights, Richard Kluger encapsulated the Glantz phenomenon: "As compulsive a worker as he was a talker, who dreamed up most of his group's arresting ideas, he had a mind both inventive and encyclopedic, raised a lot of its money, wrote its pithy newsletter (usually including his picture), and loosed its fiercest rallying cries."

For the next fifteen years, Glantz would serve as the movement's preeminent translator of the science of tobacco and disease into the public discourse of tobacco control—a master of the sound bite, not with glibness, but with the compression of complex data into an accurate, powerful metaphorical message, the significance of which could be instantly grasped by the broad public. He was a tactical treasure for a movement beginning to emerge. Most importantly, Glantz brought to the more genteel public health professionals the lesson that tobacco control is rough combat with an implacable adversary. To be successful, the tobacco control advocate not only had to stand on solid scientific ground but had to be a willing warrior. And Glantz *was* unafraid. For example, by publishing a rich cache of incriminating internal industry documents anonymously shipped to him in 1994, he knowingly risked the certain and notorious burdens of becoming the target of harassing industry legal action. On the national scene, Glantz emerged as the movement's "outside" agitator—outside both Washington and the more establishment public health organizations—or, in Ralph Nader's felicitous term, a movement "spark plug."

Round and exuberant, determinedly unkempt in his trademark orange cardigan—knitted, he insisted, by his mother—Stan Glantz flogged the languid and timid, especially the staff and volunteers of the Cancer, Heart, and Lung societies' state divisions. He pricked the pompous among the dark-suited establishment leaders in Washington and the national headquarters of the health voluntaries, delighting the feistier community-based activists around the country and gaining for himself a wide and responsive audience among them. Most tobacco control advocates—even those who relished belligerent rhetoric when safely nestled among an audience of the converted —shied away from tangling directly on talk shows with tobacco industry defenders. Not Glantz; time after time he flummoxed the most skilled of a succession of industry flacks.

But these assets alone would not have made Glantz a force Matt Myers would have to reckon with in seeking to forge a consensus behind a movement negotiating position. Glantz early recognized—and early mastered—the mobilizing power of the Internet. By the winter of 1996, he had teamed up with a deeply committed tobacco control advocate who was also a visionary Internet innovator, Michael Tacelosky. Through "Tac," Glantz had developed an e-mail network of more than a thousand of the most active and aggressive advocates, whom he bombarded with broadsides and exhortations daily, and for whom he was the preeminent guide to strategy and action. He was colorful, passionate, authoritative, persuasive—and intimidating.

Since the early 1980s, Julia Carol, now codirector of Americans for Nonsmokers' Rights (ANR), had been a trusted ally and counselor to Stan Glantz. Like Glantz, she was an "outside" spark plug—and more. Small in stature but not in voice, she often took on the lonely role at national leadership meetings of truth teller to the naked emperor. She challenged the persisting dominance of white male leadership in the movement. She challenged the lofty, undemocratic perspective of national leaders in Washington and in the national headquarters of the health voluntaries, and their chronic failure to heed the closer-to-the-earth learning of the grassroots advocates. Nor would Julia Carol hesitate to stand up to Stan Glantz when she thought him wrong.

Unlike Glantz, who did not expend any of his prodigious energy building relationships, Carol spent at least as much energy—positive and generous energy most of the time—deeply committed to the honest brokering of differences and to movement building. As a community and movement organizer, she helped expand a civic impulse initially limited to a few thousand citizens afflicted by high sensitivity to tobacco smoke when they ventured out of their homes into public spaces, into a broadly based social justice movement determined to hold the tobacco companies accountable. At Americans for Nonsmokers' Rights, leading a team of highly organized and deeply committed self-described type As, mostly women, Julia Carol pursued a collaborative, responsibility-sharing, team-centered style of leadership. And she reached out and nurtured a network of fellow advocates throughout the country.

Kluger, in *Ashes to Ashes*, captures these qualities:

> Carol served as . . . spiritual den mother, nurturing the rank and file and preaching that the struggle was not between smokers and non-smokers, but between the rest of society and the rogue vendors of cigarettes. "The majority of the public now sees the industry as pond scum," she would remark, but reserved the larger part of her fervor for cheering on and guiding those around the country she lovingly called "the movement people," the ones who had long operated out of their living rooms or garages to put the anti-smoking crusade together stick by stick.

When the Disney docudrama *The Insider* premiered, chronicling the travails of Brown & Williamson whistleblower Jeff Wigand, Wigand spoke bitterly at a press conference of how he had been left to hang and twist in the wind during his darkest days by all the prominent tobacco control groups and leaders save two: Julia Carol and Stan Glantz.

Julia Carol, Stan Glantz, and Matt Myers had grown mutually respectful of one another during more than a decade of collaboration. But Glantz and Carol would approach the questions Matt put before the November 1996 meeting with attitudes radically different from his, attitudes shaped by their very different advocacy experiences, the political environment in which they forged their successes, their strategic visions, and their temperaments. Matt, politically grounded in Washington, and Glantz and Carol, in northern California's cities and counties, each looked to very different political venues for the achievement of tobacco control objectives. Glantz and Carol had found their path to victory through local governments, which they found the most democratically responsive level of government—at least in California. They began in San Francisco, then spread city by city, county by county, across California, with a checkerboard of local ordinances now beginning to fill out across the country—even in tobacco strongholds like Winston-Salem, North Carolina, home to R. J. Reynolds. They had learned that most town councils were inhospitable to tobacco lobbyists imported from the state capital or Washington, D.C.

But higher levels of government were different. For Glantz and Carol, the state legislatures were only a lobby-infested threat to local action, with legislators physically distant and insulated from their constituents, as city council members could never be from their neighbors. Their constant nightmare was the Trojan-horse state clean-indoor-air law, crafted by tobacco lawyers and introduced by bought legislators, that offered token regulation but housed "preemption" language that prevented cities and counties from adopting strong laws. And their constant struggle was to keep timid state Cancer Society or Heart Association staff and volunteers from following the counsel of their professional lobbyists to accept meekly whatever legislative bones the lobby-locked legislatures were willing to throw them.

Washington was even more distant and threatening. Glantz and Carol both knew well the morality tale of the 1965 federal Cigarette Labeling Law: just like the preemptive state laws, the federal labeling law sheltered, under a woefully weak warning, language that barred states and localities—as well as any upstart federal agencies—from exercising their inherent public health powers to regulate the advertising and marketing of tobacco. And *that* happened under the relatively pro-consumer rule of Democrats. To Glantz and Carol, Washington was the playground of special interest lobbies, none of which manipulated Congress more effectively than the tobacco lobby. In California, on the other hand, the citizen initiative process had produced Proposition 99—the twenty-five-cent-a-pack cigarette excise tax increase directly approved by the voters—which allocated some $100 million a year to tobacco control programs, most notably, the state of California's aggressive paid industry-caricaturing campaigns to counter tobacco advertising.

All this had succeeded in driving tobacco use rates significantly downward in California. Glantz and Carol saw their state as the national model. The last message they would heed was the proverbial, "We're from Washington, and we're here to help you." As Carol was fond of saying, "We need a *national* strategy, not a *federal* strategy."

For Matt, Washington was not nearly so bleak a political environment. He had reason to have more faith in the possibilities of the federal process. Before working for tobacco control, he had been a civil rights advocate. It had been the White House and Congress—overriding the segregationist states of the South—that had responded to the civil rights movement. He had also been witness to the Nader-inspired and Nader-led national consumer movement, which had achieved in the 1960s and 1970s a series of strong federal consumer protection laws, including the auto safety law that had effectively lowered death rates from auto crashes. And Matt had been witness to the effectiveness of strong federal regulators, including the Federal Trade Commission, which he served, and which he helped aggressively challenge corporate power.

In 1984, Matt had led the first tobacco control lobbying campaign that succeeded in overcoming the determined resistance of the tobacco lobby—the campaign to strengthen and rotate the warning labels. However modestly incremental this improvement was, and despite its failure to include the critical warning of tobacco addiction, it nonetheless demonstrated to Matt that the industry was not unbeatable in Congress.

Matt was comfortable operating in Washington. He had access to effective allies in Congress, like Henry Waxman and Ted Kennedy, who could be counted upon to effectively blow the whistle and resist lobby-driven bills. He had worked with and respected both the White House staff responsible for domestic policy and the senior health policy officials at the Department of Health and Human Services. Clinton and Gore could be counted upon, he was convinced, if not to press for the strongest tobacco control law imaginable, then at least to resist any Republican Trojan horse. Matt himself had the ear of watchful and largely sympathetic journalists on the tobacco beat and editorial writers in Washington. In short, Matt was, if not optimistic about congressional action, at least less fearful of the worst than Glantz or Carol.

While Matt admired the progress California had made, he also noted that, notwithstanding the resources poured into tobacco control in that state, the percentage of teenagers who, when asked whether they had smoked a cigarette during the previous month, had bottomed out at around 20 percent and even appeared to be on the rise again. And while California, along with Massachusetts, was at the apex of tobacco control among the states, most other states lagged far behind and lacked strong advocates for change. Indeed, America was becoming increasingly divided between a handful of tobacco control–rich states and the vast majority of tobacco control–poor states, where little progress was in sight. For Matt, a critical missing link in tobacco control was FDA regulation of the safety and addictive properties of cigarettes, as well as of the industry's marketing and advertising practices—constitutionally possible only through Congress—and massive funding for national counter-advertising in all the states.

To be sure, all three advocates had worked together to mobilize support for Kessler's FDA initiatives. But Glantz and Carol had far less interest—or faith—in federal regulation. They considered Kessler an aberration in Washington, whose like would not appear again. They had no faith that Congress would do anything but gut FDA's authority if the agency ever initiated truly aggressive regulation. They had little faith that Clinton would either strongly or effectively defend FDA authority, and little faith that any future FDA commissioner and president would undertake the radical regulation of cigarettes' properties. They would happily support FDA regulation if nothing of value had to be traded for it. But if there were to be a heavy price, better by far to stay the course in the successful pursuit of local regulation than to launch a grand federal scheme that would raise false hopes and expectations and leach the energy from local campaigns.

Carol also believed deeply that the fundamental social change needed to exorcise tobacco use from communities had to come "from the bottom up," starting with a community consensus that action must be taken. For her, local clean-indoor-air or billboard-removal campaigns served a dual purpose: they were worthy policy goals in themselves, and, more importantly, they provided the opportunity for mobilizing the community to internalize the reduction of tobacco use as a shared community goal.

There were other strategic differences. Matt viewed the focus on kids as the strategic entry point that would open the political process to policies that would serve to reduce tobacco use among adults as well. Polls and politicians equally yawned at adult smoking. But when David Kessler branded tobacco use among children "a pediatric disease," he struck a responsive chord. Afterward, there would hardly be a congressional speech in support of comprehensive tobacco control legislation that did not begin with the incantation that three thousand children become addicted to smoking every day and a third of them will die from that addiction.

But Carol was convinced that decrying smoking among children is precisely the message that drives rebellious teenagers to smoke. Glantz was equally convinced that the concentration by Matt and others on tobacco use among kids plays into the industry's hands. "We don't want kids to smoke" is the constant refrain of the tobacco companies, and they had begun to offer and support various codes of behavior to reduce youth smoking, which had some surface appeal. They were perfectly willing to spend millions to trumpet the notion that "cigarette smoking is an adult habit." They would never, except under compulsion, utter the warning, "Cigarette smoking is a *killing* habit." So Glantz feared that politicians from the White House down would be seduced into accepting a glossy but ineffective industry-sponsored anti-youth smoking program, and that advocates who concentrated on the problem of tobacco and youth would be foreclosed from effectively opposing it.

There were also differences in temperament. Glantz has always been most comfortable as a guerilla warrior, not a negotiator; and needed the industry as permanent enemy. Carol has valued movement building and democratic decision making above even the achievement of specific policy objectives. Matt has been, if not more pragmatic, then more deliberative, more comfortable with incremental victories—especially large increments. Matt is lawyerly, patient. He speaks deliberately, in well-formed paragraphs. He can sound rabbinical—at worst, pompous. In boisterous contrast, words come cascading out of Glantz and Carol. (No stern invocation to Stan to limit a talk to twenty minutes has ever yielded one of less than forty, punctuated on more than one occasion by the need physically to wrest the microphone from him.) Reason is Matt's medium; passion is Carol's; passion laced with sarcasm is Glantz's. Glantz's unbuttoned orange cardigan is his badge of outsider status. Matt's fashion idiosyncrasy takes the odd form of a dedication to short-sleeved dress shirts—even in the dead of winter. But they are unvaryingly Oxford blue with button-down collars—the short sleeves invisible with his lobbyist's blue blazer covering them—conservative on the outside, with an independent core.

Carol had leadership issues with Matt, perhaps best illustrated by her reaction to my admiring account in *Giant Killers* of how Matt, in 1984, had successfully lobbied for stronger label warnings only by circumventing the cramped vision and operational rigidities of the troika of health agency bureaucrats who governed the Coalition on Smoking OR Health.

> When I go back and read your book, *Giant Killers,* where you cite Matt to exemplify wonderful leadership, I'm appalled. He went around the back of the coalition, because they were a bunch of stupid nincompoops who weren't going to go anywhere. I must confess to seeing the voluntaries that way myself on occasion.
>
> Strengthening the warning labels maybe saved a half a life, I don't know. I'll give you that much. Big deal. But the tactics that he was willing to employ, and that you were willing to applaud, go against all of my principles. Just because you're in a coalition that's marching to the beat of the slowest drummer and it's incredibly frustrating, you cannot use the name of these groups as if you've got them when you don't in fact have their heart and their soul with you. To see one man—or one woman—think that he's the lone ranger I object to.

Matt demurs: "Julia's not right. The coalition knew what I was doing, and while decision-making around what to support was sometimes the result of intense debate, I never went behind their backs. I may have been the wind that pushed their sails, but never the private deal maker."

Though Julia and Matt liked and respected one another, the seeds of future disharmony can be seen in their different visions of the right strategies for tobacco control and especially in their divergent views of the appropriate role of movement leaders. Indeed, Carol refused to acknowledge Matt as "a leader," only "a lobbyist," and a lobbyist prone to stray undemocratically beyond his mandate, at that. Matt was not embarrassed to be labeled a lobbyist. He surely considered himself no less committed a fighter for public health and justice than Stan and Julia. But he was prepared for justified compromise. Compromise was not part of Glantz's or Carol's emotional wiring.

"Everyone" Agreed!

Matt's hopes for the November 18, 1996, consensus-seeking meeting were modest: "I had no faith that the public health community was prepared to make choices or that they had thought through their priorities. But I believed, perhaps naively, that if we could cut through the rhetoric, we could develop—not a full consensus, because there's no such thing in our community—but a pretty broad consensus."

However modest Matt's goals, the meeting was not to reach them; it fell midway between a missed opportunity and a disaster.

At the outset, Stan Glantz and Julia Carol made manifest, by their body language and the deliberate way they positioned themselves at the table before saying a word, that they were there to place their bodies and souls in the path of any talk of compromise. Stan occupied the center of the table; Julia took one end. As Matt ruefully recalled, "Lest anyone be fearful about Stan's ability to dominate, Julia could drill you down at the other end." He went on: "Stan skillfully took the floor and drew very harsh rhetorical lines as an advocate: you were for good (no compromise) or you were for evil (compromise)—as opposed to a substantive debate about the issues. Stan almost single-handedly cowed others."

But Glantz and Carol did evoke a responsive chord in several others at the meeting, especially on the issue of civil justice and opposition to any liability protection for the tobacco industry. Matt was jarred by an opening salvo from the current president of the American Lung Association, a passionate volunteer who spoke of the moral imperative that the tobacco companies be held accountable at law for their crimes and that the rights of their victims not be extinguished

Such feelings were to be expected from Allison Zieve, the Public Citizen litigator, reflecting Ralph Nader's searing vision that of the three branches of government entrusted with the public welfare, two—the Congress and the presidency—had been bought and bonded by corporate campaign money, leaving the courts and the tort liability system as the single uncorrupted bulwark against corporate hegemony. And if the tobacco industry—that emblem of corporate mass murder—were to be granted any form of immunity, the floodgates would open wide to wash away legal accountability for all lesser corporate criminals. But the outpouring of such feelings from a Lung Association volunteer was a signal that a pragmatic weighing of public health priorities, and a balancing of public health against civil justice goals, was a threshold many of Matt's colleagues—not just Glantz, Carol, and the Naderites—could not cross.

In desperation, toward the close of the meeting, Matt offered a hypothetical settlement in which *every* serious tobacco control public health policy that was advocated by the movement was agreed to by the industry, in return for a large cash settlement of all the lawsuits against them. He asked if there was a consensus that such an agreement would be acceptable. Carol was the first to respond: "I can't think of anything wrong with your hypothetical." Then she paused, and added. "But I'd be against it." It was clear Carol was struggling. She had difficulty articulating precisely *why* she would be against it.

Glantz jumped in, on the attack. His opposition wasn't based on public health arguments; it wasn't Public Citizen's argument for preserving the integrity of the civil justice system. It was, essentially, the rhetoric of the successful guerilla warrior: "You fight the bastards to the bitter end, and whoever's left standing, wins." As Stan would later refine this argument:

> The fundamental reality of tobacco is that the way to beat them is to beat them, not to make a deal with them. I have never found a single instance anywhere, anywhere, where a compromise with the industry served the public health. Never. So my general strategy is to look at whatever they don't like, whatever they're fighting the hardest, and run straight at it.
>
> If you were Captain Picard on the starship *Enterprise* and searched the whole universe for the place where the tobacco industry was the most powerful, it would be under that dome downtown, in the United States Congress. They're there in large part because of the tobacco industry. And when you're a ragtag bunch of guerrillas, you don't go charging to the Pentagon if you're an insurgent and expect to come out in one piece. The reason a local ordinance strategy has worked so well is because our side has a sort of fixed small amount of resources we can muster, and it's enough to win one community at a time.

There were however, other, more tentative, voices. Nancy Kaufman of The Robert Wood Johnson Foundation, a veteran public health advocate and a shrewd observer, recalls: "There was a lot of conflict at that meeting, and as I look back, I was very conflicted. I did not speak out with a strong position, one way or the other, because one part of me was saying, 'Yeah! The benefits would be terrific.' And the other part of me was saying, 'Why would you ever dance with the devil?' "

Still others at the meeting listened quietly, keeping their thoughts to themselves. There was no formal consensus-seeking process. Dick Daynard, who had co-convened the meeting with Matt, recalls: "I don't think I expressed an opinion 'on the merits.' I was most concerned then (as now) about process and keeping the movement together, so I probably restated what I took to be the consensus of the meeting, which was 'no liability concessions of any sort, unless and until the group meets again and decides differently.' I understood that some participants were happier than others about that conclusion, but nonetheless I thought it was the conclusion that had been reached, and I most probably articulated that thought at that time."

In the following days and months, Matt would have one interpretation for what took place at this meeting; Carol and Glantz quite another.

Characteristically, Matt prepared and sent to the participants a very carefully written, one might say lawyerly, summary of the "shared consensus" that emerged at the meeting. It fairly enumerated the litany of concerns about negotiations with the industry, the inability to predict the best long-term solutions, the value of maintaining the ongoing litigation, legislative advocacy, and controversy, concluding, "All of these issues were reflected in a strong group sentiment that it is premature to be pushing a global legislative solution." But the memo contained this cautionary note: "The strong sentiment against a rush to a legislative solution was tempered but not altered by the risks that accompany the current threats to the tobacco industry. . . . It was agreed that these concerns bear close watching to be certain that the public health community does not misjudge the opportunities/risks, but that we should also avoid the traditional inclination to compromise for too little too quickly."

Matt comments on his strategy: "My notes were a political document. They were carefully crafted to strongly reflect the general sentiment and yet accurately reflect what I knew were the understated views of a large number of people at that meeting. If you read the notes carefully, you will see that they leave openings for compromise. They may be too coy, in that respect. I also didn't want to send out a set of notes that were going to prompt abusive responses. I didn't think that would be constructive at that point in time."

Stan, in contrast, was to cite this meeting with a characteristically broad sweep. Five months after the meeting, in an electronic broadside to activists, he enjoined them all: "Remember October [he meant November]: Last October, there was a meeting at which *everyone* felt that *any* kind of Congressional global deal would end up being bad for public health."

7

The Real Leadership?

Matt Myers left the New York meeting "incredibly frustrated:"

> I didn't walk away from the meeting—as Stan and Julia did—with the impression that the whole room agreed. I walked away believing that there was a significant segment in Stan and Julia's camp. But there was another significant segment who were struggling with the issues; who, but for Stan and Julia's presence, might or might not have come down in the same place, but would at least have engaged in a different dialogue getting there. This failed effort was a precursor of the power of the strongest voices to frighten everybody else to silence.
>
> I walked away from that meeting saying to myself, we're going to have a very hard time having the open, constructive dialogue that we, as a movement, have to have. I walked away realizing that, in our larger community, we were not going to be able to do that. That was the failure of the meeting, the *crime* of the meeting.

Back in Washington, Matt shared his misgivings with Bill Novelli, the president of the National Center for Tobacco-Free Kids. Novelli was impatient; he had little respect for Glantz and Carol, whom he viewed as unthinking zealots. And he thought Matt's effort to engage them in a constructive dialogue was not only futile but endowed them with more legitimacy and power than their status in public health dictated. As Novelli viewed them, Carol spoke only for an insignificant band of ragtag activists, of whom dozens, at most, were actively engaged, while Glantz, unaffiliated, spoke for Glantz.

Both Novelli and Matt agreed that the effort to stimulate a thoughtful dialogue, face hard choices, and seek a reasoned consensus had to continue. Matt recalls: "I knew we were going to have important choices to make—core questions, such as the balance between righting the wrongs of the past, and preserving lives in the future—and I felt strongly that it was an abdication of responsibility to take the easy path and do nothing but oppose. I wasn't prepared to do that."

To Novelli, the answer was obvious: the real leadership of the tobacco control movement resided with the duly constituted heads of the
major public health voluntary associations, most centrally the American Cancer Society and the American Heart Association. Each of their
CEOs was responsive to a board of trustees elected by an assembly of
delegates from the state and local divisions, and both served on the
governing board of the Center for Tobacco-Free Kids.

Matt could not disagree. The CEOs, John Seffrin of the Cancer Society and Dudley Hafner of the Heart Association, were veterans of
the tobacco wars as bloodied as Glantz and Carol—though, set beside
Stan Glantz and Julia Carol, these corporate-style chief executive officers could only be colored the conservative gray of essentially conservative organizations. In the not so distant past, their predecessors
were scorned by public interest advocates as paying lip service to advocacy while keeping the throttle only on those activities that drove
the fund-raising engine.

In the mid-1960s, when a rambunctious law student named John
Banzhaf petitioned the Federal Communications Commission to require mandatory health counter-advertisements to the then pervasive
cigarette commercials, the American Cancer Society (ACS) balked at
supporting what its leadership viewed as unseemly aggressiveness for
an organization that prided itself on being a safe haven for corporate
philanthropy—not on supporting Ralph Nader–style, anticorporate ac-
tivism. The first World Conference on Tobacco OR Health in 1966,
vigorous but decorous, was bankrolled by ACS. Banzhaf came, unin-
vited, asked to borrow a typewriter in the society's press room, then
proceeded to type out a press release excoriating ACS for its cowardly
lack of resolve. The cold response of the society's then CEO, Lane
Adams, was to decree a flat ban on *any* activist advocacy, a ban that
endured for nearly a decade.

There was little in the background or demeanor of Adams's 1990s
successor, John Seffrin, to suggest that his leadership would be any
different. While Stan Glantz flaunted his flamboyant orange sweater
on the most formal occasions, John Seffrin has been suspected of wear-
ing a tie and his dark, impeccably tailored suits to bed. His earlier professional career was as a health educator at Indiana University, a
nonthreatening vocation in the American heartland. As a dedicated volunteer for the Cancer Society, he would trek from high school to high
school, earnestly exhorting students on the risks of tobacco use. And
he wrote extensively, his papers carrying such titles as "Making Smok-

ing Education Relevant to the School-Age Child" and "Patient Education on Smoking: The Dentist's Role." To be sure, his was an early voice within ACS for placing a high priority on tobacco use as a critical issue in cancer control, but his focus was educating youth, not launching a holy war against the tobacco industry. His selection by a cautious search committee to succeed a CEO who had distinguished himself as an autocrat was seen by all as a safe choice, no threat to the nonconfrontational culture of ACS.

That proved an illusion. John Seffrin's first defining act as CEO was to take $250,000 out of a discretionary fund set aside for emergencies and send it to the Massachusetts division. The volunteer and staff leadership in Massachusetts had uncharacteristically taken an aggressive lead in support of a state ballot initiative to raise the tobacco excise by twenty-five cents and dedicate the revenues to an all-out tobacco control campaign. The tobacco lobby had allocated millions to mount a counteroffensive adverting blitz, buying up a goodly segment of Massachusetts's public relations, political talent, and airtime. The pro-initiative campaign desperately needed an infusion of unfettered cash to put the lie to the industry's propaganda. Seffrin responded and, in so doing, deliberately circumvented an ACS standing rule against paid advertising. (The society's fund-raisers, its ruling class, had feared that once the society had *paid* for advertising, the radio and television stations that gave free "public service" time for fund-raising appeals would start charging.)

John Seffrin proceeded to revolutionize the internal structure of ACS. The society had never measured the impact of its sprawling activities, from driving cancer patients to their medical appointments to distributing educational pamphlets. ACS carefully counted the numbers of pamphlets distributed, but never the *ultimate* impact of all its activities on reducing morbidity and death from cancer.

In 1994, Seffrin convened a working group of volunteers and experts, ranging from public interest advocates who had decried the society's passivity in the face of mounting evidence of the impact of heavily advertised processed and high-fat fast foods and chemical pollution on cancer incidence, to Defense Department researchers exploring the wonders of nuclear medicine and exploring the genetic map. Following the direction of a slyly subversive "futures" planner, Clem Bezold, these participants were randomly assigned to small working groups and charged with agreeing on target percentages by which cancer could be reduced by the year 2013—the one hundredth anniversary of ACS. The groups were told to list the five most effective strategies for reaching those targets—and the percentage decrease that each could reasonably achieve.

Under this concrete challenge, out the door went even the most exotic new surgery techniques, the new wonder drugs being tested in mass trials, and the imagined destinations of the genetic-mapping quest. As each group reported, the reduction in tobacco use led every list, and the estimated percentage of spared misery and death that would flow from this reduction dwarfed all the rest. The other priority strategies also reflected less glamorous—and more politically edgy—strategies, such as universal access to early screening and cancer treatment for the poor. Lane Adams would not have been happy. The priority strategies were all *advocacy* strategies.

Such futures-planning exercises are commonly trumpeted and promptly shelved. But John Seffrin made the suggested strategies a guiding light. He set about transforming ACS from a collective of bureaucratic sinecures into the infrastructure of a powerful citizens' advocacy movement, building a core of professional advocacy experts and providing the resources and commitment for mobilizing the hundreds of thousands of cancer control volunteers as a powerful grassroots force.

Seffrin enshrined policy "advocacy" as a banner headline in the ACS lexicon and, with the support of a small group of like-minded volunteers, gave it respectability. At his urging the board designated "advocacy" as one of the society's five "strategic directions," on a par with research, cancer control, public information, and even fund-raising.

When Seffrin became CEO, the American Cancer Society had a small Washington "public issues" office, a couple of lobbyists, someone to answer state division questions about legislation, and not much more. By 1997, Seffrin had ratcheted the society's overall budget for advocacy from $1 million up to $6.5 million. It would go to $8 million in 1998 and 1999. That brought greatly expanded policy analysis, grassroots mobilizing, advocacy training, strategic media, a field team of seasoned community organizers, and greater lobbying capacity. Much of the D.C. office's energy was focused on tobacco control advocacy. And if that wasn't enough, Seffrin convinced his board to commit an additional $2 million a year to support Bill Novelli's and Matt Myers's work at the National Center for Tobacco-Free Kids—a commitment that, in turn, helped convince The Robert Wood Johnson Foundation board that *their* foundation's contribution of $5 million a year to the yet untested Center would be a sound public health investment.

John Seffrin was serious about advocacy. John Seffrin was serious about tobacco control advocacy—so serious that he was prepared to stand up in support of activists such as Stan Glantz, as he did when he took the risk of alienating the chair of the powerful House Appropriations subcommittee that controlled appropriations for cancer research, denouncing the cut of a tobacco-oriented Glantz research grant from the National Cancer Institute engineered by the tobacco lobby.

Dudley Hafner had been chief executive officer of the American Heart Association (AHA) for nearly thirty years. Strong and surefooted, he had secured the unshakable confidence of AHA's governing volunteers and the dedication of AHA staff. He matched John Seffrin in his zeal for tobacco control and his efforts to light the fires of advocacy in an organization that, like the Cancer Society, had viewed its mission as raising funds for research and non-confrontational public education.

In 1980, he had taken the lead in forging the difficult but essential alliance among Heart, Cancer, and Lung to develop the Coalition on Smoking OR Health as a serious Washington counterweight to the tobacco lobby, and he had consistently supported aggressive advocacy by the coalition.

When Heart Association lobbyist Scott Ballin conceived of a plan to petition FDA to take jurisdiction and action to regulate cigarettes— a plan that most of his Washington colleagues viewed as quixotic— Hafner gave him solid support. Like Seffrin, Hafner was an engaged board member of the Center for Tobacco-Free Kids.

In December 1996, a few weeks after the cacophonous New York meeting, Matt Myers and Bill Novelli embarked on a series of one-on-one conversations and conference calls with John Seffrin, Dudley Hafner, John Garrison of the American Lung Association, Lonnie Bristow of the AMA, and Richard Hyman of the Academy of Pediatrics. Matt led the discussions but did not seek to build a consensus around a predigested formula for compromise. Rather, his goal was, as it had been in New York, to force these senior decision makers— those whom the Chinese call "responsible persons"—to *take* responsibility. Matt explains:

> I wouldn't have gone off on a crusade of my own; I absolutely wouldn't have done that—and that wasn't the goal. The goal was to say, okay, I had

tried one mechanism to get people to talk and think, and I had failed. I'm still not going to make a decision for people, but I'm going to do whatever I can to make people think through those choices. I saw this as our vital role and made it an absolute duty and obligation, because these decisions were simply too important, too fundamental, to let them be only knee-jerk reactions.

A Suspect Consensus

In a series of conference calls in December 1996 and January 1997, supplemented by one-on-one conversations, Matt Myers and Bill Novelli raised a series of hypothetical questions with the leaders of health voluntary organizations, essentially the same hypothetical questions Matt had raised in New York. Would they accept, even support, a compromise that to some extent freed the tobacco industry from civil liability for *all* its past lies and deceits, in exchange for a broad affirmative mandate from Congress that also granted FDA powers, a stiff penalty sufficient to force prices up significantly, other long-sought public health mandates, and some mechanism for holding the industry accountable for its past acts?

These conversations were intense. As Matt recalls: "In some respects I have a great deal more sympathy for how people reacted later, because it required time and energy to figure out what we really cared about, what we really thought was feasible, what our own view was of what we could accomplish, what the right tools were." The responses that emerged would have infuriated Glantz and Carol—if they had been privy to them. Matt remembers:

> It was clear from those discussions that at least the CEOs of those major organizations came at this from an entirely different approach than the sentiment that had dominated in that November meeting [in New York]. John Seffrin wasn't alone or out of the mainstream at all in advancing the notion that if there really was an opportunity to bring about major change in these core areas, that had to be seriously explored.
>
> The responses that we were getting were extraordinarily favorable. Yet what we were talking about was significantly less than what would later be on the table. To a person, the reaction at the time was euphoric on their part. And the liability issue wasn't a lightning rod at all.

To a person, that is, except for John Garrison, head of the American Lung Association, who was not so much opposed as distracted. In contrast to Seffrin of the Cancer Society or Hafner of the Heart Association, who were personally committed and deeply knowledgeable on tobacco control issues, Garrison up to that time had largely delegated responsibility for tobacco issues and followed the lead of his Washington office staff. As Matt remembers: "Garrison was fundamentally uninterested. It wasn't like he sat on the phone and later raised objections. He was just fundamentally uninterested."

By early February 1997 Matt was able to craft for the CEO group a draft titled "Statement of Core Principles for the Consideration of the Resolution of Current Outstanding Tobacco Issues." To the unpracticed eye, these principles appear identical to the principles asserted in Matt's memo memorializing the consensus at the November meeting. That is, they unequivocally warn Congress "not to cut short the opportunity for real progress by compromises that promise much, but accomplish little," as in the past. They run through the usual litany of advocates' demands, from broad FDA regulatory powers to full public disclosure of internal industry documents. And they affirm: "The rights of victims of the tobacco industry to be justly compensated for the injuries they have suffered should not be abridged and the tobacco industry should not be immunized from accountability for its own wrongdoing."

But to the wary eye, the precise wording of these principles opened a crack in the wall holding back congressional mischief in three ways:

1. The principles left room for legislation restricting civil actions against the companies—restrictions that some advocates would view as a form of "immunity" for the companies—while providing compensation for smokers and their families afflicted with smoking-caused disease, perhaps through a plan such as workers' compensation, that could be seen to "justly" compensate the victims of the tobacco industry.

2. In the text supporting the principles, the statement excoriates efforts by the industry to escape "immunity from *future* wrongdoing," leaving unsaid whether a penalty and compensation scheme might also grant the industry immunity from its *past* wrongdoing.

3. The statement contemplated the *possibility* that Congress might act. It did so by indirection, that is, by enjoining Congress not to

act *unless* a consensus could be reached that addresses all key public health goals without infringing on the rights of tobacco's victims.

As is the way of this world, as soon as Matt had circulated this draft statement to the CEOs and they in turn began to share it with their public issues staffs, the copy machines whirred, and the faxes beeped, and the e-mail surged. Glantz caught wind of the draft principles and demanded that Matt share the draft with him. Matt delayed responding. Glantz followed up, on March 14, with an e-mail note, reminding Matt that Glantz's intelligence-gathering network was a match for the CIA's:

> I am very disappointed that you have decided to ignore my request to see your principles.
>
> Two different people, neither on the distribution list, have sent them to me unsolicited.
>
> It looks to me like you are limiting distribution to people who will agree with you, not the broad consultation that everyone agreed to undertake in New York.

Two hours later, Julia Carol also e-mailed Matt:

> Matt,
> Working together as a team, yet from different coasts, and while we're all over-swamped makes it easy for miscommunication and misperceptions to happen. I'm holding on to that notion as well as how highly I respect you, your integrity, your judgment, and your work.
>
> I must say, though, that I am getting pretty frustrated. I do have a copy of the secret documents . . . I don't know why they're secret, I'm not sure I have the latest copy, and I'm not happy about not knowing why I couldn't get them from you.
>
> I also heard a rumor that you met one week ago with a bunch of AG's . . . I'd like to know what happened.
>
> I'm not sure whether you still care about ANR's position, but I've spoken with many members of my board (I recognize that this one is much too important to leave as a staff driven item and that's rare for us, but that's an indication of how strongly everyone on our board—and in OUR community—feels about this) and they seem to agree that its fine to have core principles, as long as enough minds make sure they're as air-tight as possible, but they should NOT be presented as principles we want to see if there's a global settlement. That's the wrong message.

. . . I think we should release a strong set of core principles, couched as the reason why we DON'T want a Global Settlement, making sure we're clear that we're not opposed to individual settlements. Or even settlements by all of the AG's if its just involving those cases. Basically, we want Congress to stay out of it—We don't want the FDA messed with at all, and we don't want any other public limitations on public health policy or regulation.

I know you're probably busier than ever—but there needs to be a mechanism for updates and dialogue on what's happening here. Otherwise, the tension is going to keep growing, rumors are going to keep flying, and we'll end up being very uncoordinated, with relationships at risk. I don't think this needs to happen.

I want to continue talking to you about this, whether or not we agree. It's important for our side to dialogue and debate, don't you think?

So—I consider this message going from an ally to an ally—please remove the veil of secrecy, ok?

Julia

Two days later, Matt responded:

A) I do care about ANR's position. B) I haven't ignored you or your views. I value them. C) I have been out a good deal lately due to the illness and then the death of my wife's father. D) I have been testing out a series of ideas to see what people might be able to agree upon, if anything, and have been using several people as initial sounding boards, but may never do anything with it if there is no consensus. No one will be end runned by my effort and you will not read about it first in public before you are consulted. E) I do speak with various AG's off and on about a variety of matters, generally related to their pending cases. Nothing nefarious here— just my effort to keep them focused on public health goals and to build the type of trusting relationship that I hope will keep us all in good stead when we need them. While they are by and large very good people, don't assume that they are all white knights who will fall on their swords for our issues without a lot of helpful coaxing and education.

I appreciate your concerns. To date, I have been able to stay on top of the various frightening rumors and like to think that my efforts have helped prevent them from turning into disasters for us or our goals. I don't think I have ever sold out anyone before and I don't intend to start now. I am also not so arrogant as to think I know all of the answers but do think my efforts can help make sure our views are heard effectively at critical times and that is my goal.

On March 16, when Matt wrote this e-mail letter, indeed, nothing "nefarious" *was* happening. In Mississippi, Dick Scruggs and Mike Moore continued to look for new openings for settlement, but no serious new proposals were floating; no negotiations with the industry were going on. Still, Carol was right to be wary. Settlement was in the air. And whether Matt would follow through on his pledge that "no one will be end runned by my effort and you will not read about it first in public before you are consulted" remained to be seen.

Guess Who's Coming to Dinner

The first call came in late March, just before April Fool's Day, from George Mitchell—former federal judge, Maine senator, Senate Democratic majority leader, international peacemaker, and symbol of rectitude. Mitchell had been recruited by Washington's latest bulging firm of influential "rainmakers," Verner, Liipfert, Bernhard, McPherson & Hand, which was well on its way to becoming Washington's most generously remunerated tobacco lobby. Matt was in no hurry to return the call ("I knew why he was calling, already"), but they eventually connected. The call was painful. Mitchell, who hardly needed an introduction, introduced himself. He affirmed that he had been retained by the tobacco industry, noted that he had never worked for the tobacco industry before, swore that he had no sympathy for the tobacco industry, and reminded Matt how good his record had been in Congress on tobacco issues. "It wasn't true," Matt recalls reminding himself.

Mitchell told Matt that he had agreed to represent the tobacco companies only after they had convinced him that they not only were ready to negotiate with public health advocates, but were fully prepared to accept fundamental changes in the way they did business. He asked only that Matt accept a call from his partner, Berl Bernhard.

Matt was not impressed:

I have always admired George Mitchell, but I told him I was highly skeptical; that I had been around long enough to see these tobacco industry overtures, time and time again; and that they had always been complete smoke screens designed to avoid governmental action.

This may say much about my lack of deference, my irreverence, but I also cautioned him, saying, "I'm sure you've thought about your role in this, but there have been a number of other prominent former public officials who thought they could do the bidding of the tobacco industry and accomplish something useful. And in every one of those cases they ended up tainting their personal reputations instead."

He didn't respond, and I remember thinking, "How humiliating! Here was someone of his stature, not calling to talk substance, but just calling to say, 'Will you take a phone call from my law partner?'" That may have been a terribly unkind reaction, but that was my reaction to the call. Still, I answered, "Sure, I'll talk to anyone."

Bernhard, staff director of the historic U.S. Civil Rights Commission, opened his call to Matt with what was becoming a ritual claim of personal distaste for the tobacco industry and ended with a request that Matt meet with him and a few colleagues. Again, Matt agreed. "The idea of not listening is one that's alien to me. I'm not easily intimidated; I'm not going to be easily coaxed. Why should I be afraid to walk into a room with industry lawyers?"

Bernhard arrived the next day with his partner Harry McPherson, the former right-hand advisor to Lyndon Johnson, and Jane Hickey, a veteran aide to former Texas governor Ann Richards—now, too, a member of the Verner, Liipfert firm. Once again, each began with an apology: "It was a little bizarre because they each felt the need to re-cite this pledge, how they hate the tobacco industry. Bernhard said he had convened a family meeting and explained to his family why he was doing this. It was just sanctimonious, but it was interesting that they absolutely felt the need to justify themselves."

They made their pitch. They insisted that this time the companies' overtures were indeed "different;" they were prepared to make concessions they had never before contemplated. Bernhard vowed that he would not be there representing them if he hadn't been convinced that this was true. "And besides, they're paying him a ton of money," Matt remembers thinking.

Then Matt proceeded to chronicle for them, in detail, the devious history of smoke-screen settlements that had consistently characterized all previous industry pleas for peace. He told them that he wasn't prepared to waste his time as party to yet another illusory industry "reform." And he insisted that they needed to get from the industry some concrete commitment on key issues before he'd be persuaded that this time was, indeed, "different." When he hadn't heard back from them in a few days, he assumed that his intransigence had chilled the industry's initiative—or at least canceled his invitation to participate in any negotiations. He was wrong.

Matt had been hearing regularly from Dick Scruggs, Mississippi attorney general Mike Moore's lawyer. Scruggs and Moore had remained undeterred in their eagerness to craft a settlement acceptable to all. They continued to seek common ground with the other attorneys general and the trial lawyers who also were plaguing the industry with their private class action lawsuits. And they continued to send lobbyists John Sears and Tommy Anderson, the industry's phantom intermediaries, new versions of their "term sheet," their proposed settlement outline, and to get back indirect reactions from the industry leaders. By February, these leaders had sent word that they were prepared to raise the settlement payments from $150 billion to $250 billion over twenty-five years, and to make further concessions in complying with the FDA rules. But they remained adamantly opposed to accepting broad FDA regulation.

Why did Scruggs feel it necessary to deal with Matt, after Matt had slammed his earlier proposal? Despite that conflict, they had grown to respect each other. Matt was convinced that Scruggs genuinely sought to achieve what the public health community wanted. And Scruggs had found Matt helpful in gaining the public health groups' support for the two earlier Liggett settlements.

But Scruggs also could not circumvent Matt, even if he found Matt unreasonable in his demands. As we've seen, Bruce Lindsay, the president's close advisor and the White House point man on tobacco, had been impressed by Matt's insistence that the earlier settlement brokered by Scruggs and Moore would have outraged and alienated the entire public health community—one of the few communities that had unreservedly hailed Clinton as a champion. Lindsay had told Moore and Scruggs that no new deal could be supported by the president without support from the public health community, and, to the White House, Matt Myers was the initial barometer. So Scruggs, despite his unhappiness and frustration with Matt ("I would describe our relationship as something of a roller coaster," says Matt), had persisted through the winter in bringing Matt each new marginally improved term sheet; and Matt had, just as persistently, rejected each of them as not good enough. He had told Julia Carol the truth: in mid-March, no serious negotiations were taking place.

On March 21, 1997, the industry suffered a serious setback in the second of two settlements with the Liggett tobacco group. Among other key concessions, Bennett LeBow, on behalf of Liggett, publicly admitted what all the companies had long denied—what the secret industry documents released by LeBow proved—that Liggett had all along lied to the American public, including the Congress. The three explosive lies:

- We at Liggett know and acknowledge that . . . cigarette smoking causes health problems, including lung cancer, heart and vascular disease, and emphysema.
- We at Liggett also acknowledge that nicotine is addictive.
- Liggett acknowledges that the tobacco industry markets products to "youth," which means those under eighteen years of age.

Moore was rightly ecstatic. He told the *New York Times* on April 16, "I've been a prosecutor all my life. I know what happens when one of the five turns state's evidence. We've got the goods on 98% of the industry by turning the little guy."

The settlement announcement generated almost as much celebratory publicity as if Philip Morris itself had caved in, creating the misleading public impression that the tobacco industry dominoes were all in line ready to fall to the crusading attorneys general. Wall Street again panicked, and many tobacco control leaders were giddy with anticipation.

Not Matt, and not the attorneys general's sober counselor, Jim Tierney: "The public health community saw the publicity and the apparent ease of Liggett's caving, and said, 'Hey, we've got them on the run; those AG cases must be pretty powerful.' But *we* were never fooled about the strength of our cases."

The settlement did give the attorneys general and the trial lawyers access to a treasure trove of potentially incriminating, hitherto secret, industry documents—not just Liggett's. It also gave political impetus to twenty more attorneys general to file suit, and it spooked the companies, as well as, once more, their jittery Wall Street investors. The industry pursuit of a settlement had suddenly become even more intense.

Soon after Matt had sent George Mitchell and his partners away, Scruggs called to say that White House aide Bruce Lindsay wanted Matt, with Scruggs, Moore, and a representative of the class action trial lawyers, to meet with Phil Carlton. Carlton was a former North Carolina supreme court judge, close to both North Carolina's Democratic governor Jim Hunt and White House chief of staff Erskine Bowles. In a meeting with President Clinton in December, Hunt had urged Clinton to take a more active role in brokering an agreement, and Clinton had unleashed Lindsay to bring the parties together. Much to Matt's discomfort, Lindsay had become an active advocate for a settlement, and Carlton was now officially negotiating for the industry.

Scruggs and Moore were no more enthusiastic than Matt about meeting with Carlton. Indeed, Scruggs initially refused. He believed that the industry would never agree to a settlement that would satisfy both the White House and the public health advocates, but that if he narrowed the gap enough through his indirect term sheet communications with both sides, the Republican leadership—especially his brother-in-law, Senate Majority Leader Trent Lott—would support the legislation, even without an industry sign-off. He calculated that Lott and House Speaker Newt Gingrich might view the notorious Republican affinity for the tobacco lobby and its campaign money as a political albatross for Republican candidates in the next congressional elections, as it had been for Republican presidential candidate Bob Dole. A good bill would drive away the albatross, take the lead in protecting children's health away from Clinton, and leave their tobacco political friends sullen but not mutinous, since tobacco had nowhere else to go.

Still, neither Scruggs and Moore, nor Matt, could afford to say no to a direct White House plea to meet with Carlton. And so they did meet, on April 1, at the Center for Tobacco-Free Kids offices. John Coale, representing the class action lawyers, also joined them. The meeting was stiff and awkward. It began with what Matt had begun to characterize as the "Bernhard speech"—the self-justification before the pitch. But Matt also confesses that he found Carlton less offensive because he was less unctuous than Mitchell, Bernhard, and company. "At least with Carlton I had the sense of okay, I know what I'm getting." By contrast, the others turned verbal handsprings to swear that they weren't doing this for the money, but as a public service.

Carlton was straightforward ("Southern, slow, folksy, slick," says Matt, "but straightforward"). He'd grown up on a tobacco farm. His family had been in tobacco farming forever. Jim Hunt was an old friend and colleague. Steve Goldstone from R. J. Reynolds had come down to North Carolina late in 1996, the previous fall, to play golf with Hunt, and to tell Hunt he wanted to put the industry's problems behind him. Hunt put him together with Carlton. Carlton told the group of his long talks with both Goldstone and Philip Morris's Geoffrey Bible. He noted that neither was among the notorious seven tobacco CEOs who had sworn under oath to Congress three years earlier that they didn't believe smoking was addictive. He said they were very different people from their predecessors, with different basic attitudes, and that they were prepared to accept radical changes in the way in which their companies did business. "Let me put it plainly: Tobacco wants to negotiate. We want peace."

Matt listened. He sensed there was some truth in Carlton's assertions, especially about Goldstone. He had read the transcript of Goldstone's testimony in a Florida trial the previous month and noted in it more candor, less evasiveness, than he had heard from any predecessor in a like position. Goldstone was also not a "tobacco man" from way back. A lawyer with a Wall Street firm, he had only been named chief executive officer of RJR in 1995. To Matt, Goldstone *seemed* to exhibit some modicum of sincerity. Still, Matt continued to be wary. "I just said to him the same thing I had said before, which was that I would always listen but remained incredibly skeptical. . . . The products that the tobacco industry makes kill thousands of people. You have a bad credibility problem."

By pre-arrangement, Mike Moore responded for the group. He, too, was hostile, skeptical, saying, as Matt recalls:

> I have a trial coming up in July. I don't have a lot of time for screwing around, and I'm not prepared to divert my attention from getting ready for trial—except if you're very, very serious. Given the time constraints, the only way I will do this is if you get the CEOs to demonstrate you're serious and we set this meeting up within the next forty-eight to seventy-two hours.
>
> I want to see the whites of their eyes—the tobacco CEOs—I want you to produce them. If you can bring the CEOs of Philip Morris and RJR to a meeting, and they say the industry is sincere in wanting peace, we'll take it from there.

Carlton said that he would be driving directly to New York when he left the meeting and would meet with Bible and Goldstone that very night.

The next day, April 2, Carlton called Scruggs. Bible and Goldstone would come to the table, and the meeting would take place the following day. It must, of course, be secret. Very secret. Scruggs called Matt. He and Moore had agreed to come; would Matt?

"Yeah."

Day One: Four Meetings, Two Directions

The secret meeting of Geoffrey Bible, Steven Goldstone, and the lawyers and state attorneys general who would form the nucleus of the negotiators was first scheduled for April 3, 1997, at 2:00 P.M. at the Sheraton Hotel in Crystal City, Virginia, across the Potomac River from D.C., and next to Washington National Airport, where the flock of tobacco company and trial lawyer private jets would descend. Matt Myers had promised to speak at a forum at American University at 11:00 A.M. organized by the American Trial Lawyers Association, to address the possibility of a global settlement—and whether or not such a settlement would be in the public interest. Again, Matt would take the opportunity to warn the lawyers of the dangers of a settlement rich in dollars but threadbare in public health protections. He and his Washington colleagues from the Cancer Society and the Heart Association had also scheduled a 2:00 P.M. briefing for supportive congressional staff to warn them of the threat of Trojan-horse compromises—bills that would cripple FDA—emanating from the Republican leadership.

Carlton and his colleagues agreed to move the starting time for the meeting back to 3:00 P.M. in part because they were so skittish about leaks that they feared that if Matt suddenly canceled his commitments, someone might get suspicious. Then Dick Scruggs and Mike Moore urged Matt to attend a "premeeting meeting" at noon, in Arlington, to structure their presentation and response to the companies.

It was not to be a calm and deliberative day.

Matt drove to American University, in D.C., persuaded the forum's moderator to let him speak first, then sat patiently through the second talk by Jim Tierney, standing in for the attorneys general. Tierney recalls: "My job at [the] American University forum was to provide public cover while the attorneys general negotiators were off formulating their strategy for the afternoon's session. I obviously couldn't do that for

Matt. The poor guy was all alone. The tobacco suits in the audience were so obvious and clueless that I went right after them. I couldn't help myself."

As soon as Tierney had finished, Matt bolted for the door: "I apologized, said I had something unexpected come up in my schedule and I had to leave early. I then got in the car and drove to Arlington for the Scruggs/Moore premeeting, had trouble finding the hotel where they were—you know, Arlington is just this sprawling blur."

The moment Matt entered the hotel suite, Scruggs swept him aside and warned him that the industry representatives were furious at him. They had already been briefed by their agents at the American University meeting of Matt's announcement that he had to leave early, and they were convinced that Matt had thereby blown the secrecy of the meeting.

The premeeting meeting had been electric with the bouncing egos of the attorneys general and the trial lawyers, who nonetheless had hammered out among themselves a format for responding. Mike Moore would represent the attorneys general first, followed by Stan Chesley of the "Castano group"—the most prominent of the class action lawyers. When Matt arrived late, they asked if he would respond as the representative of the public health community. Matt agreed but had to leave before the meeting was over.

I raced off to the Hill, literally raced off to the Hill, only got there literally on the minute because I was uniquely fortunate in finding a rare free parking place.

We did the staff briefing, at which we warned about the dangers of compromise with the tobacco industry; about the types of things the tobacco industry could propose that would sound good but that would really undermine fundamental change. I went through a list of specifics—what we were concerned about: the difference between real advertising reform and fake advertising reform; real youth access and fake youth access; real FDA jurisdiction and fake FDA jurisdiction.

Finishing, he departed as abruptly as was seemly and raced again to the Sheraton, where the industry meeting, inconspicuously heralded on the Sheraton Events Calendar simply as "Phil Carlton," had already begun.

Matt surveyed the meeting room. It held a formidable array of figures on both sides of the great divide. And that's how Matt found them aligned at the table.

On two sides of the square table sat the industry representatives: Philip Morris's chief executive officer, Geoffrey Bible; RJR's chief executive officer, Steven Goldstone; Philip Carlton; Philip Morris's veteran general counsel, Murray Bring; RJR's general counsel, Robert Sharpe; Philip Morris's senior vice president, Steven Parrish; two other Philip Morris vice presidents; George Mitchell and Jane Hickey from Verner, Liipfert; and a phalanx of industry attorneys: Herbert Wachtell, Meyer Koplow, and Arthur Golden. To the side, in the back, sat John Sears and Tommy Anderson, Trent Lott's nominated go-betweens. Facing them were Mike Moore, Dick Scruggs, and four other attorneys general who had played active roles in the litigation: Grant Woods of Arizona, Bob Butterworth of Florida, Christine Gregoire of Washington, and Dick Blumenthal of Connecticut. Gregoire was a prime representative of the skeptics among the attorneys general. Like Matt, she had told Moore: "I think this will be a waste of time. This industry would never agree to anything that would be remotely sufficient."

The Castano class action group was represented by trial lawyers John Coale, Stanley Chesley, and Hugh Rodham, brother of Hillary Rodham Clinton. Matt was the last to arrive. The others were already seated around the standard square conference table, with one seat open for Matt—two seats away from Goldstone.

With the help of his notes, Matt reconstructs the meeting—and his reactions:

> Two things hit me right off the bat: First, there was a far bigger crowd than I had anticipated. Second, Goldstone and Bible separately, but as solicitously as possible, came up, introduced themselves; made this pitch about how they had looked forward to meeting me; how they were looking forward to working with me; how they knew all about the work that I had done and that they respected it.
>
> That took me somewhat aback. It wasn't just, "Hi, I'm . . ." Of course, I shouldn't have been surprised. They are the CEOs of these gigantic organizations. They clearly had briefing books on everybody there.

The CEOs then introduced all their participants—introductions that had an eerie resonance for Matt. Though several of the names were unfamiliar and he would have trouble keeping them straight, others belonged to people he had long battled indirectly but never faced. George Mitchell had already given a brief, somber introduction.

The lineup was then Bible, next Goldstone. Bible began with the same theme as Mitchell: "This is a different era; we are different people." He vowed that he and Goldstone were united in their desire to find, in his phrase, "a fair, comprehensive solution." He said, "We're here in good faith. We're prepared to address all the matters that concern you. And we are prepared to make fundamental change in the manner in which we do business."

I remember thinking to myself, "He's good; he's very good. He seems incredibly sincere." It felt as if he was looking right at me, and I wondered whether everyone else was feeling that he was looking right at them.

And then I asked myself, "Now, okay, how much of this is real? And how much of this is bullshit? And how do I figure it out?"

Then Goldstone went on. My reactions to Goldstone were different. Goldstone seemed to me an extraordinarily bright, articulate but relatively straightforward guy. I had a sense of "what you see is what you get" with Goldstone, more than with Bible.

He was less flowery, less rehearsed sincerity in his voice, but straightforward. He echoed Bible's statements that they were prepared to make fundamental change. But he also posed a broader question, which was that one of the issues that we would need to come to grips with was our views on the acceptability of cigarettes being sold—so long as they were sold honestly and openly in commerce to adults. He posed that as a question that we were all going to have to figure out. His pitch was they wanted to get past the current era and enter a new era where they could lawfully sell their products, so long as they were honest about them. And he was straightforward, that was his goal.

Although I didn't write it down, I recall that he said, "We want to put behind us all of the fighting and all of the disputes of the past and move forward to a different era."

There were no specifics in what either of them said of any sort whatsoever. I later learned that was by agreement. That was the script for the day. That had been discussed in advance between Carlton and Scruggs.

Mike Moore responded firmly. Among his responses: "Don't waste our time. We want a reduction in teen smoking. We want the public health to change. We want you to tell the truth." Moore was followed by Stanley Chesley representing the class action attorneys.

But Matt was only partially listening. He was hastily scribbling notes on what he would say. He'd had no time to outline it earlier. Of course, he had been giving constant thought for months to the demands he and the attorneys general should make, but not to the dynamics of any interaction with Goldstone and Bible: "I was told at 1:00 that afternoon that I was going to have this opportunity and had not had a moment of time for reflective thought. Even during the driving time, I was late for everything when I got into the car, so I was actually concentrating on driving." Now, he reviews those notes:

> Ironically, the very first note I've got was, "No one can speak for the public health community and I don't pretend to do that." My next point after that was that I had one goal and that was long-term change, long-term reduction of tobacco use and the number of people who die from using their products. I said that while we were focused on kids as the marker, there had to be a much broader goal.
>
> I then said while I'd listened carefully so far, what I was listening for were real goals with real teeth and real ways to enforce it; that anything that didn't bring total openness and sunshine and honesty to do this wouldn't be enough; and that all of their secrets would have to come out. We'd have to find a way to wipe the slate clean of what they'd known, and what they'd done. Otherwise there would be no way to go forward.
>
> I said that I would be opposed to anything that was less than fundamental change; that each of their companies had engaged in what I thought were fraudulent efforts to give the appearance of change in the past, and that I wouldn't be a part of that. I said I brought a lot of skepticism to the table; that, while they made a point about wanting peace, there couldn't possibly be peace without a dramatic change and complete responsibility for their own acts.
>
> I finished by saying I had listened to them, that I remained highly skeptical, but that I had a moral obligation to listen.
>
> As far as I was concerned I had an audience of two, and they reacted immediately. Their body language was, again, one of sincerity, of interest. There was no wincing. Even when I said, "Your products can't both kill and addict."
>
> Still, I was disappointed in myself. I did not feel as eloquent or as thoughtful as I would have liked to have been. I wondered what I should have said that I didn't say.

Matt needn't have worried. Jim Tierney told me later, "The attorneys general thought he was terrific."

By prearrangement, Bible and Goldstone then left, assuring the others that while they wouldn't be in the negotiating room, they would be available personally to help move the process along. The task then fell to Arthur Golden, the RJR lawyer, to spell out some of the concrete concessions the industry was prepared to make. And they were stunning—especially to anyone who had spent decades fighting against the industry stonewall opposing every single policy initiative that they were now embracing. Golden responded, point by point, to a set of principles that the attorneys general had drafted previously to govern any proposed settlement of their cases. A number of attorneys general and Matt had urged the others to adopt such principles—just as he was simultaneously urging the health community to do—and Matt had been allowed to help draft them.

On advertising, Golden said the industry was prepared to tear down all its billboards and voluntarily accept all the FDA's proposed rules on advertising, even though they believed these rules would ultimately have been rejected by the Supreme Court as violating the First Amendment. Mike Moore jumped in, "Are you going to get rid of [Reynolds's] Joe Camel?" "We're willing to talk about that, too," said RJR's Golden, "but the Marlboro Man's got to go, too." Wachtell, Philip Morris's lawyer, said he'd talk to his client that evening and bring back an answer the next day.

Golden continued. The companies would accept FDA regulation through a separate chapter of the Food and Drug Law, but he gave no details of what that regulatory authority might be. They would agree to fund antismoking counter-advertising campaigns, vesting control of the messages in the hands of public health officials. They'd remove cigarette-vending machines and accept all the rest of FDA's rules restricting access by youth to cigarettes. They were open to strengthening warning labels (which meant being open to the "addiction" warning that they had strenuously and successfully resisted for more than a decade —against the best efforts of Matt and the Coalition on Smoking OR Health). They agreed to the disclosure of their still-secret documents relating to health-related research, though Golden was vague on scope and process. They would consider shutting down the Tobacco Institute, their notorious lobby. And they were prepared to pay "a significant sum" for damages in perpetuity, though they weren't ready with a dollar amount.

In return, the companies sought immunity from all present and future litigation—even full immunity from criminal prosecution—unless, said Golden, they were to commit some future egregious act like putting arsenic in cigarettes. ("It's already in," said Matt to himself.)

The attorneys general's principles included the requirement of a so-called trigger: a provision that set a percentage target by which tobacco sales to youth had to be reduced. If that target was not met, the failure would "trigger" a substantial additional penalty payment by the companies. It was not a provision that any of the tobacco control advocates had ever considered a serious possibility for acceptance by the industry.

Golden said the industry was open to the concept but didn't see how it could work in practice. He said the tobacco companies proposed, instead, that a study commission be appointed to recommend new rules to Congress in the event youth smoking rates failed to meet target reductions. (Matt scrawled a big "NO" next to his notes on this item.) Wachtell added that they would accept federal regulation establishing nonsmoking rules for workplaces and public spaces, which some tobacco control advocates had been pushing, while others—especially Glantz and Carol—feared that such a standard might well end up full of loopholes and preempt stronger state and local standards. Wachtell summarized the tobacco companies' fundamental negotiation posture: "What they want is peace, and what they are prepared to do in return is to become 'an entirely regulated industry.' "

Wachtell added something else that Matt considered so unusual and significant that he wrote it down carefully: "We have more to give than we are prepared to offer." Here was a notoriously shrewd and uncompromising negotiator, and he was signaling that his clients were prepared to make further concessions *even before negotiations had started.* This could be, Matt reflected, a sign that this time the industry was dead serious about reaching agreement.

A break followed, during which the two camps separated and took counsel. Matt says: "I remember Dick's unbridled enthusiasm and Mike's enthusiasm, and my cautioning that, while it all sounded great, we ought not to go overboard."

After the break, Scruggs was to propound a series of hard, specific questions to Golden on the details of their proposals. But before he did, he told the tobacco executives that the attorneys general would never consider any immunity or relief for criminal acts—past or future. They could discuss relief from civil liability, but not from any criminal wrongdoing. If that was going to be a deal breaker, the industry representatives should say so immediately, because that would end any further settlement discussions.

Wachtell was obviously pained but responded that they were prepared to continue. Matt comments: "I don't think Golden and Wachtell thought they would get criminal immunity in the end, but saw no harm in asking. While I was disturbed at the breadth of civil liability protection the industry was seeking, I was relieved at the attorneys general's quick and decisive response to the demand for protection against criminal prosecution."

Moore then propounded his questions. The answers arrested at least Matt's enthusiasm: "There was some good stuff there, but there was an awful lot of classic legal crap coming from the industry. The answers were disappointing, but not so disappointing that you'd say, 'I'm out of here!' "

They all agreed to reconvene the next day, including Matt, who reflects on the events of that first day:

> The very first thing I said to my wife that night when I got home was, "I wish I had known in advance that I was going to be called on to speak at that meeting because I found out about it during a day when I had not a moment to be reflective. How often will I get a chance to address Steve Goldstone and Geoff Bible face to face? And in a forum where there doesn't have to be posturing? And, because of the nature of events, I can actually say what I think? I just wish to hell that I had had twenty-four hours to sit somewhere quietly and think what it is I would say to them. In all probability, I'm never going to get to them again."

He was right. But he would get to their lawyers again. Indeed, he would spend more time over the next two and a half months face to face with tobacco's lawyers and the others (and traveling to and from these meetings) than he would with anyone else, including his own family.

One Stays, One Stays Out

Matt had agreed only to come to the next day's meeting, and to listen. He had not yet committed himself to an active role in formal negotiations. But that second meeting brought concrete concessions, path-breaking concessions. Arthur Golden opened the meeting by declaring, flatly, that the Marlboro Man and Joe Camel would go—if not the most important public health objective, surely the most powerfully symbolic objective for tobacco control advocates. Joe Camel may have seduced millions of kids, but the Marlboro Man was their true pied piper—60 percent of underage smokers smoked Marlboros (while only 25 percent of all smokers did), though they cost almost twice the price of the generic brands that better fit most teenagers' pocketbooks. The companies would agree to end the use of all human and cartoon figures in their advertising.

Matt and the attorneys general pressed forward. Matt referred to President Clinton's stated goal of cutting teenage smoking at least in half. And he pressed on the issue of look-back penalties, which Golden had skirted the day before: "We want to put in the accord that if this goal isn't met by a predetermined number of years, each cigarette maker would have to pay a steep financial penalty—a penalty in the billions of dollars."

"We can live with that," responded Golden, "but we are not going to give you a blank check."

Matt had begun to believe that this negotiation might indeed be different from all the preceding ones. And he decided to stay at the table.

By the conclusion of the discussions that Friday night, I had decided that it would have been unimaginably irresponsible to have had this opportunity to explore what might be possible, and to walk away from it. I truly saw the talks as a way to accomplish something that I didn't believe we could otherwise accomplish. Remember that as of April 1, 1997, it had been two and a half years since the last congressional hearing on tobacco.

It was clear from the very beginning that it would take hard negotiations, but what they appeared willing to give up on public health was light years beyond what anybody ever thought about getting from these guys.

So I have to admit I walked out of the first two days of those first discussions believing they were the opportunity of a lifetime for the tobacco control movement.

While Matt was wary of Scruggs's and Moore's overeagerness to settle before their Mississippi trial date on July 7, he also knew that their impulse was fed by a well-grounded fear that the attorney general cases were fragile, their favorable outcome far from certain.
As Matt saw it:

I spent a lot of time looking at the cases that we were all depending upon and the people on whom we were depending to prosecute them. I've done very large class action litigation; that's what I did for the ACLU. I had much greater qualms than those who had just read the attorneys general's press clippings.

The cases were wonderful, but only if we were able to leverage them to achieve public health goals, and that could best be done through a settlement, not trials, because trials are mostly about money—not health policy.

The more time I spent analytically thinking it through, the more comfortable I became with the nonemotional answer that these negotiations—even with the devil—could hold the key to our public health goals.

I thought that this was the right time to strike. I feared the public's interest in curbing the tobacco companies would wane over time. I saw the weaknesses in the class action cases and thought they were less likely to win than not. The time to maximize them was when the industry was still afraid of them. I saw the industry's fear of Kessler and the FDA as another source of leverage. I concluded we were at a maximum time to try and nail something down.

Matt knew that there were tobacco control advocates who did see the trials of these cases as public health initiatives—and the ultimate bankruptcy of the companies as the new Holy Grail of tobacco control. The very fact that Bible and Goldstone were at this table together made it clear to Matt that they and, more importantly, their investors, greatly feared bankruptcy—feared that the combination of two or three massive jury awards of punitive damages, totaling in the tens of billions of dollars, would throw the companies into bankruptcy.

Fear was written in the behavior of Wall Street as well. At each court ruling or verdict favorable to the tobacco foes, tobacco share prices plummeted. Even *rumors* of settlement talks freed investors from their fears. In February 1997, a report that a settlement was on the table added more than $10 billion to Philip Morris's market value. But the investors' and the executives' fear of litigation and of bankruptcy did not persuade Matt that forcing the attorneys general to try their cases was a viable strategy. First, it couldn't be done. With or without the support of the public health community, and with or without a global settlement blessed by Congress, the companies would offer small public health concessions and large pots of money—and the attorneys general would take the money and run. Sure, most of them would have liked to boast that they had reduced tobacco use, but they would not risk the politically enchanting prospect of bringing hundreds of millions of dollars into their states' treasuries in order to satisfy the most zealous of the public health advocates.

Second, even if some cases went to trial, the punitive-damage jury awards in the tens of billions that would be required to throw the companies into bankruptcy were the remotest of possibilities. Nothing like that had ever happened before. And no less a light than the president's erstwhile pollster Dick Morris had quietly polled the citizen pool of potential jurors for the attorneys general and come away with the disquieting news that there was little sentiment for punishing the tobacco companies.

For Matt, the vision of tobacco companies "brought to their knees" by bankruptcy and thereby unable to market cigarettes aggressively was a fantasy, a metaphor without substance. Matt knew that bankruptcy might bring a change in management, perhaps a corporate shuffle, a reorganization, but the aggressive marketing of Marlboros and Camels would continue unabated. Finally, even if his colleagues' fantasy prevailed, even if the companies could be wiped out and their cigarettes no longer marketed, it would not solve the tobacco problem. "Bankrupting the companies never fit my social agenda. We've got 50 million addicts in this country. It's not an answer to wipe out the tobacco companies, just as it's not an answer to suddenly ban nicotine. That's not how you solve the social health problems of tobacco use. If these companies disappeared, others would arise to replace them."

Matt had calculated that the enticement of short-term rewards for investors (and executives holding stock options)—leaping share prices —would induce them to make major concessions, even concessions that would severely depress long-term sales and profits. This is why he was not impressed by the arguments of Stan Glantz and others that a rise in tobacco share prices was necessarily bad news for public health.

Perhaps most difficult for Matt—or any of us who had fought the tobacco wars for decades—was the possibility, however difficult to calculate or prove, that beyond hard economic survival the tobacco executives simply needed to be restored to civil society from their pariah status in their communities or families. The media exposés, the grotesque editorial cartoons, and the tobacco control ads being aired in California that publicly shamed the tobacco company executives cast them further and further beyond the pale of decent society.

Chronically wary of Bible's or Goldstone's sincerity, Matt did not entirely discount the genuineness of their desire for a peace that would allow them to shed the stigma of their predecessors' contemptible behavior and be seen as the legitimate sellers of a duly regulated but legal product, playing by the rules. Matt:

> Goldstone is part cold company man. He says to himself, "I have a company that is highly leveraged. I can't afford to lose these cases. This is my best way out." But there is also Goldstone's belief that if he played by a set of broadly accepted rules, he could lawfully and *ethically* sell cigarettes, even though they killed.
>
> The reality is that this industry took more crap the year before these negotiations than you could have imagined. They wanted this settlement real badly. Whether it was for purely economic reasons or to end their pariah status for their own personal comfort level, there's no doubt they wanted to be known as legitimate business people. That's part economic and part noneconomic.

Finally, there was the reality that if Matt refused to participate in the negotiations, no one else would be there to advocate solely for the public health. The negotiations would continue. The attorneys general and the trial lawyers wanted them, the tobacco companies wanted them, and the White House wanted them. Matt knew that "there would be no one else at the negotiating table who had any real knowledge of the tobacco control movement, its history, and what it considered important. There was nobody else there who didn't have divided loyalties. I thought, here was a unique and special opportunity for the movement, to say to these tobacco guys this is what you have to do. And the notion that we wouldn't listen or that we wouldn't take our best shot at it was unfathomable to me. I mean that's what I was in the movement to do."

Jim Tierney implored Matt to stay with the negotiations:

> Unlike any other of the lawyers associated with the health forces, Matt
> was a skilled trial lawyer with a great deal of jury experience. He never
> deluded himself as to the real legal merits of the state cases. He knew that
> they were high-risk cases that could go south as easily as succeed.
>
> Matt also knew that even if the attorneys general team got everything
> we ever asked for in our cases, the First Amendment would limit our abil-
> ity to get advertising restrictions, and juries and bankruptcy law would
> limit the damages. We all knew that no jury could order FDA jurisdiction
> over tobacco. That would take Congress, and it was Matt's Washington
> knowledge and stature [that] made him an incredibly important ally for
> the attorneys general.

So Matt was in. But his solo role was deeply troubling to him. Tierney
recalls talking with Matt by phone after the initial meeting with the
tobacco companies: "Matt called me that evening and we talked at
length about how personally exposed he was by being in the room
without another representative from the health community. Both of us
had been in this fight long enough to know that his solitary appearance
was a huge risk not only to him personally, but to the integrity of the
Center [for Tobacco-Free Kids] and the process that was about to begin. We both knew he needed someone with him in the room."

At Matt's urging, Moore and Scruggs approached David Kessler,
who had just left FDA and was about to take up his new role as dean of
the Yale Medical School. Now a private citizen, he was free to speak
as an advocate in his own voice. Kessler and his chief policy aide, Mitch
Zeller, who was staying at the FDA, agreed to meet Moore and Scruggs
for dinner. Both recall that dinner, and Mitch describes it vividly:

> At dinner, Moore and Scruggs laid out their plan to David and me. They
> had no idea whether it would work, but there would be secret negotia-
> tions—this time with the blessings of the CEOs—to hammer out the is-
> sues, from the pot of money to FDA regulation to civil liability. It would
> be done in secret and it would then be presented as a done deal to the
> world, meaning Congress, the administration, the rest of the public health
> community that wasn't involved, and the general public.
>
> This evening did not go the way they planned. David and I were 100
> percent negative. We were polite, but we were negative. We both said to
> them, if your goal is to initiate a public debate, call attention to issues, get
> the ball rolling, then this is fine; then the process that you're about to em-
> bark on makes a lot of sense. If on the other hand, your goal is legislation,

this is absolutely the wrong way to do it. You can't hatch controversial comprehensive tobacco legislation without Congress, without the administration at the table, and without broader representation from affected constituencies. And we gave them examples of successes and failures.

One of the successes and one of the failures was pesticides. I told the story about how throughout the spring and summer of 1993, Bill Galston, who had been the number two person at the domestic policy council in the first Clinton administration, oversaw a very thorough and comprehensive process within the administration to put together pesticide legislation. The amazing thing that Galston pulled off was that he had FDA, EPA, and USDA in the room on almost a weekly basis for four or five months; and this one guy got agreement and consensus from three agencies on issues that they had never agreed upon before.

The problem was the administration was doing it by themselves. It was going to be an administration bill; we were having these meetings and excluding the public. There was no secret that the administration was formulating legislation, but nobody was privy to the discussions, and all the while the FDA was patting ourselves on the back because we were looking across the table at USDA and seeing eye to eye with USDA on pesticides, which in and of itself was monumental and we thought, I guess implicitly we thought, if *we* can agree then this is the hardest part.

But it was a disaster. We had a finished product, and then we told Congress, and then we told the environmental groups about it. And we pissed off everybody. So I told that story. That was pesticides, part 1. And then David told pesticides, part 2, which was how it actually got done a year or two later. The right people representing Waxman [Rep. Henry Waxman, then the Democratic chair of the House Health Subcommittee] and Bliley [Virginia congressman Tom Bliley, then ranking Republican member of the subcommittee] and the administration were locked in a room, and they did it. You had then a full spectrum of representation from the Hill and the administration.

Kessler himself recalls two reactions to Scruggs's and Moore's invitation:

First, you can do big legislation, but it takes more than one Congress; it takes years. This is just way too big. And I probably said you've got to involve Bliley and Waxman. [With the Republican House takeover in 1994, Bliley was chair of the House Commerce Committee and Waxman ranking Democrat on the Commerce Committee's Health and Environment Subcommittee.] My sense was, if you get those two guys and this was theirs, even if it was big, that was the way to do it.

Second, I didn't want to be co-opted. Perhaps co-opted is the wrong word, but when you are at the table as part of a negotiation you are a party of that negotiation. I made a deliberate decision to stay out. Knowing that there would be plenty of points along the way to be involved.

Kessler was right; Matt would keep them informed at every step of the process. "The only human beings outside the office I told about the meeting before the meeting and whom I briefed instantly after the meeting were David and Mitch."

Despite Kessler's own decision, neither he nor Zeller counseled Matt to stay out. Zeller:

> Matt had already dipped his toes in, but had not made the decision to commit to be a negotiator at the table. At that point, he had simply been asked to come to the meeting with Bible and Goldstone. That began a very intense level of communication between Matt and me on almost a daily basis.
>
> He was struggling with his decision about whether or not to be at the table. I thought it was the right thing to do. I told him that despite my total misgivings about the process that, if it was going to take place, better that he be at the table than not, because his presence could only make the package better. I also remember telling him that he had to have a very clear idea of what it would take to get him to walk away; that he should never lose sight of the point at which the deal would get so noxious that he simply had to walk.

Kessler did not advise Matt to join the negotiations, but he didn't counsel him to stay out: "I didn't say you shouldn't be at the table. I felt it was a decision for each of us to make for himself."

Nor did Kessler react negatively to Matt's initial reports on the substance of the health concessions the industry was prepared to make:

> I remember Matt calling me and laying out what the provisions were on the public health side. It was early still. It was before the negotiations were breaking in the press.
>
> On the public health side, the things he was fighting for, the things he wanted, the advertising and that stuff, all looked pretty good. I think I probably said that.

There was one person who was both passionately engaged and committed to FDA regulation of tobacco and equally close to Kessler and Myers: Judith Wilkenfeld, a highly experienced regulatory lawyer who had first worked with Matt and later led the Federal Trade Commission's efforts to restrain the excesses of cigarette advertising. In 1994, on loan from the FTC, she had joined Kessler at FDA to lead his efforts to attack the advertising under FDA's banner. Those provisions of the FDA rule that would sharply restrict such advertising were largely the product of her lawyer's craft.

She had remained close to Matt, as friend and neighbor, as well as colleague. Early in their relationship, she challenged Matt to suspend his intense work habits long enough to tend to his health, so Judith, her husband, and Matt began running together every weekend. And they did so throughout the period before and after the negotiations began.

When the previous summer's press accounts of negotiations among the state attorneys general, the trial lawyers, and the industry had surfaced, she had been instinctively alarmed.

The tobacco movement really was in trouble, because all of the wrong people were sitting at the table. I have still not developed positive feelings for the private attorneys. They just don't have tobacco control and the public health in mind; the notion of compensating the victims is one thing, but getting people not to smoke was never part of their agenda. As for the state attorneys general, what they were doing in tobacco was very much like what they had done in attacking deceptive food advertising, what they had done in bringing environmental advertising cases. The outcomes often fell very short of any meaningful restraints. They looked good on paper; they got a lot of publicity, but I'm not sure how much effect they had in the end. So I was very concerned that these guys were going to cut a deal and the public health would be left out in the cold.

Matt and I would talk about this, our misgivings about all of these people sitting down and talking. Then he told me that he had been asked to sit in. And he asked what did I think about it, and I was wildly enthusiastic from the moment it escaped his lips.

Because somebody had to be there who cared. I never had any confidence that if they struck a deal and were able to sell it, that the president could veto it. I was always afraid that politics would take over in the end. I had seen every single piece of tobacco legislation get weakened and undermined in the end by some deal. And who else could stop that? Who else could do that if not Matt?

I had met Matt back in 1980, when he first came to the Federal Trade Commission to work on tobacco, and it was clear to me that he was one of the smartest people I'd ever met. But it wasn't until after he left the commission and started the work with the Coalition that I realized how savvy he was as a political operative.

It's like Chinese water torture dealing with the industry, and Matt was the only one I could think of who could sit there and take that and not give in. His agenda was so strong that he wouldn't give in to that kind of stuff. And that agenda was public health. That was his bottom line. I knew Matt would support the things that I cared about, without selling out the other public health provisions.

He said to me one day when we were running, "So tell me, what do you really think?"

And I said, "Matt, I hate to put it this way, but none of us could forgive you if you don't do it. There comes a time when an event, the watershed, occurs and this event will happen. It's going to happen regardless, and if you don't take advantage of it then we may have lost the opportunity because we'll never get this opportunity again. Kessler has come and gone. This president has the rest of his term, and who knows what comes next. Now is the time, and if you don't do it, you won't forgive yourself. We won't forgive you. But, you know, you do what's best for you."

But I think by then he already knew that he had to do it.

The Settlement

Progress

Matt returned to the Center for Tobacco-Free Kids office late Friday (April 4), after the close of that second day of negotiations. He reported to Center president Bill Novelli on both the day's events and his conviction that the industry was prepared to make major concessions on all of the key public health issues. Bill, as he would remain throughout, was fully supportive of the Center's participation in the talks through Matt. Bill recalls:

> Matt came in and he said, "Hey, you're not going to believe this!" And he laid out how he had been contacted, and he said, "What do you think we should do?" Of course, my first reaction was why would we want to sit down and talk to these bastards? This is never going to work. Negotiation with these guys in reaching some accord, some détente, this won't work. We have to destroy these people.
>
> Well, here came the opportunity to actually negotiate, and so I had to kind of unscrew my head a little bit in order to accept it. We had all programmed ourselves to fight the enemy, and you have to change your mindset in order to go from fighting to negotiating.
>
> The more Matt and I talked about it, the more I thought to myself: (A) it can't hurt to listen; (B) we owe it to public health; and (C) I was egotistical enough to think well, who better than us?
>
> And so I said, "Okay, let's do it; but let's not do it alone, let's figure out how to keep our allies abreast of this thing. We're not the Lone Ranger; we're not freelance people here. The deal was that we had to do this in full confidentiality. We said, "We'll abide by that but we can't really abide by full confidentiality. We have got to keep a few people abreast. After all we have a board; we are accountable, we're not just a couple of guys out here on an island."
>
> So we determined that we would keep some people informed, and we chose four or five people who were not only reasonable counselors, but people who really had to know these things. We chose John Seffrin [CEO of the American Cancer Society], and we chose Dudley Hafner [CEO of

the American Heart Association], and we chose Lonnie Bristow [immediate past president of the American Medical Association], and we chose the president of the American Academy of Pediatrics, Richard Hyman.

Bill and Matt quickly set about convening the group by conference call. Matt reported, and the response was uniformly enthusiastic. The Cancer Society's John Seffrin recalls: "Matt did a marvelous job with his infamous yellow legal pad, going through exactly how far the talks had gotten, what was still on the table, what was off the table. And I immediately recognized that there were opportunities here to get things that we wouldn't get in the rest of my life any other way."

The Heart Association's Hafner confirms the enthusiastic reactions of the group: "We were very positive. This was something very, very significant and we owed it to the public to see it through. And we said right up front, Matt emphasized it, and we all emphasized it, that if this didn't work, if it didn't play out the way the tobacco execs were letting on, we could always walk away. We owed it to the public to find out."

But Matt's decision to join the negotiations—the only designated public health representative—was challenged by another confidant whom he briefed on developments, Nancy Kaufman, vice president of The Robert Wood Johnson Foundation, a veteran public health advocate and shrewd strategist. Kaufman recalls her reaction:

> I have to say I was excited about this happening. It seemed quite historic. But, I was also scared because I know how good and clever the industry is, and how they hire the best help they can buy. I felt, here was a kind of David and Goliath challenge, and I was a little bit scared about what might happen, too.
>
> I didn't like the fact that Matt would be in there by himself. I told him it would be a huge mistake. I realized that there were either tremendous strides to make in these negotiations or tremendous failures, and I didn't think that anyone personally would want to take that on his shoulders.

In the first briefing of the CEO group after those first two days of negotiations, Matt and Bill Novelli told the CEOs that they thought it important—and prudent—to ask other public health advocates to join the negotiations. They were urged to identify those they'd like to see at the table alongside Matt. This goal was not addressed by the group, however, for several weeks—a delay that would prove irremediable.

That weekend, Matt received a call from Dick Scruggs asking if he would come to Chicago on Monday, April 7, prior to Tuesday's scheduled negotiating session, to take part in a subgroup of negotiators that would address the public health issues. When that meeting took place, Matt—at that time, the only participant on the attorneys general' side deeply versed in the health issues—took the lead in presenting the public health demands, but they were supported with equal fervor by Washington attorney general Christine Gregoire and Massachusetts assistant attorney general Tom Green.

The response was remarkable. On one issue after another, the industry lawyers gradually agreed to their demands, each of which was supported by both the attorneys general and the Castano lawyers who were present. By the close of that Monday night session, Matt recalls, "We had leaped a decade forward. By the time that first day in Chicago was over, I was convinced that what was taking place was different."

Of course, not all the critical issues were addressed or resolved that day in Chicago. Many had not been discussed. The concept and mechanism for the so-called look-back penalties—the payments the industry would be forced to make if targets for the reduction in youth smoking were not met—were just touched upon, and a wide division remained between the industry's offer and the public health demand. And the central issue of nicotine regulation by FDA was not even reached. This, however, did not disturb Matt:

> My strategy at that meeting was we were making progress on a host of other items, and narrowing the potential areas of dispute with regard to the FDA in a very substantial and serious way. It seemed to me to be useful to keep going down that path.
>
> It was clear from the very beginning that it would take hard negotiations, but what they were willing to give up on public health was light years more than anybody thought the industry would be willing to concede. You wait until later in the process to figure out where their bottom line is. You don't find the bottom line; they don't give it to you, right off the bat. You don't find it 'til you've pushed for it.

The negotiators put aside, for the time being, the central issue of FDA regulation, including the FDA's authority over the nicotine yields of cigarettes. Matt reflects on the decision to delay discussion of the nicotine issue:

Nicotine regulation was never an issue I would compromise on. But in that first week, when we hadn't yet talked about nicotine, from a pure strategic standpoint I thought that wasn't bad. This was a process that had to evolve and that everyone needed to be deep enough into, with enough promise that there was an end goal that could be achieved, before we got to the really hard issues. And for me, control of the tobacco product itself, including nicotine and look-back, where there was a huge gulf, fell into that category.

What Matt did find significant—indeed, startling—in the Monday premeeting was the apparent *desire* of the tobacco companies, especially Philip Morris, to grant FDA authority over the tobacco product itself. As Matt observed this, he began to sense a shift in the future marketing strategies of the industry giants—at least for the U.S. market—strategies that had profound public health implications:

> I thought then, and thought throughout the negotiations, that Philip Morris, first and foremost, and to a lesser degree, RJR, actually envisioned a next generation of products—less hazardous products. They were prepared to move there but couldn't figure out how to get there. And they understood from the Premier and Eclipse experiences—where their efforts to market less hazardous cigarettes only raised a firestorm of skepticism and suspicion—that it was going to be a very hard transition; they needed the backing of regulation. And they were willing at that juncture to agree to a process that would give FDA the broad authority to evaluate and require change in both their traditional products and their new so-called less hazardous products, including testing requirements, product standards, and marketing.

The negotiators reached agreement that FDA would have authority over both ingredients added and other constituents in tobacco—even though they didn't expressly discuss nicotine—and they agreed the FDA decisions would be dictated by science. Following the FDA model for other products, they agreed FDA would be allowed through its own mechanisms to appoint an independent scientific advisory committee to make recommendations on tobacco product regulation, an important safeguard Matt had pressed for to guard against future industry attacks on proposed FDA regulations as "unscientific," *and* against political backsliding by a weak future FDA commissioner.

Something else that took place in that week's negotiating sessions also reinforced Matt's growing sense that the industry negotiators were serious and their concessions real: the industry negotiators who'd participated in the public health working group told the truth for a change. They actually reported accurately to the next morning's full negotiating session the concessions they had agreed to.

In all my prior dealings with them, even when we negotiated the '84 health warranties, we never had a conversation with them, even a thirdhand conversation, which didn't come back to us totally distorted. So my assumption this time, again, was that they would distort and screw around with what we had agreed to, and we'd be into a fight almost instantly. But they didn't do that at all. There were one or two points that I disagreed with and said so; but they gave a very straight description of what they had agreed to.

Bill Novelli recalls:

Matt and I would talk two, three times a day. I remember one night he came back to the office and said, "You're not going to believe this. I put on the table the whole 1994 Waxman bill that went nowhere about restricting smoking in public places and work sites. And I think they're going to buy it." Well, we danced a jig at that point.

Three things gave me heart: One was that the attorneys general adopted our public health initiatives; they weren't just in there grubbing for the money. Second was that some real progress was being made. And the third thing was that the brain trust we were reporting to kept encouraging us and kept saying, "This seems to be going somewhere; keep it up; keep after it." That's what kept us going.

But very shortly, only two days into negotiations, the negotiators came to an impasse—not on the public health issues but on the damage payments the industry would be forced to pay, and the extent of relief from liability in court they would gain in return for their concessions. Matt: "When I left Chicago on that Wednesday night, we already had the ultimate conflict posed. It looked like they were prepared to give enormous amounts in terms of real—I mean truly real—public health changes, without the traditional loopholes. Yet there was this time bomb sitting on the discussions—the liability issues—without any apparent way out of it. I already knew, from the public health point of view, this was an extraordinary opportunity, but at what cost?"

Betrayed?

Matt left Chicago that Wednesday night, April 9, 1997, to make his expected appearance at the Center for Tobacco-Free Kids' first annual Youth Advocate of the Year gala, and to play an active role in the next day's series of national events skewering the tobacco companies—the Center-sponsored "Kick Butts Day." The negotiations were still secret, and Matt told the other negotiators that his absence from these signature events would raise eyebrows—and suspicion: "I said to them, if I don't show up for these two things, somebody's going to ask awkward questions." The negotiating sessions were scheduled to resume the next week, back across the river from Washington, in Arlington.

Then came the leak. On April 16, two and a half weeks after the secret talks had begun, Alix Freedman and Suein Hwang of the *Wall Street Journal* had the story, and, with one critical exception, it was accurate:

> The nation's two largest cigarette makers are in secret talks with tobacco plaintiffs about a sweeping settlement that would cover virtually all the industry's liability for smoking, in return for strict advertising curbs and an enormous payment that could total $300 billion over the next 25 years.
>
> While both companies have voiced interest in a possible settlement before, they are now for the first time negotiating the details of some long-unthinkable concessions, including accepting regulation by the Food and Drug Administration, banning cigarette billboards and ceasing to use pictures of people—such as the Marlboro Man—in ads.
>
> In return, the cigarette makers are seeking shelter from the mounting threat of liability lawsuits, through a novel mechanism that would require an act of Congress. The plan under discussion would set up a regime somewhat akin to workers compensation whereby smokers could seek payments from a big industry fund, but generally would be forbidden to sue the cigarette companies.

After cataloguing the cast of participants, they characterized Matt's role: "Another influential figure at the table is Matthew Myers, a lawyer for the Coalition for Tobacco-Free Kids and long-time crusader against cigarettes, who could help deliver the valuable support of public health groups."

But the authors were dead wrong in suggesting that Matt and his negotiating colleagues were prepared to give up FDA authority to regulate nicotine, an inaccuracy that would predictably startle and enrage most tobacco control leaders—and raise grave doubts about Matt's role at the table. "The industry appears to be gaining a crucial concession on its most controversial ingredient: nicotine. Although nicotine is widely believed to be the addictive component in cigarettes, the current proposal would leave nicotine outside the FDA's purview. The industry has been alarmed that the FDA might try to force it to lower nicotine levels."

Who leaked the story? Certainly not anyone supportive of the negotiations. Knowing fingers pointed to Minnesota attorney general Hubert Humphrey III, who had a strong case under Minnesota law, a responsive judge, and able and aggressive attorneys. Humphrey had every incentive to try to win his case in a dramatic trial on the eve of the Minnesota primary elections for governor, in which he was a strong, but strongly challenged, candidate.

Humphrey and his legal team, led by Minnesota trial lawyer Mike Cerisi, had been angered to learn—only the previous week—of the negotiations. They were deeply ambivalent about participating, and later they would choose to resist fiercely both the process and the settlement agreement itself. "Bullshit!" exclaimed Cerisi to the charge that the Humphrey camp had leaked the story.

Later, David Kessler's confidant and counselor, Jeff Nesbit, implied to me with a lifted eyebrow and a shrug that it was he who had leaked the story. But the *Journal* story contained details of the negotiations that Nesbit did not know at the time.

So Humphrey and Cerisi may have been unfairly blamed—or there may have been more than one leak. In any event, the leak cleaved a division between Humphrey and the negotiators that would widen and deepen as the settlement unfolded.

Matt was awakened by a 3:00 A.M. *Good Morning America* phone call the morning the *Wall Street Journal* article appeared, asking him to comment on the *Journal* story and to appear on the next morning's show:

I knew instantly this was a complete disaster. I couldn't have predicted what it was going to be, but I knew this was not going to be a good day. There was no game plan in the event of a public disclosure, and I had no idea how people would respond. All my internal instincts said, "Oh, shit! This is going to be awful."

I went out to the talks, walked into the hotel, and was confronted for the first time in my life by a camera chasing me, demanding comment. I went to the meeting and everyone was talking about how to respond and whether to go forward with the talks that day. Finally, I said, "There is no way we can meet; no way I can stay out here. If we have any chance of dealing with this, I've got to go back downtown and be in my office and begin dealing with the people in the public health community." The attorneys general agreed and decided they needed to reach out as well.

Late that afternoon, the Center put out a statement quoting Bill Novelli and Matt jointly:

Our objective in participating has been to ensure that the views of the public health community are expressed. The principles of the public health community have been critical to these discussions. Our goal has been to ensure that the opportunity for fundamental change not be lost or compromised away, that nothing be done to weaken the FDA rule to protect children from the marketing and sale of tobacco products or to weaken FDA authority to oversee the tobacco industry. We have consulted with the leadership of the American Cancer Society, the American Heart Association, the American Academy of Pediatrics, the American Medical Association and the American Lung Association in formulating viewpoints for these discussions.

There were, of course, many more who had *not* been consulted. They would be, variously, stunned, hurt that they had not been consulted, perhaps envious that *they* had not been invited to sit at the table, and outraged. Among the outraged, Stan Glantz led all the rest in advancing a bulging portfolio of arguments against the settlement process, Matt's role in it, the emerging terms of settlement, and the need for or the desirability of federal legislation. In the weeks following the leak, Glantz's arguments poured forth both in media interviews and in his stream of messages to tobacco control advocates through his e-mail listserv. As Glantz progressively honed his arguments, their keen reasoning and rhetoric, finely attuned to the latent suspicions of activists outside of Washington, would carry great weight:

- The negotiation process is deeply flawed, and Matt's participation in it is illegitimate.

In negotiating with the industry, Matt "chose to ignore a consensus among public health groups not to enter a deal with the industry," and once he entered negotiations, he refused to share or debate the principles on which his negotiating was based with anyone who disagreed with them: "Participation in the decision making process has been kept to a small circle; history shows that broader involvement serves the pubic health. The process has been kept secret; history shows that secrecy favors the tobacco companies. The process is designed to centralize power; history shows that decentralized power favors public health."

Glantz spoke directly to the activist's sense of disenfranchisement. He called for "a wide-ranging debate to develop a consensus as to what, if any, non-judicial resolution would be in the public interest."

In any event, he argued, these negotiations are the wrong forum. Those who are leading these discussions (the tobacco industry, the attorneys general, the trial lawyers, the White House) all are driven by "a vested political or financial interest in the process"—not a public health interest. Non-governmental organizations should lead, not follow: "The public health community has the power to control the venue and scope of these talks by insisting that they be limited to the litigation at hand. . . . The public health community has a tremendous amount of power to control the current negotiations because it would be politically impossible for Clinton to support a deal without the support of the health groups."

Even if an appropriate settlement were to be reached, settlement now is premature, since "important information is coming out of the discovery process in the attorneys general cases and we do not even know the full extent of the industry's wrongdoing or liability. A resolution at this time would stop this important process. The industry documents may never see the light of day. We may never know the true extent of the industry's wrongdoing."

Further, a settlement will "disenfranchise" unions, consumer groups, and health insurers not party to the negotiations. Matt's presence at the table will serve to co-opt all of those groups who oppose the settlement; his participation gives free rein to those pressing for the settlement to claim the support of the public health community. "The Center has been quite consistent in representing itself as speaking 'for' the health groups more literally than the facts justify."

Negotiations with the industry can't produce sound results. "The only way to beat these guys is to beat them . . . when the history of this period is written, I fear that it will be one more time that the public health community let the tobacco industry off the hook because of the need to be reasonable."

- The emerging terms of the settlement constitute a victory for the tobacco industry and a loss for tobacco control.

"The best indicator of the damage to the public health that this deal will do is the stock market. Every time settlement rumors heated up, tobacco stocks went up. . . . Smoking costs society $100 billion a year in medical and related costs alone. The industry is getting off for pennies on the dollar. . . . The business community clearly thinks that this deal is good for tobacco. And what is good for tobacco is bad for public health."

A comprehensive settlement will be enormously complex, and complexity opens opportunities for industry mischief. "We do not want a large complex bill . . . public health does better with a series of clean, simple steps." Moreover, the settlement's youth focus—like all the other activities of the Center—plays into the industry's hands by neglecting policies that will address adult smoking.

Without quite saying so, Glantz implied that the Center—and others soft on settlement—had entered a collusive relationship with the industry: "It is worth noting," he noted slyly, that the same groups who focus on kids also support "cutting a deal with the tobacco industry."

And the tobacco industry will be free to expand its markets in Asia, Eastern Europe, and elsewhere. "Even if fewer Americans die as a result of this deal, it will be at the price of more deaths overseas."

- The settlement will subvert justice.

It will undermine the vital role of tort liability in restraining corporate wrongdoing: "If tobacco companies can get away with murder, then this will set a precedent for other companies that harm people or pollute the environment to escape accountability." And it will violate basic "tenets of justice . . . to sacrifice a person's right to recover damages against the tobacco industry without fair compensation. . . . The tobacco companies will simply pass these costs through to their victims, leaving management and investors untouched. . . . The likelihood that industry officials and lawyers will face criminal prosecution drops."

- As weak as the terms of the settlement will be, Congress is sure to do far worse.

Congress can't be trusted. The tobacco companies, "the largest sources of soft money for the Republican Party," own the Republican majority. "It is simply inconceivable that Trent Lott and Newt Gingrich will do anything that seriously burdens the tobacco industry. . . . One can be certain that, as bad as this deal looks today, what emerges from Congress will look worse. The tobacco lobby is strongest in Congress; weakest with local governments." Relying on Congress risks "a repeat of the errors of the 1960's," when a flaccid label-warning bill let the industry continue its marketing aggression for decades.

- The White House can't be trusted.

  Clinton is too eager for a "Rose Garden Ceremony" bringing together the Congress, the public health leaders, and the tobacco industry to celebrate historic legislation.

- Even if the terms of the agreement were to provide some modest health benefits, these would be outweighed by the loss of advocacy energy at the local level, where the public health benefits are greatest.

An air of complacency will likely set in after a settlement is reached, and the efforts toward public education will be more difficult. Moreover, the public health interests will also lose the public health benefit of "having the tobacco industry continuously under the microscope of the press and the subject of daily headlines. The lawsuits have proven to be a valuable tool to educate both individuals and policy makers."

As the story of the secret negotiations leaked, Glantz's first expressions reflected not only his well-wrought arguments and concerns but his untrammeled rage as well. In an interview with the Nader-supported *Corporate Crime Reporter* on May 5, 1997, Glantz called Matt a "fool" who was being "misled" in negotiating with the industry:

Myers thinks he's going to go into the back room and cut a deal—a deal so clever that it will solve the problem. But that deal will go into Congress and it will be torn to shreds, and Myers won't be able to stop it. And we're going to have to live with the outcome for the next thirty years.

. . . The tobacco control community now has a real opportunity to end the tobacco industry in this country. If that opportunity is lost it will be because the National Center for Tobacco-Free Kids lost it for us.

How could Glantz explain how Matt, a colleague who had fought alongside him for many years, had suddenly become an agent of evil?

"He's been taken over by aliens. It is very troublesome. . . . It is very disheartening . . . [the result of] ego, stupidity, or . . . hanging around Bill Novelli for too long."

Glantz sent Matt an uncharacteristically brief e-mail note shortly after the *Corporate Crime Reporter* article appeared, apologizing for calling Matt a fool—but not for any of his other quoted sentiments: "I just saw *Corporate Crime Reporter* in which I am quoted (accurately) as saying you are a fool. I gave this statement as I was waiting for the plane to Chicago and was (and am) very upset with you and the way you are handling this entire situation. Nevertheless, I regret calling you a fool and want to apologize."

Matt e-mailed back:

While we disagree about whether I should be at any discussions with the industry, and you clearly feel strongly that I am wrong, I am disappointed at your name-calling and the way you have conducted yourself during the debate. There are substantive issues worthy of serious debate, but I don't challenge your motives or your intelligence and would have expected the same decency from you. To disagree, we need not vilify the other. Name-calling is not a strategy, nor is it a way to make a meaningful point.

I continue to believe I can do more good being in the room than outside. I also believe that the attorneys general's motives are good and that we have already gained from the publicity over the industry's concessions. I share your concern about what Congress would do with any agreement, but that will be one of many factors we all should take into account at the right time in determining our position on what, if anything, comes out of the process.

The brief summary you received last Friday of what has been discussed and the position that we at the National Center and the AG's have taken at the meetings concerning the so-called immunity issue have not been accurately reflected in your rhetoric. Have the debate, but use the best facts. If an unacceptable resolution of this important issue is reached, I will join your opposition, but I will wait to see where these talks are going before I make up my mind. I also believe that I have a greater chance to prevent a bad outcome if I participate in the debate. It may be easier to throw bricks from the safety of the outside, but it is not more effective.

The issues discussed at the talks concerning the remainder of the public health issues are impressive. If adopted they would not be preemptive of state and local activity and would result in funding of state and local tobacco control activists so that local activity could increase not decrease. . . . The FDA discussion will not produce a result unless FDA's full authority ends up intact. I am not embarrassed by what is on the table as the result of our efforts—just the opposite.

Don't confuse my willingness to talk with my endorsement of any particular result or with any naiveté about the Hill, but if I am convinced at the end of the day that we can do more to produce long term change that will drive down tobacco use and tobacco deaths through the talks, I will have the courage of my convictions.

Glantz did mute his rhetoric after this exchange. To Sheryl Stolberg of the *New York Times* on June 4, 1997, writing a profile of Matt under the lugubrious headline "Beleaguered Tobacco Foe Holds Key to Talks," Glantz judged more in sorrow than anger, though his words were hardly comforting: "I view him as a tragic figure. He's spent the last 15 years working on this issue and he's going to go down in history as the guy who allows the industry to slime off the hook again."

Julia Carol and Stan Glantz may have been twinned in their outrage and opposition to talks and the settlement, but their responses to the leaked story of the settlement negotiations reflected their differing temperaments. Stan's was a single-minded focus on wrecking the talks; derailing the settlement; and discrediting Matt, Bill Novelli, and any other leaders inclined to support them.

Julia felt personally, deeply betrayed.

She had left the November meeting in which Matt posed his hypothetical settlement equations wary of him, and she and Stan had mobilized opposition to any settlement:

I came away from that meeting convinced that Matt was up to something. The lights were on, and he was beginning to get the oven lighted up for some cooking, and it worried me greatly. I don't think he had it all laid out, but I assumed that if he thought he was seeing an opportunity coming along, he would position himself as the person who might be able to investigate that opportunity.

I think that a fire was lit, a fire was lit in Matt's brain that perhaps some big fancy thing could be pulled off and he would be the big hero of the world.

So she had determined to "stay on Matt:"

I talked to him often; e-mailed him often, and Matt consistently said one of the following things:

"Why are you asking *me*? Who am I? Nobody," was a line that he used often.

"Nothing is happening, and I promise I'll tell you. You'll be one of the first to know if anything happens."

He was very evasive, continued to be evasive. And I continued to implore him not to do anything without consulting. Why don't we have the group that met in November meet again? How come we haven't heard any communication? We need more discussion as a movement as to what our options are. I started pushing at that time for some education on what is immunity and is it a public health issue.

"Don't worry. I'm not going to sell anybody out, and you know I'll keep you informed."

Now those were his famous last words.

Julia's feelings of betrayal were understandable. I asked Matt about Julia's conviction that he had lied to her. His response was that at the times he told her he was not engaged in negotiations, he was not. To be sure, Scruggs kept sending him new, marginally different versions of the previous summer's settlement proposal, but Matt had rejected them and did not think the interaction was going anywhere. He did not enter into what he viewed as serious negotiations until the call came from George Mitchell. After that he did not communicate with Julia until after the leak. So he didn't lie to her, but he had certainly failed to keep his pledge to her: "You'll be the first to know."

14

Slings and Arrows

Stan Glantz's thunderbolts and Julia Carol's expressions of betrayal stung, especially where they struck a responsive chord in Matt's own ceaseless self-questioning. Glantz's diatribes were a harbinger of deep trouble ahead, when his picador-sharp rhetoric and his disdain for the significance of the public health gains in the emerging settlement terms would harden the hearts and shut the ears of the network of activists— small in numbers but prepared to wage relentless war against those he fingered as apostates. Matt had expected no less from Glantz.

But he was not quite so ready for the harsh response of public health and public interest leaders with whom he had worked in harmony and mutual respect for many years, most prominent among them former surgeon general C. Everett Koop, Henry Waxman, and Ralph Nader. As did Glantz, each raised valid concerns about the risks of Matt's participation in the negotiations. Especially telling was their warning that Matt and the Center's apparent representation of all public health interests at the table would be taken by the press, Congress, and the White House to confer the blessings of the public health community on any settlement that emerged, and give wings to swift congressional action before the terms of the settlement could receive essential line-by-line scrutiny.

Neither would they spare a kind word for the landmark concessions Matt and the attorneys general already appeared to have exacted nor acknowledge that there were also risks to public health interests in letting the negotiations go forward *without* a knowledgeable public health advocate like Matt at the table. Dr. Koop had been instantly critical of the negotiations to PBS. On April 18, he asked and then answered his own rhetorical question: "Why should those people have immunity? I just don't believe they should."

But Matt was convinced that Koop's concerns would be mollified once he had the opportunity to brief him on the nature of the public health gains he was making:

Dr. Koop had said to me on more than one occasion that he was open to the opportunity for a trade-off. He had said to me that to him the idea of saving lives in the future was far more important than lawsuits, which he said he saw as mostly addressing what has already happened. So after the first public announcement of the settlement, when Koop had been initially very critical, I called him immediately. He had an angry tone in his voice, and I said to him, "You know, we should get together; we want you to understand exactly what's going on, and bring you fully, 100 percent up-to-date."

Dr. Koop came to the Center and we spent two or three hours talking. I apologized for not having kept him fully informed and brought him up-to-date on everything I knew. And Dr. Koop couldn't have been more clear at the end of that meeting that he thought the trade-offs that were being talked about made perfectly good sense, that he didn't see litigation as a solution.

I believed Dr. Koop, in part, because he had openly favored tort reform in the context of medical malpractice. He felt very strongly, as a physician and public health leader, that it was critically important to look forward and not backward, and he saw litigation as a backward-looking effort. He expressed no objection to the idea of negotiating with the industry, none whatsoever.

Then Matt told Dr. Koop he would brief him every few days on the state of the negotiations. Nevertheless, Koop's public utterances on the negotiations would remain harshly critical. Matt was and remains perplexed by this. So were the attorneys general. Jim Tierney recalls: "Everyone in the attorney general world worked hard to keep Dr. Koop informed and on our side, but the good doctor never seemed to say the same thing twice in a row. We were completely flummoxed as to what to do about him."

I gained some insight into Koop's attitude toward Matt and the negotiations when I interviewed him almost two years later, in the fall of 1999. Koop was still seething with resentment at Matt for what he saw as Matt's deliberate effort to shoulder him aside as a leader of the tobacco control movement, a resentment that had its origins in the fall of 1996, before the negotiations. Koop told me that he then had come to Matt and a group of other tobacco control leaders and offered to lead "a new national campaign to try to keep us from taking the curse of smoking into the next century."

After a series of meetings, he found the group inexplicably cool to his overtures, and he determined, he told me, that it was Matt who masterminded the rejection. He had become convinced that Matt did so because he himself was determined to become the "deal maker and the kingpin." Matt's subsequent emergence as the sole negotiator in the secret settlement talks left him "absolutely aghast" and confirmed his worst suspicions. Matt acknowledged the rejection, but not the motive:

> Dr. Koop had come to a number of us in 1996 just as the Center was getting started and we had a series of meetings that had not panned out. He had contacted a number of us to say that he believed that there was no one bringing people together and that there needed to be a super-coalition headed by him. Those of us who worked with him saw him as a courageous and charismatic leader, but did not see him as a grand strategist. By and large he had absented himself from the front lines of the tobacco battle for a long period of time, and the world and the tobacco control movement had changed quite dramatically while he was gone. While he could play an incredibly important role, his best role was never to be the grand strategist for the movement. Each of the major organizations agreed. So no one had moved forward on his proposal—no one. Nonetheless, I was delighted that he wanted to get involved again, and Bill and I looked for alternate ways to give him a prominent role, but that opportunity wasn't what he wanted.

Congressman Henry Waxman, another long-term ally, was outraged at Matt's effrontery in undertaking to negotiate *legislation* with the industry—a role that Waxman viewed as grossly inappropriate for an advocate. He and his staff lashed out bitterly and personally at Matt. Waxman later told me:

> When legislation is put together, it is important for those of us in the Congress to be able to say that the advocacy groups won't accept anything less than whatever you're fighting for. Now I've had experiences over the years—happily rare—where the advocacy groups decide that it would be a lot more fun to make the deals. When that happens, invariably, they undercut the position that they advocate.
>
> I was critical of Matt Myers and whoever else was in there. They didn't coordinate with their colleagues in the advocacy world; they didn't coordinate with their allies on the Hill.
>
> I remember Matt Myers saying that everything we ever had on our agenda legislatively we were going to get: FDA jurisdiction, certain kinds of advertisement on billboards, and places where kids would see it, and a whole bunch of other things. But the world changed, the world was different than the things that he was advocating as an antismoking lobbyist for

many, many years. The world had changed. And we were really looking at a different world where I think that we needed to do something much more radical. There should have been others negotiating who were much more knowledgeable and knew this issue better than Matt.

It's arrogance that you think you can go out and make the deal, and you also think you know all the answers. You don't have the benefit of all the information that you should have. Certainly the tobacco industry consulted with each other.

Matt found Waxman's indignation at the inadequacy of the industry concessions particularly disturbing and surprising. Only a month earlier Waxman himself had proposed negotiating a compromise with Virginia congressman Tom Bliley that would have eliminated any claim of broad FDA authority over tobacco products or their ingredients such as nicotine.

When the Waxman staff had called Matt to discuss their proposals, Matt had told them that he thought they were asking for too little. In response, they had told him that they didn't think it was possible to get full authority for FDA from Congress at that time.

Matt knew Waxman and his staff would be angry that they had not been informed of the discussions—justifiably angry, he felt—but he also thought they would be pleased at the concessions made by the industry, based on what they had said to him. He was wrong:

> I had worked closely with Henry Waxman for over a decade and saw him as the most crucial leader in the House. I knew nothing could be accomplished without his help and support. My faith that he would force changes in any agreement that did not go for enough was one factor that had led me to enter the talks. But I misread him. I saw the calls from his staff as a sign that he was prepared to seize the moment to pass legislation and, if anything, saw the need to compromise even more that I did. Having been unable to move legislation for years, I also thought Henry would welcome the opportunity to break the gridlock if an agreement addressed the issues he felt were important.

Also galling were critics who knew better but nevertheless fueled the perception of the Center for Tobacco-Free Kids as shunning consultation on the negotiations. For example, John Garrison of the American Lung Association complained of the secrecy of the negotiations but failed to acknowledge that he had been among the group of CEOs briefed by Matt earlier in the year, before the negotiations had become a reality, and invited to participate with the Cancer Society and the

Heart Association in the ongoing consultations. He had listened passively, offered no criticism of the process; then chosen to withdraw—not because of any expressed unhappiness with the Center's role, but because ALA was uncomfortable with the very idea of discussions with the tobacco industry.

Ralph Nader knew and greatly respected Matt's earlier tobacco control work, he told me. He had appreciated the account of Matt's skillful lobbying against the tobacco industry in *Giant Killers*. But on May 2, 1997, he issued a statement: "The role of the National Center in the negotiations is doing serious damage to the public interest and imperiling decades of work by committed public health advocates to curb the ravages of the tobacco corporations."

A Nader-related advocacy group, calling itself the BASIC's (Battle Against Sin in Corporate Society), picketed the Center, handing out broadsides with Bill Novelli and Matt's picture framed in black as fugitives from justice, emblazoned "WANTED FOR SELLING OUT THE PUBLIC'S HEALTH."

Among the charges:

> Negotiating with the tobacco industry for such immunity is immoral and threatens to undermine decades of work by committed public health activists to curb the ravages of the tobacco corporations.
>
> We say: No immunity. No deal. Let the prosecutions commence.

Unlike Stan Glantz and despite her bitter disappointment, Julia Carol did not abandon Matt—or all sense of proportion. Carol and her equally steadfast codirector at Americans for Nonsmokers' Rights, Robin Hobart, deplored BASIC's demonstration. They issued this statement through the Internet:

> We are aware that a group calling itself the BASIC's (Battle Against Sin in Corporate Society) is holding a protest of the National Center (we're not going to help them by publicizing the date and time) this week. They have also released a WANTED poster with pictures of Bill Novelli and Matt Myers saying the National Center is WANTED for selling out the public's health.
>
> While ANR strongly and publicly opposes a global settlement brokered through Congress at this time (and especially opposes any legal immunity for the tobacco companies) we are posting this note to let you know that we are not endorsing the protest of the National Center and do not believe that the tactics begun by the group the BASIC's are going to be helpful or effective at this time.

But Carol and Hobart were among the very few opponents of the settlement who balanced their passion and hurt with civility. Others fed, and fed on, rumor and distortion, and Glantz's sometimes reckless outbursts, until a harsh, crudely distorted composite portrait of Matt and the Center's perfidy coursed through the activists' e-mail lists, growing uglier with each exchange of mutual outrage.

In addition to the personal attacks on Matt for his alleged egotism and arrogance, they included the charge that Matt and Tobacco-Free Kids' support for the settlement was not driven by genuine concern for children but by self-interested greed; and that Matt was maneuvering to structure the settlement to make certain that the funds to be paid by the industry for counter-advertising would flow directly into the coffers of the Center itself—whose president, Bill Novelli, they charged, was at heart an advertising man ready to serve any client who could pay.

As soon as these charges floated to the surface, the Center issued an unequivocal statement that it would neither seek nor accept any funds generated by the settlement. The denial was simply ignored.

One voice on the Internet stood out for its recklessness, that of Bill Godshall, an advocate from Pennsylvania, a former Cancer Society staff member who had been unjustly restrained, then fired, in the early 1980s for his too vigorous tobacco control advocacy. He soon emerged as a tireless, self-supporting lone advocate, often strategically insightful and justly critical of the weak-willed health voluntaries. But he also railed unceasingly against the timidity of most government or nongovernment "bureaucrats."

"The Center," he charged, in e-mails broadcast widely, has "demonstrated that it is dishonest, has no principles, and has no credibility." And, again, "The Center's role in this entire process seems very similar to the public relations role served by Hill and Knowlton in the 1960's by promoting tobacco industry protection legislation as public health legislation."

No less indignant was Michael Siegel, a physician dedicated to tobacco control, first in California, then at the Centers for Disease Control in Atlanta, and now as a professor of public health at Boston University, working on Massachusetts's strong tobacco control program. Siegel added his voice to the Internet broadsides:

> This is an issue of integrity, both of individuals and organizations. It is about making commitments and breaking them. It is about saying one thing and doing another. It is about assuming a mandate beyond that given by

the people one represents. It is about selling away the rights of other people to try to gain individual and organizational advancement. It is about participating in power elite decision-making. It is about ignoring the overriding sentiment of public health practitioners in our communities and making decisions for them. It is about restricting yet another institution to control by a few individuals, almost exclusively white males, and almost exclusively attorneys. It is about putting political and organizational advancement and economic gain above principles and values, above individual rights, and above the pursuit of social justice.

Matt would later reflect:

All of my instincts told me that we would face a firestorm among some advocates. But I didn't anticipate the ferocity, the nastiness, the viciousness, nor did I anticipate fully its impact on the large organizations that I believed supported what we were trying to do. I knew who would oppose what we were doing. I underestimated their ability to frame the debate, largely because I had guessed that we would have key allies who would speak out strongly in support, but who did not do so. It was not our opponents who surprised me, it was the people and organizations whom I assumed were allies.

15

With Friends Like These . . .

The fury of Matt's critics was matched by the tepidness of his defenders. Where were the *public* voices leaping to Matt's defense from those public health leaders who had encouraged and supported Matt's presence in the negotiations from the very beginning—and continued to do so *privately?* Muffled. Where were the public voices of those others who had privately responded with awe and enthusiasm to Matt's accounts of the breakthroughs at the negotiating table? Silent.

All had their reasons.

David Kessler, who had held back from participating in the negotiations, but had not urged Matt to do the same, nontheless participated in a press conference with Congressman Henry Waxman to denounce the negotiations, but he avoided any direct criticism of Matt and tried to temper the harshness of others' attacks. He acknowledged in an interview with PBS's *Frontline* that he had been invited to join the settlement talks, but he had decided "not to go to the negotiating table. I didn't want to be captured. I wanted to be able to evaluate it for what it was. I wanted to have some distance to be able to look at it and see whether I thought it would be in the public interest." This was certainly true. But Kessler also chose not to dampen the characterizations of Matt as the arrogant loner at the table. He *could have* disclosed that Matt had kept him informed directly and indirectly through Mitch Zeller nearly every day of the state of the settlement talks, constantly seeking guidance on FDA matters.

Nor did Kessler volunteer in Matt's defense that, while he himself had chosen not to participate in the negotiations, he had never counseled Matt to do the same.

Mitch Zeller, who remained at FDA, could not speak out in defense of Matt's participation because to acknowledge their exchanges might have compromised FDA's independence from the settlement, though privately he was convinced Matt had to be at the table: "I was then, and I remain now, an unabashed supporter of Matt's decision to participate in the process. Having said everything that I said about how the process was doomed to fail, if there was going to be a process, and if Matt was willing to participate, I thought that was the right decision for him, the right decision for the public health."

To be sure, there were sound strategic reasons for downplaying—even suppressing—the fact that Matt had indeed not taken it upon himself to go to the table, but that he had gone with the fully informed, constant, enthusiastic backing of the duly constituted leaders of the major public health organizations: the Cancer Society, the Heart Association, the American Medical Association, the Academy of Pediatrics.

As much as John Seffrin at Cancer and Dudley Hafner at Heart were personally inclined to stand up in Matt's defense—and they were—their senior lobbyists urged them to distance themselves from Matt and the negotiations in order to preserve their ability to maintain independence from the terms of the settlement, and freedom to press for narrowing the concessions to the industry negotiated by Matt and the attorneys general. Seffrin's and Hafner's readiness to defend Matt was also chilled by staff concerns at the small but venomous stream of protests against the negotiations from volunteers and staff members in the field—skillfully inflamed by Stan Glantz and Julia Carol.

This strategic distancing was fueled by the affronted Linda Crawford, the Cancer Society's new Washington lobbyist. She had been kept totally in the dark by Seffrin and was forced to acknowledge to the media, when first confronted with the leaks, that she knew nothing—the last confession a lobbyist ever wishes to make. And there was an unmistakable whiff of envy and resentment that it was Matt, not she, who was at the center of the national stage. She got even. Two days after the *Wall Street Journal* broke the news of the negotiations, she unabashedly added her voice to that of Kessler, Koop, and Waxman in a *Los Angeles Times* story denouncing the reported settlement plan. She also orchestrated the release of a statement by ACS volunteer president George Dessart, which proclaimed: "Present and future victims of tobacco-related diseases must be allowed to seek their own day in court. The settlement as it stands now would be good for tobacco, but bad for the American public."

At Crawford's insistence the Cancer Society, despite Seffrin's misgivings, ran ads in major newspapers on April 24 warning that the deal, as outlined in the leaks, would "let the tobacco industry walk away the winner."

While not overtly critical of Matt's role, the warnings carried clear implications. As the *New York Times* reported: "To some extent, the health groups' resistance to a deal is a rebuke to the role played by The Center for Tobacco-Free Kids and its preeminent anti-smoking advocate, Matthew Myers, who has been the main public health advocate in the secretive talks."

As they continued their customary weekend runs, Matt's friend and counselor, FDA lawyer Judy Wilkenfeld, could see the physical and emotional toll taken by the pressure and demands of the talks and the attacks, and, worst, the sense of abandonment by those, like David Kessler, whom Matt had most admired and trusted:

> He was working around the clock meeting the demands that were being made at the negotiating table. He grayed rather badly during this period, and the lines in his face increased. You know one's physical well-being is affected not just by the hours one puts in but also by one's ability to feel good about oneself. He hadn't had a decent run since the beginning of the negotiations. He got tired in the middle, had to stop sometimes. He was a wreck.
>
> I've never seen him so unhappy about what he was doing. Personally almost devastated, like all the joy had gone out of life. At one point he said, "I never thought I'd say this before; but when this is over, I don't want to have anything more to do with the tobacco movement."
>
> And I said, "I can't believe that. Wait until it's over."
>
> He said, "I will, but the hurts are just too great."
>
> And you could see it. That just wasn't right.

16

The Line Hardens

Just as the first leaks of the negotiations were fueling activists' distrust and anger, Bill Novelli's earnest entreaty to a meeting in Washington of state tobacco control advocates, was, in essence: "Trust us, we're talking to your leaders." They didn't. They thought *they* were the movement's leaders.

By the end of April, as antagonism mounted within the tobacco control movement over the negotiations, the Center and its quiescent allies in the leadership of the Cancer, Heart, AMA, and Pediatrics groups were finally roused to respond to the criticisms.

At Bill Novelli's and Matt's urging, the Cancer Society's John Seffrin and the Heart Association's Dudley Hafner convened a meeting in Chicago of voluntary health organization heads to shape a response to the complaints of Matt's perceived lone-ranger role as a public health negotiator. They intended to broaden the representation of public health groups at the table, and Matt was anxious to share the load—and the opprobrium. The plan was to offer a seat at the negotiating table to each of the major organizations, and to create for Matt and the other negotiators a technical advisory committee of veteran tobacco control experts, as least some of whom had voiced concerns about the terms of the negotiations.

The Lung Association had already made its decision to cast its lot with the dissidents, not with its former allies Cancer and Heart. Its Washington lobbyist, Fran Dumelle, alerted Congressman Henry Waxman to the meeting. He demanded to be invited but was turned aside on the grounds that this was to be a meeting only of nongovernment advocates. Defiantly, Waxman, Stan Glantz, and Julia Carol crashed the meeting, trailed by a crowd of cameras. They demanded to be heard in opposition to the continuation of *any* public health representation at the table and proceeded to attack the process and the tacit support that the groups were seen to give to a negotiated settlement.

When the intruders left, the group leaders, including John Garrison

of the ALA, solemnly weighed the benefits and risks of Matt's continuing participation and of sending more representatives to the table.
Ultimately, all except the AMA decided that it would be prudent to
keep their powder dry and wish Matt and Bristow well—leaving themselves maneuvering room to denounce or make demands on the terms
of any settlement ultimately negotiated.

Only the AMA had, in Dudley Hafner's words, "the courage" to
join Matt. The group designated as its representative its past president,
Dr. Lonnie Bristow, long a strong advocate for tobacco control as a
senior volunteer within the AMA, who was nonetheless not seen as an
independent advocate by the activists. In truth genuinely supportive of
Matt's leadership from the onset, Bristow worked closely with Matt,
and rarely, if ever, did they disagree. As time went on, Bristow joined
with Matt, Washington attorney general Christine Gregoire, and Massachusetts assistant attorney general Tom Green to take the lead in
negotiating the public health issues.

Seffrin and Hafner at least insisted that the group make clear that
Myers and Bristow were at the table with their full support, if not their
proxy, for the terms of any settlement the two might agree to. Even
John Garrison agreed that he did not object to Matt's and Bristow's
participation in the discussions. And Seffrin instructed his Washington staff to develop a balanced position paper on the settlement talks
that recognized the potential benefits of the settlement as well as the
need for careful scrutiny. But that position paper took two months to
develop and distribute to ACS staff and volunteers—reaching them two
weeks after the settlement was announced, and too late to temper res-
tiveness about ACS's role in the negotiations.

Bill Novelli believed that little was to be gained from responding to
or debating the Center's critics. On the one hand, he looked to the AMA
and the other major health voluntary organizations as the crucial constituency, whose support would determine the fate of any settlement
coming out of the negotiations. On the other hand, he saw a chorus of
dissident voices, representing no organized constituency, that would
only be inflamed and emboldened—and given unwarranted legitimacy—by his or Matt's efforts to respond to them. Stan Glantz, especially, he saw as a tar baby—the more one struck back at him, the more
enmeshed one became.

The next effort at reconciliation was at least a draw—but it was a
draw between hardened, polarized combatants, not colleagues within
a movement.

"So, you're going to convene a fight—and hope a meeting breaks out!" With this wry quote from an anonymous invitee, the AMA's tobacco control staff leader Tom Houston welcomed the seventy-five or so advocates convened, this time by the AMA, for a May 28, 1997, "Tobacco Advocacy Caucus." "Another way to look at it," Houston hastily added, "is our hope that what we have managed to do is convene a wide a set of representatives—a cross section of tobacco control in the United States . . . in an attempt to get the widest variety of discourse and discussion related to the issue at hand: the so-called tobacco control settlement discussions that have been going on." He was right. *Everybody* was there, including health organization leaders supportive of the negotiations, as well as many of Matt's harshest critics: Garrison, "lone advocate" Bill Godshall, and Alan Morrison, Public Citizen's leading litigator, representing Ralph Nader.

Julia Carol was represented by Robin Hobart, her codirector at Americans for Nonsmokers' Rights. Robin, like Julia, was no hater; and like Julia, she deplored the personalization of the attacks on Matt. But she was a deeply convinced and strategically adept campaigner against the settlement, and her priority concern, she e-mailed back to Julia and her colleagues, was "not to be marginalized as a bunch of screaming mimis."

There was no scarcity of flame-throwers—and no complaints that *this* crowd was stacked with settlement supporters. Tom Houston expressed the hope that "today we will be willing to disagree, but willing to disagree in a civil way that leads to positive steps as we go on in tobacco control." But Robin and her colleagues saw this meeting only as an opportunity to mobilize opposition to the settlement. She had convened the night before with Jerie Jordan, a passionate settlement foe within the Cancer Society—and one of those who, early on, led the buzz of outrage as word of the negotiations leaked out.

In her e-mail communiqué to Julia and her other colleagues, Robin wrote:

The plan that Jerie, Paul [Billings of the American Lung Association] and I developed was:
- Get ALA a slot to present on the morning agenda, to go last after all speakers.
- Circulate the ALA position for organizations to endorse, for later release to the press.
- Make sure some key questions were raised during the afternoon Q & A session.

- As best as possible, make sure the opposition stayed calm, cool, and collected.

Their theme was printed in a lapel pin that they passed out and pressed their colleagues to display: "No Moore Sellout."

At the opening of the next day's session, Mike Moore played unwittingly into the conspirators' hands. Robin scornfully dismissed his presentation in her e-mail notes home to Julia as:

> a used car salesman/motivational speaker approach, which was received in lukewarm fashion. This lukewarm reception was heightened when, about 10 minutes into his talk, the press (which was kept out of the room) literally burst through the doors and started filming. Although they were shepherded out by AMA staff after a few minutes, the damage was already done (fine by me). Regina Carlson [a veteran New Jersey activist] stood up toward the end of his remarks to say that she had come to the meeting under the impression that she was going to be updated, and that Moore was failing to do so (Yeah, Regina). BTW—Moore very cleverly got his hands on the label by Anne [Donnelly, a label that attacked Moore] and our yellow button—and put both on while he spoke.

The Minnesota team came next, with Assistant Attorney General Doug Blanke, the able sparkplug of his boss Hubert Humphrey's initiative, hammering away at the overriding importance of nicotine regulation—not immunity:

> When it comes to health issues, we think the starting principle is: whoever controls the nicotine, wins. Whoever controls the nicotine, wins. So look for the devil in the fine print on nicotine because, in one sense, that's what this is all about.
> . . . The essence of controlling tobacco is the nicotine.
> Last week the *Washington Post* said that FDA regulation of nicotine content in cigarettes is "one of the company's worst fears." Well, we think the *Post* got it almost right, but we don't think that federal control over nicotine is just *one* of their fears; we think it's their *worst* nightmare.
> When all is said and done, whoever controls the nicotine, wins.
> Think about the famous investor, Warren Buffet, and what he had to say about why these companies are so profitable. He said, "I'll tell you why I like the cigarette business: it costs a penny to make. Sell it for a dollar. And it's addictive." So I'll say it again: whoever controls the nicotine, wins.

Matt couldn't have expressed his own priority pursuit of FDA regulation of nicotine and other cigarette ingredients more eloquently. Ironically, however, Minnesota trial lawyer Mike Cerisi deployed the
nicotine regulation issue to inflame the sentiment of the meeting participants against Matt and the negotiations, proclaiming, "On April 13th,
nicotine wasn't on the table, it was off the table; it was off the table,
and I know it."

In truth, he *didn't* know it. Matt says he told Cerisi directly at the
time, and the industry negotiators subsequently confirmed directly to
Humphrey, that at no time was nicotine "off the table."

But the Minnesota presentation pleased Robin Hobart. She wrote to
her colleagues back in Berkeley: "Mike Cerisi, the lawyer who ran
class actions against Dalkon Shield and Union Carbide, (VERY SHARP)
. . . made the point that if an agreement is eventually hammered out,
'He who controls nicotine wins.' All three speakers scored big points,
and about 1/2 of the audience stood to applaud each of them after they
spoke."

Matt followed. He did not challenge Cerisi or other critics of the
negotiation. Hobart characterized Matt's talk as "very low key . . . saying he wanted to defuse the emotionalism of the room."

Hobart grudgingly acknowledged the contrast between Mike
Moore's approach and Matt's: "He largely limited his remarks to his
thinking when first approached about the negotiations, and what goodies
are currently on the table. This was a good strategic move, as it moved
folks (even those opposed to negotiations) from a frame of 'Why negotiate?' to a frame of reference of 'What are we getting/what should
we get?' "

Robin's late-night "final thoughts" to her colleagues back home:

I don't think anyone can claim that their agenda "won" at this meeting:

- Mike Moore and Matt got a clear message that much of the field is at
  best deeply concerned about, and many opposed to, the negotiations.
  They also maybe got the message that they can't back down on the
  immunity issue AT ALL and keep the public health community on board
  (and AMA also got that message).
- Moore damaged himself, as did Bristow. Matt probably came out about
  the same he went in.
- ACS and AHA are clearly not going to move off the fence, they are
  now taking a "wait and see what comes out of the talks" stand and only
  reiterate their commitment to the core principles.

- I think most participants got the message that Mike Moore and the other AG's have a different agenda, that they may sell us out to settle if they think they can get away with it, and regardless of what folks thought about the question of global settlement, everyone agreed we shouldn't rush to settle.

Matt had done his best. There were no new cries of "arrogance." But, like Robin, those who were already set against the settlement were little moved. If anything, they left Chicago determined to redouble their efforts to sink it.

A Divorce in the Family

To be sure, there were a few respected tobacco control veterans who had the conviction and courage to stand up to Stan Glantz and others.

One was Russ Sciandra, for many years a strong and skilled tobacco control advocate within the New York State Health Department, until forced out by the political appointees of newly elected Republican governor George Pataki, whose election campaign had been generously supported by the tobacco companies. He had rebounded as the director of New York's Smokeless State Coalition. In straight-talking e-mail messages, Sciandra challenged the arguments made by Stan and others against the emerging settlement:

> There are two ways to reduce deaths from tobacco: lower consumption and foster the use of less dangerous products (harm reduction). They are not mutually exclusive and harm reduction promises to save many lives in places like the third world, which are far behind us on the denormalization curve.
>
> The global settlement, if FDA power is made explicit, sets the stage for both.

Another defender was Ken Warner, professor of public health at the University of Michigan, without comparison the leading tobacco control public health economist, as well as a deep-thinking movement strategist and an authoritative advocate with fierce integrity. He was not intimidated by Glantz or the morally affronted physician advocate Michael Siegel:

> We should all recognize that what divides us are those judgments about trade offs, and not some ill-conceived and damaging assessment of who are the "good guys" and what former "good guys" have become "bad guys."
>
> So the ultimate value of a negotiated settlement depends entirely on its terms (obviously) and on what would otherwise transpire in the future. The ALA position may well be the right one. But I see no basis for con-

cluding with certainty that it is. I guess I'd rather learn the terms of a "deal" and then bring the full force of the tobacco control community to either support or defeat it (although, realistically, it looks most unlikely that we would be able to achieve unanimity even once the terms were explicit).

But these sober voices were drowned out by the chorus of damnation. And, as Sciandra dryly noted later, while Glantz did not lash out at him, he also didn't share Sciandra's e-mail rebuttals with his own Internet audience.

Most others who were privately either supportive or open to the settlement were tongue-tied by rationalization, distaste for confrontation, fear of ostracism, ambivalence, preoccupation with other parts of their lives, or just plain inertia.

So the critical voices led by Glantz, Godshall, Siegel, and a few dozen others came to dominate the electronic billboards and exchanges on which more than a thousand advocates lurked silently. The result was that Glantz and Carol and those who agreed with them were able to insist that there was a broad "consensus" within the movement of opposition to the settlement—and that Matt Myers and anyone else who supported the settlement were violating that consensus and defying the will of "the movement."

Still, among local and state tobacco control leaders, not all minds slammed shut at first word of the leak. Perhaps more representative than Stan Glantz or Bill Godshall of the people who worked in tobacco control was Karla Sneegas. In the late 1980s, Sneegas, as a low-level public health worker in the South Carolina Department of Health, displayed the temerity and guile of a guerilla fighter in launching a vigorous state tobacco control program in that tobacco-indentured state. She then moved on to become the heart and strategic compass of a recalcitrant Indiana's increasingly aggressive and effective coalition of non-government tobacco control advocates.

Warm-hearted, fair-minded, though no less deeply committed an advocate than Matt's critics among her colleagues, she had always held great respect for Matt. Sneegas would nevertheless become increasingly wary of the negotiation process.

She told me: "Matt had always been accessible to people like me. I had this doubt—everybody was shouting the doubt in my ear. But, on the other side, I had this enormous respect for his work, and I couldn't imagine that he would be doing the wrong thing."

Sneegas believes that many advocates in the field, especially those who, like her, had worked with Matt, would have been open and responsive to a candid explanation of the unfolding events from him, and would have at least suspended judgment until more could be told. She believes strongly that Bill Novelli and Matt and their colleagues at the Center could have reached out effectively to many in this core group of state leaders: "Even if Matt and the Center had no choice but to sit at those negotiations and not tell anybody about them because those were the terms, there was a lot they could have done after the leak to reach out to people systematically. That would not have changed the minds of those people who were instinctively negative, but it might have neutralized the opposition of many people who just followed the lead of people like Stan because they weren't hearing the other side."

Sneegas felt this silence was a serious strategic mistake: "I can understand the crisis communications strategy of not responding, but our best weapon in tobacco control has always been our ability to communicate with one another and work together, because we can't compete with the industry dollar for dollar. But when the Center was silent, Stan filled the void."

Russ Sciandra, though he supported Matt's efforts, agrees: "I thought the Center took a very arrogant and standoffish position towards all the people that were screaming out in the field. I think what they really didn't understand was that most of the people, the vast numbers of troops, didn't know what to think at first, and they allowed people like Stan to seize the soapbox completely and shape opinion, at least within the small world of tobacco control."

This was precisely the experience of Tim Filler, a young community organizer new to tobacco control, who had just been hired by ACS to lobby for the Indiana tobacco control coalition. Filler was struggling, as were many others, to comprehend and judge the unfolding events.

> It was just after the first leak that I got my first e-mail message from "the list."
>
> I had heard about Stan Glantz. People were talking about this guy who wears the orange sweaters to the conferences and probably would have a tie-dye suit. But he can put a blue suit on and talk about epidemiology and clean up for the court trials. So I viewed his statements with a little more seriousness because he had some credibility. But I just remember from the beginning, the people who were opposed got organized fast, and they got organized because of the e-mail. And they came up with a multitude of reasons why the settlement was bad, even before the settlement pack-

age had been presented. And then it seemed that they made the reasons fit with the settlement package.

I also heard from them that part of the settlement would give money to a foundation that looked a lot like the Center, so that money was going to go to the Center right from the settlement. I also heard that maybe Matt still had an involvement with his old law firm and maybe the law firm was involved with these other law firms and he was getting kickbacks that way.

I heard all the personal negatives that you could even think of. It was as negative as any political campaign I've been in.

Meanwhile, I was waiting to hear something from our ACS national office. But it was months later before they put together a large packet. That information was great, but there wasn't a statement, there wasn't a directional statement that says, "This is what we support."

I was waiting for them to fill the void. I got the e-mails from the people who were opposed to the negotiations. That probably didn't really sway me directly, but it made me understand their perspective first. So I was more inclined to be skeptical when I finally did get the ACS package.

For Sneegas, as for others who were deeply conflicted by the negotiations, the polarization of the movement was now irreparable—and deeply painful: "It was either you were going to go with those bad guys in Washington, or you're going to stick with us real, committed activists. It was really uncomfortable. I felt that I was in the middle of a divorce. Mom and Dad have split, and these are the two people I had trusted most for giving me my marching orders, helping me to know what was the right direction—and all of a sudden, they hated one another, they didn't agree on anything. Yet I had allegiances to both of them, and I didn't know what to do."

18

The Nicotine Fix

Whatever his inclinations, Matt had little time and less focused energy, as the negotiations moved into May 1997, to reach out to disturbed but still open-minded activists in the field like Karla Sneegas and Tim Filler; no time to explain patiently how he had come to be at the negotiating table, why he had proceeded as he had, and within what constraints he was forced to work. His primary focus was on the negotiations themselves, which had reached a critical, demanding stage.

In Matt's view, three issues remained either unresolved, or deeply troubling, as the negotiations moved into May and early June: Assuring unrestricted FDA authority over nicotine; developing strong lookback penalties—the penalties the companies would have to pay if they failed to meet the established percentage targets for reducing teenage smoking; and preventing any agreement on industry liability that would amount to immunity.

As if these issues were not difficult enough, in the last weeks of the negotiations, Matt found himself fighting them on separate fronts simultaneously.

Outside the negotiations, he was fighting to get expert help in the FDA negotiations from a silent David Kessler and a stonewalling Department of Health and Human Services and FDA. *Inside* the negotiations, he was fighting to get the strongest possible authority for FDA to regulate and eventually to move the market to a position where either the health risks were virtually eliminated or nicotine levels controlled to minimize addiction, based on the best available science and technology. He realized that he did not know the right scientific answer, but he wanted to be sure FDA had the authority to get that answer and act on it.

Outside the negotiations, he was fighting those critics who considered *any* concessions to the tobacco companies on liability unacceptable. *Inside* the negotiations, he was fighting to restrain the attorneys general, the trial lawyers, and the White House—all so eager to reach settlement they were prepared to make concessions on liability that Matt held unacceptable.

Within his own Center for Tobacco-Free Kids, he was wrestling with the entreaties of the younger lobbyists who worked most closely with him. They, with increasing fervor, were urging him to walk away from the negotiations. They feared that the attorneys general and the trial lawyers were so eager to reach agreement that they would override Matt's objections and accede to the very industry demands that Matt held unacceptable—leaving Matt to face the accumulated wrath of all those who already expected the worst from the negotiations.

In the early weeks of May, the negotiations had come to a standstill. The negotiators remained far apart and obdurate on the liability issues. They had yet to tackle the most critical public health issues: nicotine regulation and the form and formula of the look-back provisions. And, as Matt recalls, "All sorts of games were being played among the negotiators; people were very angry at each other as well as the other side."

At that moment, Matt was called by Dick Scruggs and asked to join Scruggs, Mike Moore, and some others, including Washington State attorney general Christine Gregoire, in a small meeting in New York with a few of the industry negotiators to see if a way could be found to jump-start the negotiations.

During a break at the meeting, Matt pressed for resolution of the nicotine issue: "I privately spoke, separately, to Steve Parrish and Meyer Koplow [the principal negotiators for Philip Morris]. I said we had to solve the nicotine problem; we weren't anywhere near close to agreement; we couldn't dance around it any longer. And I said that I couldn't bring back any deal without nicotine regulation in it."

The next evening, at Parrish's invitation, Matt and Chris Gregoire had dinner in a private room in a private club atop Grand Central Station with Parrish and Philip Morris lawyer Marc Firestone. The elegant setting was "a little bizarre" for public interest advocates, recalls Matt, "but Chris and I talked candidly about our determination to give FDA complete authority to regulate tobacco products, including nicotine. They talked about their fears of de facto bans."

As a result, when the larger negotiations resumed on May 19, the negotiators set up several smaller working groups. Gregoire took the chair of the negotiating group on the remaining public health issues, joining with Matt and Massachusetts assistant attorney general Tom Green. Massachusetts attorney general Scott Harshbarger was the first of the attorneys general to rely on his own legal staff to develop and prepare his case, and Tom Green had led his team in developing legal filings that became models for successive states. Dr. Lonnie Bristow, as the AMA's public health representative, also joined the group frequently. Representing the industry were Philip Morris's Steve Parrish and Marc Firestone, along with Tommy Griscom of R. J. Reynolds.

Gregoire would continue to be a forceful partner for public health in pressing hard for both strong nicotine controls and look-back provisions. It had been clear to Matt from the earliest meetings with the industry negotiators that Gregoire was as skeptical of the industry and as committed to strong public health provisions as he was. The bargaining hand of the Gregoire negotiating team had been significantly strengthened by the unexpected April 25 decision by federal district judge William Osteen. Judge Osteen, seated in Greensboro, North Carolina, the tobacco lawyers' handpicked judge in their handpicked court, surprised the negotiators and all the knowing experts by accepting FDA's claim that its broad authority over drugs and drug products could indeed be stretched to cover tobacco products. He did rule against the government's contention that FDA's authority over tobacco products extended to the advertising of those products, but he affirmed FDA's power to regulate the tobacco products themselves.

Since all the negotiators had assumed that Osteen would rule for the companies, his decision provided a jolt to the FDA negotiations. Matt had never contemplated as acceptable anything less than full FDA authority over tobacco, but the decision hardened the resolve of others, too, and made it much harder for the industry negotiators to resist.

The attorneys general's counselor, Jim Tierney, comments: "Those at the table realized immediately that Judge Osteen's opinion would give our side a window of opportunity in the negotiations, and Matt Myers, Chris Gregoire and Tom Green drove the wedge as deep as they could. Our own internal research, however, showed us that the chances of ultimate victory on the FDA issue in the Supreme Court was less than 50 percent. We never shared that, of course, and at the table stated that with FDA jurisdiction 'assured,' we should get additional concessions."

When the industry negotiators met with the Gregoire committee on May 19, they did not resist the basic demand that FDA authority include the power to lower—and even eliminate—the constituents in tobacco products, including nicotine, but they raised two sets of questions, the first being scientific.

Matt and Kessler had had extensive discussion about the science behind regulating nicotine. Kessler and other experts acknowledged that they simply did not know enough about the consequences of mandating reductions in nicotine on other components or constituents of tobacco products—and were years away from having sufficient data to make scientifically sound judgments. They couldn't be certain that sudden or radical reductions in nicotine levels wouldn't propel millions of nicotine addicts seeking their "fix" into a new black market. They doubted whether the technologically sophisticated tar-reduced—but nicotine-delivering—cigarettes from Philip Morris and RJR actually reduce the risk of disease, and they worried that they could be even *more* hazardous than conventional cigarettes.

It is true that some behavioral psychologists held to a powerful vision of progressively lowering nicotine levels to zero to "unhook" most present smokers and to spare children and others who experiment with smoking from any risk of addiction. But there were no experiments or pilot tests that could assure that such radical action would in practice provide the imagined public health benefits. In short, however promising in theory, in 1997 not enough evidence existed to justify mandatory nicotine reduction or other tobacco-produced change.

The second set of questions raised by industry negotiators at the May 19 committee meeting related to the time full FDA authority would take effect. The industry wanted time—as much as it could extract—before sacrificing its addictive hold on its current customers, before entering the radically new marketplace of nicotine-free tobacco products.

But the industry saw the future and was prepared to alter its marketing strategies to seize it. Matt was taken aback by a casual conversation with Philip Morris's Parrish. During a recess in the FDA negotiating sessions, Parrish told him that Philip Morris had calculated that it would take the company twelve years to develop a line of non-tobacco nicotine delivery products—so-called nicotine inhalers—that would be attractive enough to addicted smokers to enable Philip Morris to compete effectively in the marketplace with SmithKline Beecham and the other drug companies that had thus far dominated the rapidly growing nicotine replacement market. They could do it. They would do it. But they needed time, and they needed to be forced to abandon their traditional profitable product line.

Gregoire, Green, and Myers found these concerns understandable but knew that the devil was in the details. They insisted that FDA should have the immediate authority to begin to mandate fundamental changes in current products, including the authority to reduce and, where feasible, eliminate harmful components found in the product and in its smoke. They also insisted that FDA should be allowed to require reductions in nicotine if that would reduce the number of people harmed by tobacco products. But when it came to the authority to completely eliminate nicotine, they compromised. They ultimately agreed that for twelve years FDA could reduce but not fully eliminate nicotine from cigarettes—and could do so only after establishing that "a preponderance of the evidence" showed that the reductions: (1) were technically feasible, (2) wouldn't create a significant black market, and (3) would produce public health benefits. At the end of the twelve years, FDA would be empowered to eliminate nicotine altogether and would be able to do so by meeting a lower standard of evidence.

Matt was not as troubled by the twelve-year delay in the potential elimination of nicotine as he might have been because of his conversations with David Kessler:

> David [Kessler] had told me it would be four to five years before FDA would even be able to get to a level of sophistication on nicotine to be able to formulate a position on its removal. And then, he said, any position that they would formulate certainly would not lead to the elimination of nicotine in less than another five years. When the industry argued for a period of time in which FDA could not eliminate nicotine, I was thinking we would be fine if we kept it to ten years. So, I actually took the ten-year period straight from what he had said to me in private conversations.
>
> I was still troubled by the twelve-year limitation, but I didn't think that was going to be a lightning rod. I thought calm heads would prevail. As compromises go, if that's the price we had to pay, it was a pretty good one.

The issues relating to the procedures, such as the difficulty of establishing any real evidence of the absence of a potential black market, were "a struggle" for Matt. He was an experienced, able trial lawyer, but he was not an expert in the labyrinthine corridors of FDA law, layered as it was of a series of complex laws interpreted by decades of court decisions. What precise burden of proof would FDA have to meet in order to justify regulating or eliminating any constituent, including nicotine, from cigarettes under existing FDA law and the court precedents interpreting that law? He keenly felt his lack of expertise—especially since the industry had engaged a team of past FDA general counsels who knew well every nook and cranny of the law—and every shading of the court decisions.

Matt wanted and needed to know what procedures and burden of proof would govern FDA's action to mandate the removal of changes in tobacco products under *existing* law—if the Supreme Court ultimately upheld FDA's general authority over tobacco products. But he couldn't get a straight answer from David Kessler. Moore and Scruggs had pleaded with Kessler to join the talks, but Kessler chose not to engage in discourse over the terms of the settlement, only to listen passively to Matt's day-by-day briefings. "Having not gone to the table," Kessler told me, "I couldn't have it both ways. I'm sure Matt asked a question or two, especially at the end, but I really took this informatively, not as an advisor."

Nor could Matt get an answer from Kessler's former lieutenant at FDA, Mitch Zeller. Zeller's lips were sealed by edict from the FDA department heads that the agency would not participate in any way in the negotiations:

Matt had asked for help from the administration. But the official administration position was that since we were not a participant in the talks, we could not even be in a position to provide technical assistance to the few public health people that were.

I couldn't do it because the administration had said publicly that it was not a negotiator and it was not a participant. And, to keep our word with the public, I couldn't be a backdoor participant by phone. On the other hand it was important that I be kept informed of what was happening, and the negotiators knew they could trust me not to tell anybody where these talks were going.

I always had to be careful about how Matt and I held these conversations. I would ask a question. Matt would give me an answer. I would ask him another question. He could tell from my questions that he was in quicksand. And that happened a couple of times."

He never lost sight of the fact that he was in an impossible position, being just one person and trying to figure out the ins and outs of all of these issues. He was looking for help too, and he had one hand tied behind his back. And I had almost two hands tied behind my back. It was very hard.

Matt pleaded with the deputy secretary of the Health and Human Services Department, Kevin Thurm, to designate an FDA expert to join him at the negotiating table—to no avail:

> I even asked Bruce Lindsay at the White House the same thing: Take the draft language and have FDA review it for us.
>
> I told FDA and HHS that they were welcome to participate, talk to me on the record or talk to me in total confidence. They chose not to talk to me at a time when their advice could have made all the difference on the FDA section. Chris Gregoire was prepared to go to the wall for a very good FDA section, and I am convinced we would have gotten whatever they had asked for.

Gregoire, Green, and Matt nevertheless got it—mostly—right, with the sympathetic underground help of Judy Wilkenfeld, the experienced regulatory lawyer and Matt's friend, who had been borrowed from the Federal Trade Commission by Kessler to design much of the FDA's tobacco rules. It turned out that, even under existing law, the FDA would indeed have had to develop "substantial evidence" in exactly the way the negotiators had agreed—though this requirement would subsequently be attacked by the agreement's critics as "gutting" FDA authority. As Matt would observe: "I tried to model what we were doing as closely after what appeared to be the best authority of what they would have to do *anyway*. The court burdens that were ultimately criticized came straight from the FDA provisions that would have been applied under existing law!"

Matt reflects on the compromise:

> I did not get it all right—I wish I had. I got the basic standards right, but I made some important mistakes, especially agreeing to language which appeared to mandate a formal rule-making process.
>
> Some of the criteria to be used to make the final nicotine decision were judgment calls that could have been contested, but we carefully avoided those that David or Mitch said were most problematic and tried hard to soften the others—on that score, I think we reached a fairly reasonable compromise.

Chris Gregoire, Tom Green, and trial lawyer Joe Rice also teamed with Matt to hammer out the other major remaining public health issue: the look-back penalties. This had already been the subject of lengthy discussions and negotiations. At the May 20 meeting of her committee, Gregoire finally proposed that the targeted reduction be 60 percent in ten years, and that the penalties the companies paid be equal to the lifetime profits from the sale of cigarettes to every youth smoker in excess of the target. The industry agreed but insisted that there be a cap on the overall penalties for which it would be liable. The industry negotiator, Meyer Koplow, offered to set that cap at $1.4 billion a year. Gregoire, who had planned to insist on a cap of $1.7 billion, jumped her demand on the spot to $2 billion, and the industry negotiators reluctantly agreed.

The broad outlines of most of the public health issues were essentially resolved—though much hard work remained in drafting and filling in crucial details, and hard bargaining was still ahead on such issues as the mandatory public disclosure of secret industry documents and national rules restricting indoor smoking. From Matt's viewpoint, they had achieved a remarkable advance.

But, as Matt had said earlier, what principally remained was "the price to be paid."

The money issues remained unresolved, and immunity issues moved front and center.

19

"I Say It's Immunity, and I Say the Hell with It!"

The tobacco control advocates were unified in opposing immunity for the tobacco companies, and sharply divided in defining precisely what "immunity" meant.

Indeed, embedded in the core principles that Matt had drafted, and that even those most open to settlement had embraced, was this anti-immunity plank: "The rights of victims of the tobacco industry to seek compensation for the injuries they have suffered should not be abridged and the tobacco industry should not be immunized from accountability for its wrongdoing."

Matt had fiercely opposed the attorneys general's lawyer Dick Scruggs's earlier settlement proposal for its blanket grant of immunity to the tobacco industry. On December 11, 1996, Matt had written Scruggs a strong, detailed memo challenging the immunity provisions of the agreement that Scruggs was then prepared to put forward. Matt complained, "As drafted, the proposal gives the industry a license to misbehave that cannot be justified."

Yet Stan Glantz and other die-hard opponents of any settlement would sharply divide the tobacco control community into anti-immunity faithful and pro-immunity apostates.

Why this apparent contradiction? Because "immunity" came to mean different things to different advocates at different times; and, because the war cry "No immunity!" was to become so disconnected from its basic meaning—that the tobacco companies should not escape accountability for past and future crimes and misdeeds—that it became a political bludgeon, not a tool of analysis.

During the first days of the settlement negotiations, the tobacco companies demanded total insulation from criminal, as well as civil, actions for any past or future corporate or individual wrongdoing. *That* insulation would unambiguously have constituted immunity. Without internal dissent, the attorneys general and their colleagues insisted that immunity from criminal prosecution was "off the table," nonnegotiable. After some grumbling, the industry negotiators gave up this demand, and it was never again considered.

But Stan Glantz was not given to fine distinctions, and advocates in the field who relied on Glantz's broadsides from the settlement wars would have been forgiven for concluding that the attorneys general were supinely prepared to scuttle all the pending criminal investigations as well as all civil litigation. In this example, Glantz evokes the fresh wounds of the Oklahoma City terrorist bombing: "A jury has voted the death sentence for Timothy McVeigh because he killed 168 Americans. The tobacco industry has killed 10 million Americans since 1964. No attorney general or politician even considered letting McVeigh cop a plea; the same should be true for the tobacco industry."

"Cop a plea" is the language of criminal prosecution, not civil-damages actions.

Most tobacco control advocates, including Matt, also considered any settlement that would relieve the tobacco companies from class actions for future wrongful acts, another demand of the tobacco negotiators, to be an unacceptable grant of immunity.

But an agreement by the tobacco companies to set aside billions of dollars in a compensation fund for tobacco's victims in exchange for the uncertainties of litigation was seen by the attorneys general and trial lawyers as reasonable compensation for liability claims, not immunity from those claims—with respectable congressional precedent, such as the legislation that progressives fought for to provide a compensation fund for coal miners who succumbed to black-lung disease. Matt did not necessarily disagree, but he fought fiercely against any immunity from potential *punitive* damage awards against the companies for their deliberately wrongful acts.

But for Ralph Nader and others, any settlement that intervened in the trial of any or all civil claims for damages against a tobacco company defendant constituted immunity.

Nader wrote to the Center on June 19:

> The effort to draw a bright line between "immunity" and the various schemes of limited liability is misleading and dishonest. Indeed, the prospect of "immunity" may well have been floated by the tobacco companies just so they could switch to a position of disguised immunity and appear to have retreated.

Proponents of the settlement must at the very least honestly acknowledge that the agreement would in fact restrict victims' rights and effectively shield the industry.

The critics of immunity through settlement—who assailed the Center's willingness to embrace any agreement to limit liability—relied on at least four distinct rationales.

One group, led at various times—though not consistently—by Congressman Henry Waxman, David Kessler, and Dr. Koop, was convinced that liability concessions were unjustified because they were politically unnecessary to achieve public health goals. They were convinced that the political tide had turned so powerfully against the tobacco companies that the Congress was prepared to enact tobacco control laws beyond the recent imaginings of even the most optimistic tobacco control advocates. And they were confident that media scrutiny of the tobacco companies and resultant public outrage could only wax exuberantly, not wane.

Thus on June 29, Waxman wrote in the *Washington Post* "Outlook" section:

> In some ways, the tobacco industry's position reminds me of Paul Newman and Robert Redford's final moments in "Butch Cassidy and the Sundance Kid," when the duo are trapped in a market square by the Bolivian Army. They have no place to go; no place to hide.
>
> Instead of the famous shootout, imagine the movie ending with a legion of lawyers negotiating a settlement. They propose immunity for Butch and the Kid: Incriminating evidence about the pair's past will remain secret, and the outlaws will be free to rob more banks, especially in other countries. In exchange, the pair promise to share their loot with the authorities and to lower their public profile.
>
> That's the deal the tobacco industry is offering. It makes for bad cinema—and even worse policy.
>
> . . . If this were a once-in-a-lifetime opportunity, the argument for the deal might be stronger. But many of the same restrictions can be established without having to concede immunity.

So Waxman condemned the settlement: "This is a Faustian bargain. We don't pay polluters not to pollute, and we shouldn't offer immunity and regulatory relief to get them to stop addicting our children."

In March, Kessler had commented in a similar vein in an interview with PBS *Frontline*: "Congress doesn't have to make a deal. It can accomplish everything in that settlement without giving the industry special legal protections. . . . The industry would love you to think that, gee, you have to give us immunity. We're not going to give that up. . . . Why do you need a settlement? Why do you need to give the industry immunity?"

A second rationale fueled Ralph Nader's opposition. In a meeting I had with him shortly after the negotiations became public—and he had harshly criticized Matt for participating in such negotiations—he laid out what was, at that time, a compelling alternative scenario. He first pointed to the revelations of even deeper, darker industry secrets—the "smoking howitzers"—promised by Minnesota attorney general Humphrey in his upcoming trial. Those revelations, predicted Nader, would fuel the five ongoing Justice Department criminal investigations of tobacco company conspiracy and other crimes, leading to explosive criminal indictments. The indictments, in turn, would generate broad public demands for congressional action. The Republican leadership of Congress itself, fearful of being tied to the tobacco companies through their open-armed embrace of tobacco's ill-gotten millions in campaign contributions, would rush to enact strong laws to insulate themselves from voter retribution in the next elections.

But Nader's objections to liability concessions went beyond the others' arguments that these concessions weren't politically necessary. In this second rationale, Nader believed that *any* concessions to the tobacco industry on liability were a greater threat to the public interest than could be offset by the public health gains—even unfettered FDA regulation of tobacco products. If Congress were to loosen the rules of liability for this most culpable of corporate wrongdoers, responsible for more preventable death and disease by far than any other industry, that would surely signal that the Congress was prepared to provide future relief from liability for any industry whose wrongdoing, however egregious, wrought less havoc than Big Tobacco's.

Nader was prepared to face the possibility that the refusal to provide any liability relief might jeopardize the fate of the public health provisions. He no longer held any faith that a future FDA, subject to control by a corporate-funded and -indentured White House, would take bold regulatory steps, no matter how theoretically broad its authority. He believed that maintaining the integrity of the tort liability system ultimately held greater promise for corporate accountability than did shaky regulatory schemes.

Stan Glantz offered yet a third argument against liability relief for the companies. He harbored a nonlawyer's blissful confidence that the attorneys general's cases were certain to be victorious if only they were allowed to proceed to trial. So he argued in a June 23 *Los Angeles Times* op-ed piece that unfettered tort liability was *itself* a far more efficacious public health strategy than laws and regulations:

> What is the alternative to this deal? Finish the job that the attorneys general started. Finish the discovery so that we know the full extent of wrongdoing. Take a few cases to trial and let the public decide what the real liabilities are. I am confident that, given patience and hard work, the tobacco industry will lose enough of these cases to be brought to its knees.
>
> What should we accept in such a settlement? We should take the tobacco business, all of it, including foreign subsidiaries, as part of an agreement to let these companies keep their cookies, cheese, and beer. We should let the government make plain cigarettes available (no fancy brands, no advertising, no nicotine boosting additives, no campaign contributions) for smokers that can't quit. We should take the money from the sale of these cigarettes and use it to help tobacco workers and farmers retool and to run big, aggressive anti-smoking campaigns (modeled on California's successful campaign) to reduce smoking as quickly as possible. Since we will own the overseas business, we can simply close it so that America can no longer be accused of exporting death.

Fourth, there were those, like Michael Siegel, who considered fundamentally unethical any trade-off of tort claims for public health laws, no matter how many lives might be spared nor how tenuous and unlikely ever to be realized in the courts: "The real question is now, and has always been, whether or not it is right for US to sacrifice the legal rights of present and future victims of tobacco products. . . . There is truly a moral issue here. I do not think it is right for us to sacrifice the legal rights of present and future generations of people."

As the negotiations proceeded into May, the industry continued to insist on virtual immunity from civil liability for any past or *future* wrongdoing. Some of the attorneys general and all of the trial lawyers for the class action plaintiffs, as they saw the settlement—the recovery of vast sums of money for state treasuries *and* colossal attorneys' fees—slipping away, softened their resistance to the industry demands.

The talks, which now shuttled among New York, Dallas, Arlington, and D.C., focused on liability issues and, says Matt, "got worse." The lawyers for the major class action cases, the Castano group, included several past presidents of ATLA—the American Trial Lawyers Association. The association—representing the thousands of trial lawyers who were not part of the negotiations—was among the fiercest opponents of any liability relief for the tobacco companies. But the former ATLA presidents among the Castano lawyers were hell-bent on settlement. "There was nothing they wouldn't say yes to on the liability issue," laments Matt. "They gave away punitive damages in a minute, gave away class actions in a minute. The attorneys general were different. Many were troubled by the concessions but felt they were necessary to get an agreement."

In exchange for their multifold concessions on public health issues, and their agreement to pay hundreds of billions of dollars in damages, the industry negotiators sought two critical "immunity" concessions:

1. No punitive damages could be awarded by any jury for any past or future industry wrongdoing. Ordinary damages in tort liability cases were limited to the actual, calculated costs to the victim of the injuries caused. But punitive damages were unbounded. In theory, juries were free to set a figure high enough to *punish* the defendants for their wrongdoing. The worse the behavior of the companies, the freer the juries were to raise the level of such penalties. And the richer the companies, the higher such penalties could be in order to inflict real punishment. Since the tobacco companies were among the world's richest, and their corrupt practices among the worst imaginable, the companies—more concretely, their Wall Street investors—feared that one, or two, or even three such punitive-damages awards could present the companies with instant liabilities payable at once, in the tens of billions, throwing the companies into bankruptcy, thereby eliminating the value of all the tobacco stocks held by investors. So long as that threat, even theoretically, hung over Wall Street, tobacco share prices would remain severely depressed.

2. No new class actions could be brought. Class actions, in which many individual claims are aggregated in a single lawsuit, provide trial attorneys with enormous economies of scale and potential rewards, an attractive investment to groups of lawyers who pool their resources to bring and prepare such cases. Individual cases are almost as expensive to prepare; invite harassing, cost-burdening tactics by industry lawyers; and have low odds of suc-

cess. Lawyers will often shun them. This is precisely why the industry negotiators sought to eliminate both present and future class actions—even for future wrongdoing

Though the liability talks were discouraging for much of the negotiations, Matt remained patient, building support quietly with those allies among the attorneys general who shared his resistance to the industry's demands—a group of about a dozen litigating attorneys general led by Iowa attorney general Tom Miller, Connecticut attorney general Dick Blumenthal, and Florida attorney general Bob Butterworth. Matt recalls:

> Relatively early on I decided that the best chance of a decent result on liability was just to stick it out, knowing that the liability provisions would probably be rotten for a long period of time, but that I had a shot at making a significant change in them if I was patient and quietly worked with them. I spent lots of time talking to attorneys general—trying to create allies, convince them that too much had been given up on the liability issues, and urge several of them to be spokesmen on the issue.
>
> The liability discussions went on, and they were almost always pretty bad. They inched better—just inching better and better. I was constantly striking a balance between pushing but not letting Mike Moore or Dick Scruggs think that if they made this provision just a little better, that would suddenly be okay with me.
>
> Mike Moore was concerned and sympathetic but absolutely convinced that the liability concessions were necessary and that they were a price he was willing to pay for the public health concessions. Dick Scruggs and Joe Rice had trouble understanding why the public health community cared so much about liability issues if the agreement was a public health success. Several attorneys general agreed with me but were hesitant to blow up the discussions over these issues.
>
> Then, in Dallas, the whole talks did break down over the liability issues.

At this point, the industry negotiators asked for a separate, late-night meeting with three of the lead attorneys general—Moore, Butterworth, and Arizona's Grant Woods—and Matt. They wanted to know why their proposed liability formula was unacceptable. Matt went third and responded with what he recalls with some pride as

> a social justice speech that would have made even my harshest opponents happy. But I was not alone. Butterworth and Woods were eloquent in stat-

ing their opposition to broad liability protection, and Mike Moore tried to make the industry understand the attorneys general's position.

We broke up with real rancor. That was really hard. Dick Scruggs and a couple of others were very angry, and I was high on the list of whom they were angry at. They thought the agreement was amazing from a public health standpoint and had lost their patience with our community. Despite the personal support they had given me throughout the discussions, I left that night thinking that these guys would never speak to me again.

But in that low moment, an unlikely conversation took place that gave Matt reason to think the negotiations might not be over:

Parrish [Philip Morris's senior vice president] came up to me afterwards, actually with his hands shaking. It's the only time I'd seen Parrish not seem composed. He said, "Don't quit; there are people on our side of the table who have staked their careers on these talks succeeding, who don't agree with the position the industry is now taking." I shouldn't quit the talks; I should stick with it.

Parrish is very bright and clever. It was clear he wanted to keep me at the table at a point when it looked like I had no choice but to quit. At the same time, I thought he was sincere.

But just as Parrish was urging Matt to hang in, the Castano trial lawyers were increasingly unhappy with Matt. Matt:

At one meeting in New York, Russ Herman [one of the Castano lawyers] waved a copy of a newspaper ad our Campaign [for Tobacco-Free Kids] had just run opposing immunity from punitive damages. He had carefully circled the names of several organizations who had sponsored our ad. He went through them, pointing out that their state divisions had testified in support of state laws eliminating punitive damages. Then he turned on me, yelling, "What the hell right do you have to come in here and say you won't yield on this?"

They stopped inviting me to the sessions where they were talking about liability. Actually, I didn't want to be part of each of those negotiation sessions. But I not want to relinquish my right to object or offer alternatives, so I spent a huge amount of time negotiating with attorney general after attorney general to build alliances. Several agreed with me, but I had little success with those who disagreed with me, and those who seemed to agree were hesitant to take on the others.

As Jim Tierney points out: "Many states had effectively abolished punitive damages. It was pretty hard for an attorney general such as Chris Gregoire to hold out for punitives when her state didn't have them!" But Matt's pleading struck a responsive chord among the small but influential core group of the attorneys general who opposed immunity, led by Jim Tierney and Iowa's Tom Miller. Tierney persuaded the only Republican at the table, Arizona's Grant Woods, to join them. On May 18, Gregoire, Woods, Butterworth, and Blumenthal confronted Moore and Scruggs, expressing their solidarity with Iowa's Miller and with Matt. Matt recalls:

> I am told they went in and said to Mike Moore, "You know we've got to meet with the industry; we've just got to say to them this is not acceptable to us. We've got to start over again on this because it's just not acceptable."
>
> Mike was beside himself and upset; Dick was beside himself with anger. Mike was convinced that we needed to make these liability concessions to get a good deal on the public health issues and was certain that those who disagreed were wrong. But Mike is a leader that doesn't lose his troops. He knew he had to step back for the moment, but I am sure he hoped it was just temporary. He then went in and led, not with his heart, but rather than lose the troops, he did lead them. And they went in, presented a united front, and the industry walked out. "It's over! Done! We're through with you guys!"
>
> That brought one of the few moments of absolute relief during the whole negotiations! I remember Blumenthal and Butterworth coming to me and saying to me, "You know, this is the first time in weeks we feel good."
>
> No one wanted to see the negotiations fail, but a number of us felt there needed to be enough of a halt to make the industry believe we were serious. Mike and Dick disagreed. They feared that everything could fall apart; they did not want that to happen. Almost immediately, there was a conversation between Mike and Dick and the industry. They agreed to take a few hours off, let both camps caucus, before they would just totally call the talks off. What happened at that juncture was that the industry came back and said this is miserable and rotten but we'd like to keep talking.
>
> That was really unfortunate, not because I wanted the discussions to fail, but because it would have been good for the process for everyone to take a break and gain some perspective. But Mike was never willing to let that happen. He believed we had to keep going if the talks were to have any chance of success.
>
> Then we came back to Washington. We were in the last couple of weeks

of the discussions. Initially, the attorneys general held tough on most of the liability issues.

The negotiations had paused for only a few hours. They resumed almost immediately in New York, then, for the last weeks, back in Washington. For a while, the attorneys general held the line against further liability concessions. But their frustration at the lack of closure, and their anxiety that the talks might fail, wore them down. They gave in to relief for the companies from class actions—but continued to hold the line against barring punitive damages.

At that moment, one front caved in. Moore and Scruggs, with a small delegation of industry attorneys and trial lawyers—and no Matt—sought mediation on the punitive damages issue from Bruce Lindsay at the White House. Lindsay forged a compromise on the spot. The industry would have to come up with an additional lump payment— a preemptive punitive-damage payment—to compensate for any possible future jury awards of punitive damages. "Come up with some bright, shining thing," Lindsay told the industry lawyers. And that "bright, shining thing" ended up being $60 billion.

Matt had lost. The attorneys general had agreed to a bar on future class actions and on punitive damages. Matt:

That was the one time where the White House undercut my leverage on the negotiations—on both class actions and punitive damages.

The punitive-damage concession was made physically in the White House. I got a call that something very significant was going on while I was meeting with tobacco control leaders, including Koop and Kessler. But it was a fait accompli. I was angry, and that was a point where I probably should have just said, "You've gone one step too far; you've lost me, I'm going."

But Matt didn't walk. Instead he turned to another key unresolved issue—the full disclosure of all secret industry documents.

After I'd gotten over being angry, I said, "Well, if you're doing this on punitive damages, there's no longer any justification for hiding any tobacco industry documents—even the privileged documents have all got to be made public. There's got to be nothing held back, everything has got to come out in public, 100 percent." Several attorneys general were quietly supportive of my position, and Ron Motley had been working on a proposal to free up as many documents as possible. This issue tied them up for about twenty-four hours.

It was at that point that [New York attorney general] Dennis Vaco, who had often been an ally on public health issues, was heard screaming down the corridor, "We're a bunch of attorney generals. What the fuck are we doing, letting one little public health guy hold up our whole agreement?"

In the end, trial lawyer Motley worked out an agreement that would have put more documents into the public domain than later became available through the Minnesota trial, but it fell well short of total disclosure. It was the best we were going to get, and I knew it.

"When to Walk Away"

As the negotiations moved into their final hours, Julia Carol offered Matt unsolicited advice by e-mail:

> If I were Tokyo Rose and could sing to you as you went about your business, I'd be singing the Kenny Rogers song about the gambler:
> "You gotta know when to hold 'um . . . know when to walk away . . . and know when to run."

And Matt replied:

> I like your counsel—even as I feel like I am going up in flames—at least with you it is because you have been fighting the good fight and have thought the issues through. With too many others, it is because they like to grandstand, but not do the hard work.
> Don't be surprised if I end up on your side of the battle when all is said and done, but it will be because the key AGs failed to hold firm on important issues. I hope they don't give me a reason to oppose what they are doing because, if done right, I do believe the talks have the potential to move us along further and faster than the alternatives. Only time will tell.

Carol's wasn't the only friendly voice urging Matt to walk away from the negotiations. The two staff members who were his lobbying team at the Center, Anne Ford and Michael Kirshenbaum, became increasingly insistent that it was in the public interest—and his own interest—to walk.

Anne Ford was Matt's right hand in lobbying the Senate. She had worked for five years on the Senate Agriculture, Nutrition, and Forestry Committee for the ranking Democrat, Tom Harkin of Iowa, before joining Matt at the Center. She could be a passionate advocate but had little patience with those critical of any compromise with the industry: "I came from the Hill. I don't understand pure. I had no sympathy with those who said, in effect, 'I'm going to be pure as the driven snow no matter what public health we can get out of it.' And I would provoke heated arguments with them."

So Anne had not questioned Matt's participation in the negotiations until Mike Moore, Dick Scruggs, and their colleagues began to edge toward agreeing to limit the industry's liability for future wrongdoing:

> I have a vivid memory that we were going beyond what had seemed acceptable earlier. And my sense was we were getting caught up in the rush to the end. I began saying to Matt, "I don't understand why we don't take a step back and think about where we are, take an assessment, walk away from it."
>
> His response was, "Fine, Anne, I'll walk away. We lose whatever voice we have. I might be able to actually stop some bad stuff from happening. This is going to happen regardless of whether I'm there or not there."

Anne was not persuaded: "I said, 'Let them continue, but they won't have you there.' "

Michael Kirshenbaum was a young, able, politically populist idealist—in other words, highly skeptical of the political process, distrustful of the president and Congress, appalled at the thought that the "system" would force the choice of trading off the industry's full liability for its misdeeds in exchange for essential public health policies. "Right or wrong, it was horrible; it truly is a horrible thing. And it shouldn't be that way."

But he nevertheless supported Matt's decision to participate in the negotiations:

> I accepted that he saw this as a strategic opportunity where there had been no hope for any type of national tobacco policy before.
>
> If I had believed that Matt got involved in all this for other motives than what he thought was the best way to advance tobacco control policy and make public health gains, then I would have been disillusioned with him personally. And I wasn't.

Ford, Kirshenbaum, and the Center's veteran tobacco control consultant, John Bloom, all argued that the liability negotiations already were infuriating the movement. They felt that the provisions, which seemed to undermine the full authority of FDA, would be a lightning rod for David Kessler and the other tobacco control advocates who were already inclined to oppose the settlement. Michael argued that the Center should distance itself from the settlement:

We tried to alert Matt to the potential controversy that was coming. The additional burdens placed upon FDA were significant and unpredictable, and, once the door was open on changing FDA authority, the potential for future congressional mischief seemed enormous. Psychologically, it had the effect of a very questionable compromise on what had become the Holy Grail of tobacco control. I told Matt repeatedly that if the settlement didn't get FDA right, then it would set off a firestorm within the community.

This internal controversy came to a head the evening of June 19, the day before the settlement agreement was to be announced. Anne Ford describes the tension—and her disappointment:

By the end of the process, I had become very frustrated with Matt and the Center, in general. My most vivid memory of the settlement was the night of June 19, the day before the settlement was announced.

I was very concerned about where the public health community was. And so what I was pitching was: there's absolutely no reason we can't say, "We participated in these discussions because they presented an opportunity to get great public health concessions. But now it's time for the public health community to take a close look at the final settlement. We need to do the same thing, and we need to listen to our colleagues and talk to our colleagues and make a decision and go from there."

Matt was in and out of the room and had no patience for our point of view at this point. The only concession we won is when Matt agreed not to appear with the attorneys general on the podium. But I was advocating that we don't do a press conference at all.

It was one of the most contentious, heated meetings that I have participated in. I was frustrated because I no longer had Matt's ear. So was Michael. I think Matt was just so caught up in the settlement; he was excited about it. I think he felt a tremendous obligation to the attorneys general, especially Chris Gregoire. I don't know about the others, but I certainly felt his personal loyalty to Chris and his feeling that he needed to stand with her.

I treated him a little bit like a member of Congress, where a staff member needs to say, "You've got to watch out for your political future here, and you've got to weigh the risks pretty carefully." And I remember him telling me, "I don't want you to be a staffer to me. You're not here to protect me."

Matt reflects back on those final weeks of the negotiations:

Early on, I had made a decision that the potential of the talks was so great that, even if I was unhappy with the direction they were heading at any given time, I wanted to see them reach completion so that at least there would be an opportunity to debate the outcome. But if the talks never reached a completion, the opportunity just dies.

I was constantly measuring (a) leverage and (b) potential outcome. And when I was prepared to walk out at different times, I continually came back to the concept that walking out had to be a gesture designed to strengthen the agreement, not to end the talks. I was convinced that an agreement offered an extraordinary opportunity that could be lost if I walked out, given the frenzied opposition. The agreement contained so much that was good. I was convinced it needed to be improved but not killed.

Should I have walked in the end? The answer is yes. At the level of liability protection they were talking about the answer was yes, because it would have protected them to a great degree against future wrongdoing. And the level of liability protection they were talking about also would have sent the wrong message to other industries about facing the consequences of past wrongdoing.

Ironically, there was a time early on when I briefed Gore's staff on the state of the negotiations. I told them, "It's too risky for you get in there!" I cautioned them against the vice president getting too closely attached to the settlement, because the liability issues were going to blow up.

I was right, but not wise enough to take the advice on my own. I often wondered whether I allowed myself to get emotionally attached to the negotiations, making it hard to abandon the process, or whether I was right when I told myself, "You have to stay in to give the process a chance to succeed." Because I was convinced that it was a unique set of factors that would not last and had led to the concessions we obtained.

In fact, Matt did "walk" from a negotiating session, not in protest but for a personal matter involving his close family friend and FDA lawyer Judy Wilkenfeld. Judy recounts:

Matt never lets his work stop him from doing what's right. And when my mom died, he insisted upon coming to the funeral.

I had said to Matt, "I don't care what they're saying. If you weren't there we'd really be up the creek. You're the only thing that keeps this from becoming a true Donnybrook. I mean, everybody's criticizing the settlement. Can you imagine what it would be like if you weren't there?"

I said, "If you walk out of that meeting, you're going to leave the wolves there alone." And when I saw him at the funeral, I said, "Matt, you shouldn't have come."

21

The Two Ks to the Rescue

As the promise—or threat—of a concluded settlement drew nigh, Jeff Birnbaum of *Fortune Magazine* told me he had concluded that legislation embodying the settlement would pass only if it drew the support of at least two of the "three Ks"—Kessler, Koop, and Kennedy. Ted Kennedy was the Senate's preeminent public health advocate. Kessler and Koop were the public health statesmen whose prestige and public trust dwarfed those of all the others.

As we have seen, Kessler's and Koop's openness to the settlement had waxed and waned as its general outlines had become known. The two were alternately awed by the extent of the industry's concessions and outraged at the process of dealing with the devil and the need to make any concessions at all.

But Henry Waxman, Kennedy's House counterpart and ranking Democrat, had remained fixed in opposition from the first news leaks. Now Waxman had grown increasingly fearful that the coming together of the industry, the attorneys general, the White House, and a respectable—if unrepresentative—segment of the public health community would create irresistible momentum toward swift enactment of the negotiated legislation. Waxman recalled:

> The idea behind this whole agreement was that if Scruggs and Dick Morris and Bruce Lindsay and Trent Lott all signed off on a mega-agreement, they were thinking they would put it through quickly on some kind of reconciliation bill, there would be no dissent. How could anybody fight against an agreement with that much force behind it?
>
> And if there were some people that fought against it? Well, it's a Republican-controlled Congress, and they'd lose. And the White House would be standing behind it, so they'd lose big. And if they could get some public health groups to give them some support, they'd have strength in their position. So I could see the steamroller coming.

Only the combined moral force of Kessler's and Koop's unequivocal opposition, he reckoned, could arrest this momentum. So, consulting with his key allies in the resistance movement, especially Fran Dumelle of the Lung Association, Waxman called Dr. Koop and asked if he would agree to convene and co-chair with David Kessler an advisory committee of public health representatives to scrutinize the settlement and render its judgment to the Congress.

Waxman knew that Koop and Kessler were both skeptical of the negotiations, if not hardened in a position against the settlement. He also calculated—correctly—that even though a request by a handful of minority Democratic House members to form an "advisory committee to Congress" was hardly an official imprimatur, the combined public prestige of Koop and Kessler would assure that any such committee would instantaneously assume quasi-official status, a high media profile, and an arresting influence, at least on the White House, which remained highly sensitive to the goodwill of the public health community. He anticipated that a committee broadly representative of the public health community would provide a pulpit for those most hostile to the settlement. And he also knew that, in such a committee, with Koop and Kessler at the helm, the group pressure to unite in an unequivocal stand against the flaws in the settlement would silence or mute the moderating voices of those who privately favored the settlement, and stiffen the resistance of the rest.

As Waxman later reflected:

> We [Waxman, Kessler, and Koop] were in synch with each other as to where we were going with the agreement and what the pitfalls were. It seemed to me that the biggest problem we were going to have legislatively was to have the public health advocacy groups split. If we were going to get any changes in the agreement, we needed to have that agreement scrutinized very carefully.
>
> So we got members of Congress who have been advocates and fighters for tobacco control to ask our advocacy community not to go off in different directions, but all come together. I didn't want to split anybody off. I wanted them all together. Let them all sit together and give us an honest evaluation from their point of view, from the public health point of view, what the deal is all about and what we needed. It just seemed to me an idea that made a lot of sense, and it just leapfrogged over a lot of the division.

Waxman first approached Koop, who readily agreed. Then he called Kessler. Kessler was reluctant. He had already delayed by three months his scheduled move to New Haven to assume the deanship of the Yale Medical School, with a waiting agenda of new challenges. But he did share Waxman's deep skepticism about the negotiating process. He feared the erosion of the FDA powers he had asserted and fought fiercely to defend; and he knew that he was more versed in the arcane complexities of tobacco regulation than the somewhat removed and Olympian Koop (who also had conflicting commitments, including scheduled knee surgery). He was persuaded that only he could set a clear course and give the committee day-to-day direction.

Kessler had found his departure from the government liberating. As FDA commissioner, he had to submit to the discipline of collective decision making and the authority of the White House. But now, "I was learning I could have my own voice!" He was also emboldened by the surprising decision of the supposedly tobacco-friendly trial judge to uphold his claim of FDA authority to regulate cigarettes.

The Center's Bill Novelli, for one, was highly skeptical about the committee—and Kessler's role. In an e-mail message to his colleagues, he voiced his fears: "It could work well, or it could be a nightmare. I do not have a great deal of confidence right now in David's political judgment (I used to think he was a political genius!), based on what he has been saying of late. And I think Chick Koop [Koop's affectionate nickname, for "Chicken Koop"] is, or has become, an unknown who can be swayed. The media and the vocal opposition to a 'deal' will be all over this committee. Its hearings will surely be public, and games will be played, there will be a circus atmosphere."

Matt's feelings were more mixed. He was intrigued by the possibility of the committee's setting the bar of public health acceptability high enough to force Congress to address the most significant shortcomings in the settlement agreement; but he feared that it would adopt utopian goals and such fierce rhetoric that "it would make passage of a bill, no matter how good, impossible. Ultimately, the key would be how it was used."

Kessler told Waxman he'd agree to co-chair the committee, but only on condition that he recruit Jeff Nesbit, a former FDA associate commissioner, who had worked closely with him in the evolution of the FDA tobacco control initiative, as the committee's chief of staff. Nesbit had joined the FDA as its spokesperson in 1989, two years before Kessler.

Describing himself as an idealist in the Nader tradition—and having suffered the loss of his father from smoking-caused cancer—Nesbit had begun agitating among his colleagues at FDA for the agency to assert authority over tobacco. He continued when Kessler came in 1991, and though Kessler set other priorities, he promised Nesbit, "This is something the FDA can and will do someday." When Nesbit left FDA to become communications director for Vice President Dan Quayle, he kept calling Kessler to remind him of that commitment. Kessler credits Nesbit with being the pied piper who first led him to his tobacco initiative.

To form the Koop-Kessler Committee, Kessler and Nesbit reached out for a broad cross-section of tobacco control organizations and leaders, including both Matt and Bill from the Center, John Seffrin of the Cancer Society, and Dudley Hafner of the Heart Association. Whatever their private reservations might be, such an invitation from Kessler and Koop was not an invitation to be refused. "It was obvious," recalls Nesbit, "that to make this thing work, we needed to get just about everybody who was anybody to join in without breaking the bank, to keep the process manageable, and get everybody behind something that they could all support. That was the concept: for there to be as little division as possible, yet still press for substantial change."

"Breaking the bank" would mean bringing to the committee the most contentious and divisive of the activists. Kessler and Nesbit avoided this by restricting membership to the formal leaders of organizations. Thus they could and did exclude Stan Glantz and Bill Godshall as lone activists. But they could not and did not exclude Julia Carol, representing Americans for Nonsmokers' Rights, or John Banzhaf, who headed the advocacy organization Action on Smoking and Health (ASH), and whose signature mode of discourse was scorn for all lesser advocates as insufficiently aggressive.

The committee met three times. It first convened June 5 and constituted itself into five task forces. Then it met on June 18 to review the reports of the task forces, and to approve the combined task force reports as a comprehensive "blueprint for the future of tobacco policy and public health." The task force reports took no overt note of the settlement, but on June 25, five days after the settlement was announced, the committee met for the third and last time—this time to review and react to the settlement.

Dr. Koop opened the first meeting with an acknowledgment that all was not harmonious within the tobacco control community, and he sounded the call, as he would time and again, for unity:

The tobacco talks have produced trying times for some of us. Most of us felt poorly represented or inherently distrustful of the tobacco industry and knew only what we read in the papers or saw on television. Rumors abounded, but never really clarified the issues. If anyone was in charge, we did not know who it was, and even those of us who are in contact with many of the players did not know as much about what was going on as we would have liked to have known.

Now, unfortunately, as sometimes happens, these circumstances, frustrating as they were, have given rise to some hostility, and again, as sometimes happens, that hostility is directed not at those who deserve it, but at others.

If you prefer a milder term to hostility, we could say "unhappiness," or "discomfort," has divided some of us from others of us, and this in a time that the public health community must present a united front. There is severe danger in splintering the public health community; indeed, it could be a tragedy. If we don't present that united front, the other side, I think, would find a chink in our armor and we would be wounded.

He also sounded the theme that the role of the committee would not be to react to the settlement, but rather to craft an independent blueprint to guide the White House and Congress, a "plan to improve the health of this nation." Nevertheless, Koop also signaled his openness to a settlement with strong public health provisions—even at the expense of liability concessions to the industry:

When [the settlement] comes, and no one has sold out to the tobacco industry, and the health of the public is considerably or much better [under the agreement, than the status quo], I am going to look at it very carefully, and with as little prejudice as I can under the circumstances.

I do know that weighing the gains to public health against any less desirable aspects of a settlement may be far better than any alternative, which would be business as usual, with no settlement at all. An emboldened tobacco industry could say, "We tried, and they refused."

Let me also say that there is a natural tendency for those who have fought in the tobacco wars to see the culprit, the tobacco industry, punished. I know some of us believe we have the upper hand, and to the victor belongs the spoils.

But it is very likely that if a settlement is reached, and perhaps even if it is not, that we will have an unprecedented opportunity to participate in the biggest and most effective smoking-cessation campaign in history.

To do that successfully, we must pull together, remembering all of the many things that we hold in common, instead of concentrating on some differences.

... My plea to all of you around this table today is, let us be allies to the extent possible, in order to enable this rare opportunity. But if that seems unlikely, let's go on to win at least as co-belligerents.

He enjoined the committee to draft its blueprint realistically: "We can be visionaries without indulging in fantasy, and we can present the Congress with a vision of what tobacco control could be."

Koop expressed no hostility to the emerging terms of the settlement. Indeed, later that same day, Koop would tell *Bloomberg News* that he was astounded at the public health provisions emerging from the settlement talks: "In my wildest imagination, I never thought they would go this far."

Kessler followed Koop's opening statement with his own, in which he did not even mention the settlement negotiations but called upon the committee "to set out a blueprint that policy makers, legislators, can use to set the tobacco control agenda for this country in the next several decades." But he, too, cautioned: "We, this group, will only be influential if what we come up with makes common sense, is eminently reasonable to the American public, is credible, and realistic."

When his turn came, Matt embraced the charge of the co-chairs but emphasized the cautionary note:

We must be looking at a framework that provides the most fundamental change in how tobacco products are sold, manufactured, and promoted in the history of this nation; and if we do anything else, we will have failed. . . .

Nineteen-ninety-seven will in fact probably be the most important year in how this nation deals with tobacco in the last forty.

If we realistically look at our policy options, not in a narrow sense but in the broad sense, ask the right questions, bring realism to the debate, drop the rhetoric and the sound bites for real substance, we have the opportunity to do something very important—to provide the Congress and the citizens of this country with a real road map and one that tells them not only what those goals are, but how we get there.

Too often in the past, it's been too easy to set agendas because we didn't have the power to achieve them. . . . We have both the opportunity and responsibility this time to set an agenda, with the power to achieve it if we do it right.

John Seffrin, of the Cancer Society, added a muted call for pragmatism: "May we remind ourselves of the words of the late Arthur Ashe, who said, 'If you want to achieve greatness, if you want to make a difference, if you want to do the right thing, start where you are, use what you have, and do what you can.' "

Koop and Kessler generally achieved their goals of civility and surface unity within the committee, but unity was achieved at the expense of pragmatism, as a group dynamic set in that drove the participants to compete for and embrace a common vision of perfection—not of the achievable. At moments, the committee confirmed Bill Novelli's apprehensions that "there will be a circus atmosphere" and supplied a resounding Yes! to his early question to Matt, "Will this end up as a utopian policy statement which neither a settlement proposal nor anything else can come close to meeting?"

Ironically, at the very moment that Matt sat listening as his fellow members of the Koop-Kessler Committee, prodded ever higher by the scornful Banzhaf, kept raising the bar for acceptable tobacco control legislation, the attorneys general, across town, were yielding to the industry's demands to eliminate their punitive-damage exposure. David Kessler recalls: "Matt had to leave. He had just learned that the attorneys general had basically sold him out. He was literally in torment on the punitive-damages issue."

22

The Deal Is Struck—and Stricken

It was late in the day, June 20, 1997, when the negotiators reached final agreement and convened a press conference. The tobacco industry negotiators stayed away from the public announcement, fearing they would sour the public reception with their tainted presence. Mike Moore, Chris Gregoire, and the other negotiating attorneys general made the announcement. They did not lack enthusiasm. Mike Moore led off: "We are here today to announce what we think is—we know, we believe is—the most historic public health agreement in history. We wanted this industry to have to change the way it did business, and we have done that."

The attorney general of Florida, Bob Butterworth, boasted: "The Marlboro Man is riding off into the sunset on Joe Camel."

Where was Matt? He recalls the intense debate in the Center's offices in the hours leading up to the signing and the announcement:

> The attorneys general and the industry wanted me to sign on, even though I wasn't a participant in the lawsuits. Indeed, they all wanted me to appear on the podium with them. I had very mixed feelings. I felt defensive about the settlement, with all that had been achieved in it and all the work I'd put into it.
>
> But my respect for Chris, Mike, and the negotiating team was enormous. There was a real bond—and that was emotional. I disagreed with Mike Moore. I disagreed with where he drew lines, but never with his intent, his well meaning, his motivation—and the phenomenon of what he pulled off. That was emotional.
>
> But people at the Center, most thoughtfully Anne Ford, felt incredibly strongly that it would be an enormous mistake. Anne and I debated it pretty intensely, as we did many issues. And she was right; even then I saw she was right. I thought it begrudgingly, but in retrospect she was brilliantly right—although I took a lot of flack for it within the group of negotiators.

Bill Novelli and Matt had decided that they would not appear with the attorneys general, but separately—immediately after the announcement—supportive but visibly independent, short of an endorsement of all the settlement's terms.

Novelli spoke first:

> The agreement goes well beyond the provisions of the FDA rule in terms of reducing youth access to tobacco products and curbing tobacco marketing. It also provides for getting secondhand smoke out of the workplace and other public places, improving health warnings on cigarette packs, funding a sustained public education and counter-advertising campaign, funding state and local tobacco control activity, setting up programs to help the fifty million adult smokers to quit, and monitoring the tobacco industry's corporate behavior. . . . Our partners in the public health community, and indeed the American public, will now begin their very important review. We will assist them in every way possible.

Then, Matt added: "This agreement isn't perfect. You only make perfect agreements when you don't have to face real reality. However, while there are things in this agreement that I would prefer to see changed, and there are things in this agreement that anyone can find to criticize, if you look at the overall, comprehensive scope of this agreement, it represents the single most fundamental change in the history of tobacco control in any nation in the world."

The terms of the agreement were described and distributed—but not reduced to the precise language of either the formal agreement or legislation—in a sixty-eight-page summary, which had been fine-tuned over the preceding days by several attorneys general, their staffs, and Matt; gone over with the subtle pens of the industry lawyers; and reviewed by the other negotiators. The actual legislative language, the precise terms embodying the agreement that Congress would need to enact, remained to be drafted.

Given the three-month stream of leaks, there were few surprises in the broad terms of the settlement. Measured against the history of tobacco control policy in this country, the public health provisions were truly extraordinary. Measured by Wall Street, Stan Glantz's trusted barometer, the settlement was no victory for the tobacco companies. Reuters headlined the story "Tobacco Stocks Fall as Deal Tougher Than Expected." But measured by the enlarged expectations and demands of the members of the Koop-Kessler Committee, the flaws in the settlement provisions were an affront.

Matt had called Kessler a week before the settlement agreement was announced and briefed him in detail on its key provisions. On the twentieth, Kessler commented positively on the public health provisions of the settlement as presented by the attorneys general. But in the next forty-eight hours, he grew increasingly outraged, as he—and Nesbit—reviewed the lawyerly language of the summary statement.

"I really got angry over the weekend at all those loopholes, at the lawyering," Kessler told the *New York Times* on Sunday, June 23, after reading the agreement over the weekend and consulting with Nesbit and others. Part of that anger was generated by what appeared to be a recurrence of the customary industry double-dealing. The agreement, as summarized, would have required FDA to establish its evidence in a formal rule-making proceeding—a requirement that would have given industry lawyers strong leverage to overturn any FDA nicotine-removal initiative on appeal to the courts. This language was subtly drafted by the industry lawyers and missed by Matt and the attorneys general in the mass of material they were drafting and reviewing under intense time pressure.

Once this language surfaced, Matt immediately reached Chris Gregoire and the industry negotiators as well, who readily acknowledged that no such formal rule-making procedures had been agreed to by the negotiators. Indeed. Matt: "David was adamant, so we went back to the industry negotiators, and they readily agreed that this was not the intent and agreed to change the language. David was right to leap on this language, though he continued to hammer on the issue long after it was resolved."

The Koop-Kessler Committee held its final meeting on June 25, five days after the settlement was announced. One by one the committee members denounced the settlement. Even Dudley Hafner of the Heart Association, who had been one of the negotiations' most steadfast supporters, denounced the plan as "totally unacceptable." He called the FDA provisions "a deal killer."

Koop arrived late, and Kessler summarized for him the group's consensus: it would be "absolutely unacceptable for the terms of the settlement to go forward." Koop replied that he was "delighted" with that judgment, adding, "I don't see how you could have come to any other conclusions and have been true to yourselves."

The next day, John Schwartz of the *Washington Post* reported: "After the morning session, Kessler told reporters that he would personally 'like to see a resolution, but not the words of this settlement.' He bristled at suggestions that attempts to change the terms too much could cause the industry to walk away and the chances for a legislated solution to tobacco issues to collapse. 'This notion of "take it or leave it"—if that's the notion, this is dead,' Kessler said."

Only John Seffrin spoke in favor of fixing—not abandoning—the settlement. "I have no doubt that this document can and will be improved upon, but that, even in its flawed state, it could still effect 'a sea change' in tobacco use."

In the end, the committee had no kind words for the settlement. Instead it adopted a statement decrying multiple flaws in the agreement, all fatal. It gave no priority to any of them.

In Nesbit's view, he and Kessler had managed the committee process responsibly—they had not asked for the moon and had sought genuine consensus: "We pressed for as much consensus as possible on a handful of very important issues. That was our strategy and that's why we narrowed our demands to five areas of the settlement. The end goal was to try to get as much unanimity as possible and make it simple."

But Matt lamented to John Schwartz of the *Washington Post* that the committee had not taken a "comprehensive or balanced view" of the settlement. "It's important that this group, as well as others, look at the big picture."

Just as the committee was ready to adjourn, Bill Novelli entered a final plea for pragmatism. He warned his colleagues, "The tobacco industry is not on the canvas." By demanding "utopian" legislation, the committee would only succeed in driving the industry and its congressional allies away from any agreement. "It will not serve the public health if we all go back to trench warfare."

Viewing the committee's list of grievances against the settlement, Mississippi lawyer Dick Scruggs commented sarcastically, "We look forward to seeing what their proposal is, and we hope they can enact it."

Meanwhile, in the Senate, the third "K" had been heard from and was no more enthusiastic than Kessler and Koop—at least publicly—about the settlement. Senator Ted Kennedy's central complaint was that the settlement didn't include funds to compensate the federal government for the cost of smoking-related illnesses that Medicare had been forced to pay. Kennedy argued: "Congress should not approve any set of proposals that do not include compensation for those enormous federal costs. This proposal is clearly underfunded."

Privately, in talks with the Center, he indicated his willingness to work toward a compromise. But he wanted to use his leverage to strengthen the settlement.

The White House didn't rush to endorse the settlement either. Responsive to the concerns raised by the Koop-Kessler Committee, the White House set up its own internal administration review committee.

Fortune's Birnbaum had been right: no matter how historic the industry's concessions were, opposition from the "three Ks," supported by a vocal chorus from the public health community, had arrested momentum toward enactment of the settlement. As the summer wore on, and time ran out on the legislative year, Senate Majority Leader Trent Lott warned: "It's kind of like a budget agreement. A magic moment comes and if you don't get it, it's gone. I think they're on the edge of losing it just because they've let it drag on too long."

Looking back, there are two sharply opposed views of what the Koop-Kessler Committee was all about. Jeff Nesbit thought

> there was a need for a vehicle to strengthen the settlement; it was that simple. Whenever you put a bunch of very well-paid lawyers from the tobacco industry in a negotiating room, as well as some brilliant political strategists, it was inevitable that they were going to get a whole lot in the settlement. That didn't reflect on anybody's negotiating skill, but it was inevitable. There was going to be a lot in there that would need to be fixed or corrected or changed or altered or moved to another place in the document. And so the committee would be a vehicle to name that and articulate it.

By contrast, Nancy Kaufman of The Robert Wood Johnson Foundation echoes Bill Novelli's concern and cynicism about the Koop-Kessler Committee. It is a far darker view than Jeff Nesbit's.

> It was a political sham. It was co-opting of the highest order, as well. It was political grandstanding. I think this was something that Waxman cooked up to defeat any possible agreement. It was an undercover operation from Henry Waxman's office—his staff and ex-staff were running things up and down, feeding lines to Kessler and Koop, manipulating the people at the meeting.
> It was done in a very fast, slap-dash fashion for a reason: to be able to say that you've brought all these groups together, and put the imprimatur

of their organizations on what Kessler and Koop really wanted—and, in the process, to throw a major kink into the settlement.

If you are really against something but want to look like you're really for it, what you do is to take a Christmas tree and overweight it with as many ornaments as you can to satisfy all possible constituents that would have an interest in it. But your endgame is that the ornaments will over-shadow the tree, and you won't be able to get the tree through the house anymore.

Ironically, both were right. Jeff Nesbit was right that the committee had set a standard—a unified standard—of strength against which the terms of the settlement could be judged, and on which demands for its improvement could be based. But Nancy Kaufman was also right: those, like Waxman and the American Lung Association's Dumelle, who initiated the committee with the overriding goal of stopping the growing momentum toward settlement-driven legislation had also succeeded. Whether stronger legislation or *no* legislation would be the final result, however, remained to be seen.

Part
III

The Rise and Fall of the McCain Bill

23

The Struggle for Clinton's Nod

Bruce Lindsay at the White House had been briefed in person at every stage of the negotiations and knew every detail of the settlement's terms; now he reviewed the actual drafts of the settlement agreement. There were no surprises to the White House. With this information, Lindsay promised Mike Moore that President Clinton would speak out supporting the settlement within twenty-four hours, a promise Moore says was repeated the week the settlement was announced.

Yet Clinton's first words after the settlement was announced displayed, instead, wariness, a distancing from the settlement, which reflected the turmoil within the public health community and among congressional Democrats like Henry Waxman and Ted Kennedy—and the force of the Koop-Kessler Committee's disapproval. To be sure, Clinton praised the attorneys general and other people working with them, including public health advocates, for "their hard work in negotiating this agreement in a way that seeks to advance our struggle to protect the health of children against the dangers of tobacco. They deserve our thanks for doing so."

But the president cautioned:

We must now carefully consider whether approving this proposed settlement will protect the public health—and particularly our children's health—to the greatest extent possible. Until now, we have not had the opportunity to review the actual terms of the settlement, and we have not concluded whether it is in the best interests of the public health.

Over the next several weeks, we will undertake a thorough public health review. I am asking Bruce Reed, my domestic policy advisor, along with Donna Shalala, Secretary of Health and Human Services, to engage in extensive consultations with the public health community and others to subject this agreement to the strictest scrutiny. They will report to me on whether this agreement represents the best means of protecting the public health interests.

As the *Washington Post*'s John Harris characterized them, Shalala and Reed were "an odd couple . . . the twin poles of a roiling internal debate about tobacco. She loathes the tobacco companies and wants to punish them; he regards them with detachment and mild disdain, but is eager for a compromise."

Matt viewed the struggle to establish Clinton's position on the settlement as a tug of war between those, like him, who viewed the settlement, for all its flaws, as a foundation on which to build, and those who sought simply to drive a stake through the heart of the settlement so that it could not survive in any form: "The Lung Association, right out of the box, took a very aggressive role, attacking the agreement harshly, challenging anybody who said anything either positive about it or talked about building on it, rather than just destroying it, with no middle ground. This was Stan's strategy. And there were those like Bill Godshall, whose rhetoric was filled with vitriol and hate— attacking anybody who says, 'Sure, the settlement is flawed, but it's an opportunity to do something, to build on something.' "

So, for the next three months, Matt would be the informal "outside" partner to Reed, making the case for fixing, not interring, the settlement—zeroing in on curing the flaws in FDA authority; significantly (though not recklessly) raising the look-back penalties; curbing the excessive liability concessions to the industry on punitive damages and class actions; assuring that all useful secret industry documents would be made public expeditiously. Matt knew that the industry would fiercely resist many of these "cures" and would threaten to abandon the agreement. But he also believed that the industry was now so committed to peace down the road that it would ultimately swallow these important but restrained demands as the price for the support of the White House and the mainstream health organizations, who would follow Matt's lead in this. Matt would pursue the negotiator's ideal objective—to leave his adversaries "sullen but not mutinous."

Shalala, by contrast, would make common cause with the harshest of the settlement's critics and seek to derail the entire settlement process. "Strictest scrutiny" it would surely be—at least from Shalala and her advisors. Shalala's reaction to the settlement announcement was tart: "All we know at this point is that the tobacco industry is satisfied." She was not at all concerned that the industry might abandon the settlement if the administration's new demands proved excessive: "They're not going to. . . . They wouldn't have come this far if they were not determined to strike a deal and avoid future court battles." She vowed to conduct "a very tough-minded review."

Though Shalala was instinctively hostile to the settlement, there were those among her senior advisors, such as Deputy Secretary Kevin Thurm and Chief of Staff Bill Corr, who were hostile neither to Matt's efforts nor to the broad terms of the settlement itself. They were nonetheless deeply concerned that the settlement agreement was only a blueprint for legislative language—not the fine print of legislation itself.

They feared, not unreasonably, that the tobacco-indentured Republican leadership of both houses of Congress would readily invite the phalanx of industry legal draftsmen to earn their astronomical fees behind closed Capitol Hill doors. They would insert subtle but debilitating language in the bills to be maneuvered by that leadership through both houses and in a final slippery Senate-House conference committee report.

Judy Wilkenfeld captures the bitter flavor of FDA's approach under Shalala's mandate:

> I got to write a whole bunch of parts of the administration critique. They were things that would have been cleaned up in drafting the bill itself. A lot of it was cosmetic. But at that point, our approach was: Don't give an inch. As far as we were concerned, we had full powers under existing law, so that anything that was seen as withdrawing from that was seen as having given too much. On the other hand, nobody would look at the risks we were running in the courts as far as the breadth of our jurisdiction, or as far as how many years we were going to be in court. That was the political part of it.

The FDA's Mitch Zeller argues that he offered Matt "moral support," that the FDA was engaged only in "substantive criticism," not "cheap shots," and that Matt had a fair opportunity to present the case for the settlement.

Matt responds:

> Yes, I had an opportunity to explain my reasoning at a White House meeting. The atmosphere was tense and cold, particularly given my relationship with these people, but not intimidating or vicious. It was not a collegial interchange, nor did I sense that there was any chance to really change anyone's final positions, but it was not an inquisition either. I got to speak my piece, and as an advocate that is all you can ask. I did not feel bad

about the meeting but felt bad about the coldness and the distance between me and people who I had worked so closely with.

I think Mitch always meant well. At one point he called me and told me that we might disagree seriously, but that he did not want it to spoil our friendship. He meant it. He felt he needed to do what he needed to do, and I respected that. He was always careful not to personalize the disagreements. I credit him with enormous civility.

In Atlanta, at the Centers for Disease Control, there was a much more balanced view of the settlement and the opportunities it presented. Michael Eriksen had been the director of the CDC's Office on Smoking and Health for nearly a decade. A former volunteer board member of Americans for Nonsmokers' Rights, and thus an early ally of Stan Glantz and Julia Carol, Eriksen displayed uncommon bureaucratic spine in a visible and vulnerable role. Like most tobacco control advocates, he was galled by the prospect that sound and evident public policies, which Congress should have enacted decades ago, might only be achieved through litigation concessions to the industry. But he and many of his colleagues grasped the enormous potential of the settlement for their health goals:

> Matt and Bill came to CDC in Atlanta about two weeks before the settlement was finalized to brief us. We convened a meeting in the CDC Directors Conference Room with a diverse group of people from the CDC—not just folks from the Office on Smoking and Health.
>
> When Bill and Matt laid out with specificity what they were getting from the tobacco industry and what the industry was being provided in exchange, there was a spontaneous round of applause.
>
> I was the last one to comment, and what I said basically was, "What you have got from them is significant—it's exactly what should have been achieved through appropriate public policy. It's just too bad we have to pay for it. It irks me to have to allow an industry to misbehave and then to buy their way out of their misbehavior, because it was the only way we could achieve that because of their power." But there was no anger in the room at what Matt and Bill had achieved.

Nevertheless, as soon as the settlement was finally announced, and President Clinton ordered an exhaustive review of all the provisions, there was pervasive departmental hostility to it. As Eriksen recalls the atmosphere, "Clearly, it was poison for any of us to view the settlement at all favorably or even a balance of good and bad."

Throughout the summer and into September, Matt, on the one hand, and Koop, Kessler, and Nesbit, on the other, would seek to frame the debate and shape the president's posture. They lobbied the White House staff directly. They lobbied key members of Congress. They—Kessler and Koop together—testified before the Senate committees that had begun grappling with the settlement.

On June 26, the day after the Koop-Kessler Committee's trashing of the settlement, Matt testified before the Senate Judiciary Committee. In subtle ways, he distanced himself from the settlement agreement, asserting that his goal in participating in the negotiations had simply been to ensure that the public health issues "remained the primary focus of the discussions." He described the settlement as an agreement among "the state Attorneys General, private lawyers, and the tobacco industry"—*not* the Center for Tobacco-Free Kids. And he characterized the agreement not as a fixed end point, but as "the first part of the process" and ripe for fixing:

> It is the view of the National Center that the comprehensive scope of this agreement represents a unique opportunity for change. It offers the best opportunity to drive down the number of children in our nation who smoke over the next decade.
>
> Like all agreements, the negotiations even over the public health aspects of this agreement reflect an intensive give and take in an effort to come up with an overall solution that was in the public interest. The agreement has flaws and they need to be carefully reviewed and debated, but at the same time the agreement's accomplishments make this an agreement that has the potential to significantly reduce the number of our children who become hooked on tobacco over the next decade. Many of these changes would have been unimaginable only months ago.

Then he addressed the need to fix it—placing priority focus, as Koop and Kessler would not, on the FDA provisions:

> While this agreement contains extraordinary public health advances, it is clearly the result of a long and difficult negotiation process and is far from perfect. Dr. Kessler and Koop and the Advisory Committee directed by them have expressed particular concern about whether the provisions that relate to the authority of the Food and Drug Administration to require the tobacco industry to modify their products is a curtailment of FDA's current authority. Their legitimate concern is that the Agreement may make it more difficult in the future for the FDA to truly protect the public

health. . . . These concerns need to be addressed and carefully considered because it was not the goal of the participants to cut back on the authority of the agency or to make it more difficult for the agency to act in this area.

Matt followed up, three days later, with an article in the *Washington Post*'s Sunday "Outlook" section. He addressed directly the assumption that time and momentum were on the side of tobacco control advocates:

> The debate about this agreement needs to be placed in perspective.
>
> Today, many retailers still sell tobacco products illegally to children, and they do it with impunity. While the FDA has announced rules to make it more difficult to sell tobacco to kids, its budget request to enforce these rules was slashed by the House Appropriations subcommittee that oversees the FDA. Rules that are not enforced do not bring about fundamental change. . . .
>
> . . . A decade after the Surgeon General pointed out the health hazards of environmental tobacco smoke, and six years after the Environmental Protection Agency declared environmental tobacco smoke a Class A carcinogen, we have no nationwide rules to protect citizens from these hazards. . . .
>
> Some people have said we should wait before entering into any agreement with the tobacco industry—perhaps a decade—in the hope that the current court cases will force the tobacco companies out of business or result in the nationalization of the industry. This is not realistic.
>
> It would be a mistake to enact this Agreement into law without addressing the concerns of Kessler and Koop. But it would be even more tragic to allow our desire for vengeance against the tobacco industry or our insistence on perfection to derail this agreement.
>
> The American Cancer Society has estimated that if the goals of this agreement can be achieved, 1 million children alive today will be saved from a tobacco-caused death. Do we need any other reason for concluding that this agreement represents an opportunity that we cannot pass up?

By contrast, Kessler and Koop hammered away at the settlement. In testimony on July 31 before the Senate Commerce Committee chaired by Senator John McCain—the committee that would ultimately shape the Senate legislation—they urged that the Congress set the settlement aside as hopelessly flawed and start from scratch to shape legislation following the Koop-Kessler Committee blueprint.

Koop, who had earlier praised the public health provisions of the settlement as going beyond "my wildest imagination," now scorned these same provisions. He told the committee, "The settlement gives the tobacco industry everything it wants, but shortchanges the public health."

When the first details of the concessions the industry was prepared to make leaked out in April, David Kessler commented: "It's very striking how far the tobacco industry has come, from fighting almost every provision to agreeing with every position. What Philip Morris offered up just a year ago is Mickey Mouse compared to what they've just agreed to." And as late as June 23, Kessler had told the *Wall Street Journal*, "Some of the elements [of the settlement] are wonderful and I support them, but other elements have to be re-written." But by July 31, he exhorted McCain and his committee members: "You don't need the industry's money. You don't need the industry's permission. You can accept the settlement, tinker with it. That will make some difference but keep the industry booming and profitable. Or you can do right without ceding an inch to those forces that have lied and killed for years."

Kessler held aloft a copy of *Spin* magazine that displayed a series of new ads for Camel cigarettes. Having been forced to retire Joe Camel for appealing to young children, he noted, RJR had a replacement campaign underway that seductively targeted the critical eighteen-to-twenty-four-year-old market. "Where is the moral outrage?" he asked the committee. "History will not look kindly on your timidness."

What was the motivation now for such unalloyed hostility to the settlement? Jeff Nesbit offers insight into the Koop-Kessler strategy:

> I had been arguing for years that the tobacco industry's legendary clout on the Hill was just that, legendary, and that there would come a moment in time where it would become very apparent that they didn't have the horses that they claimed they had, that their hard-core supporters had narrowed to a handful of tobacco states. Given the right framing of the issue as a public health—a public health *kids'* issue—there would be enormous public support.
>
> We wanted to see how far we could push the frontier; what the market would bear all across the board; how far could you go before the industry balked; how far you could go before the Republicans balked; how far you could go before the Democrats balked; how far you could go before the White House balked—you know, the whole nine yards. How far you could go before the public health community balked or walked or whatever.
>
> This was a unique moment in history, where you didn't want to miss the opportunity. We were engaged in the art of the possible.

The citizen movement in this country succeeded much more than they ever dreamed they could have. They moved tobacco to the center of the stage, where all the big institutional players were now waging this war in public and you had to recognize that.

Looking back, Nesbit insists that he never thought it would be possible to enact legislation against the opposition of the tobacco lobby. He told me: "I don't think that's realistic, I really don't, because the industry does have enough clout that they can block things. They don't have the clout to push legislation through, but they do have the clout to block. And that's obvious." But he didn't believe the industry would walk away, even from a bill that was far stronger than the settlement:

> I was not afraid that the industry would walk away from the table. They were never going to do that, whatever table you're talking about: the congressional table, the White House table, the lawyer's table—whatever table, they were not, they could not walk away from the table.
>
> Because they have to compete in America, they have to sell their product in America, and the institutional members now involved in the negotiations are the folks who control commerce in America: Congress and the FDA and the White House and the lawyers—to a certain extent—and the attorneys general.

The strategy of pushing the envelope paid off on at least one important front: it won the support of Commerce Committee chairman, John McCain, a conservative Republican who had previously exhibited neither great interest, nor his famed rectitude, in dealing with the tobacco industry. Indeed, McCain had accepted $19,500 from the tobacco lobby in his last Senate election campaign.

Nesbit and Kessler met privately with Senator McCain following that first hearing and found him bristling at the mendacity of the tobacco companies. To their delight, McCain vowed that he would take on the tobacco lobby, shape legislation the public health community could support, and make this stand against the tobacco industry, along with campaign financing reform, the matching centerpieces of his forthcoming presidential campaign.

But McCain was struggling with the framing of the issue. Nesbit:

> He's asking, "How can I support taking hundreds of billions of dollars from the industry, a lot of this going to the trial lawyers, which is anath-

ema to Republicans, and hundreds and billions of dollars going to support for more bureaucracy, which is anathema to the Republicans?"

I don't remember whether it was David or me, but one of us replied, "Senator, the amount of money that's on the table is not what's important. What matters is what works. For instance, we know that if you add $1.50 to the price of a pack of cigarettes, that'll reduce the number of kids who smoke. You can talk about what works!"

It was like a light went on in Senator McCain's head. He got it immediately, and then we started going in that direction, and again this question of what works really began to emerge.

It was this opening that led Kessler, in his next public testimony—this time before Senator Richard Lugar, chairman of the Agriculture Committee—to highlight the importance of steep price increases: "I believe this body should set real targets, real goals for youth reduction. . . . How do you get to that goal? I think it's going to require a $1.50 to $2.00 increase in the price of cigarettes. Either you can do a $1.50 per pack increase, or I think you can do a fifty-cent per pack penalty, by company, by year . . . the best data that I have suggests that if we're in the $1.50 to $2.00 per pack [range], we have a real shot at reducing [teen smoking]."

What had brought about this shift in focus from trashing the settlement to offering a concrete set of public health proposals? Again, Nesbit offers insight into what, from a distance, seemed to be a somewhat discordant approach to the settlement. This is how he describes what was taking place beneath the surface of hearings and speculation:

As we started to have discussions with McCain and other Hill leaders, David and Dr. Koop continued to have many, many conversations with White House officials. The White House aides constantly wanted to know what Dr. Koop and Dr. Kessler could live with, that was the constant message—Lindsay and Reed and Shalala and all their core staff.

The White House was always working for what would it take to get Dr. Koop and Dr. Kessler's blessings.

Our strategy for them was, "Don't be shy; make this a public health document. We don't believe you can scare the industry away." You know it was a calculated risk, but that was our constant message to them—it was that constant message without actually saying here's what we support.

In mid-August, Dr. Koop confronted the president while they were both vacationing in Martha's Vineyard. His focus, now, was on the secret documents. Koop recalls:

> I had been talking to Bruce Reed [the president's domestic advisor] and I kept saying to Bruce that the president had said he will not get ahead of Koop and Kessler on this. I would love to talk to him.
>
> Bruce Lindsay sees me and says, "Oh, Dr. Koop! The president's inside with the first lady and Chelsea. Would you like to come and see them?" I said sure. So I ducked under the rope and I went in with my hostess and my wife, Betty. And I caught them with a glass of orange juice and a bran muffin. He was stuck.
>
> He's always been very pleasant, and he listens to me. He doesn't always do what I say, but he listens all the time. And I said, "Mr. President, you've been very good about not getting ahead of Kessler and me on public health things. But I'm asking you to do one more. Right now, Skip Humphrey is in one of the fights of his life with the courts to try to get the exposure of those thirty million documents that are held spuriously under trade secret privilege.
>
> By that time Hillary had come up and Chelsea had come up, and we were standing there together and I said, "If you will assert the principle that those documents belong in the public domain, the public will be so outraged at the industry that you will get the legislation you want." And Hillary poked him in the chest and she says, "Bill, he's right!" So, that was it.

By early September, Nesbit and Kessler had developed a sense of the possible—of how far they thought they could push the Congress and the president. They sought a meeting with Waxman and his staff and Humphrey's principal deputies. In a three-hour session, they hammered out together what they had not been prepared to embrace earlier—their "bottom line" for acceptable legislation.

Nesbit reduced the elements of their agreement to the following outline:

1. $1.50 per pack
2. Absolute targets [for reduction of under-eighteen teenage tobacco use]:
   - 30 percent after three years
   - 50 percent after five years
   - 60 percent after seven years
     Substantial penalties
   - 50 cents per pack
     Penalties must be company by company

Full disclosure, including trade secret documents
Independent settlement review board, with subpoena power
- Possible future penalty is raising minimum age to 21

3. Industry granted immunity for past actions, with a cap on financial obligations. No limits on future civil liability—however, plaintiffs need to prove "misconduct" like:
   - Hiding research on safer cigarettes
   - Marketing to kids
   - Knowing failure to make a safer product
   No exemption for restaurants on secondhand smoke
   Tobacco producers given the option of a buyout
       or money to switch crops
   Full, unfettered FDA authority
   Tobacco industry agrees to change behavior. It will not:
   - Encourage smoking
   - Ignore safer technology
   - Deceive the public

In the next few days, with this outline in hand, Waxman met with Vice President Gore privately. Kessler and Nesbit met with Bruce Reed and his staff and quietly circulated the outline to other key White House staff members. Kessler also met with Senator Kent Conrad and the tobacco task force he had been designated to chair for the Senate Democratic caucus.

And he reached out to Mike Moore. Under the heading "A Pleasant Surprise," the *Wall Street Journal* reported on October 23:

> On September 10, Dr. Kessler arrived at the posh ANA hotel here for dinner with Mississippi attorney general, Michael Moore. An architect of the pact and an ardent supporter of the agreement's passage, Mr. Moore was frustrated with the White House's delays and with Dr. Kessler's public opposition to the deal.
>
> But this time, Dr. Kessler presented Mr. Moore with a pleasant surprise. "I want to be for something rather than against something," Mr. Moore recalls Dr. Kessler saying. He could support a deal if tobacco companies raised prices by $1.50 a pack, thus reducing demand for cigarettes, particularly among cash-poor kids.

Meanwhile, Shalala and her senior advisors were pressing their White House colleagues not to endorse the settlement itself, even with specific changes, for fear that embracing the language of the settlement would provide an open door for Trojan-horse bills crafted by the industry lawyers, steered and controlled by the Republican leadership, ostensibly implementing the settlement—which the White House would then be hard-pressed to oppose. Instead, they urged that the president enunciate a broad statement of principles against which the administration would test any legislation emerging from the Congress. Kessler and Nesbit also lobbied hard for such a statement, embracing the broad outline they had developed (secretly) with Waxman and Humphrey. Nesbit, again: "Shalala was very ambivalent about the settlement at all; Bruce Reed was for fixing it; Lindsay was for it. Amazingly, and I'm still not sure how this happened, all three of them chose to go in and brief the president on a unified stance."

They went in and said, "You know, we all want to be where Koop and Kessler are."

Unity under Clinton's Umbrella?

President Clinton unveiled a broad policy statement embracing "Five Principles" on September 17, in a press statement followed by a White House ceremony, surrounded by the lead attorneys general and virtually all the prominent public health leaders.

The principles:

1. A comprehensive plan to reduce youth smoking, including tough penalties if targets are not met
   - Tough penalties and price increases to reduce youth smoking
   - A public education and counter-advertising campaign
   - Expanded efforts to restrict access and limit appeal
2. Full authority for FDA to regulate tobacco products
3. The tobacco industry must change the way it does business
4. Progress toward other public health goals
   - Reduction of second-hand tobacco smoke, expansion of smoking cessation programs, strengthening of international efforts to control tobacco, provision of funds for health research
5. Protection for tobacco farmers and their communities

In reporting on the day's events, the *Washington Post* characterized David Kessler as "exuberant." He pronounced to the *Post*: "The President hit it on the head today. He stood up for children. He stood up for public health. The differences, certainly on the public health side, have vanished."

Privately, Matt was deeply disappointed and fearful that the legislative initiative propelled by the settlement would lose momentum:

There had been a debate within the White House and in the administration. There were those like us who wanted the president to be quite concrete and to lay out exactly what needed to be done to fix the settlement. And there were those most opposed to any agreement, who feared the White

House getting concrete and specific because they suspected the White House would have come down closer to what we were advocating. This would have been a disaster for those who wanted to kill the settlement and start over completely. Internally, Donna Shalala and David led that charge.

Then, as was so often the case with this White House, they came right down in the middle. They came out with a compromise that contained such generalities that it papered over, but did not resolve, any of the differences. Their principles said nothing whatsoever about liability, one way or the other. This allowed the White House to bring together most of the competing parties. But it was an illusion of unity because it didn't confront any of the issues that divided.

Publicly, Matt had little choice but to join Kessler's chorus of unity. His September 27 press release embraced the President's position: "The broad principles that the President has articulated will help the public health community and Congress work together to achieve strong legislation that saves lives and protects children from tobacco addiction. In the coming months, we look forward to joining with the President, the Congress, and public health advocates to enact a tobacco control policy and plan that finally attacks tobacco addiction in this country."

Indeed, all the supporters of the settlement gritted their teeth and hailed the president. "The President's support for congressional action enables us to take another giant step forward," said the Cancer's Society's John Seffrin. The American Medical Association, also supportive of the settlement, "stands with President Clinton," said Vice Chair Randolph Smoak.

Opponents of the settlement were perceptibly more effervescent. From settlement foe John Garrison of the Lung Association: "The American Lung Association thanks President Clinton for taking a big step forward to protect children by not endorsing the 'global' tobacco settlement that proved woefully inadequate in addressing this nation's tobacco-related problems." Minnesota attorney general Hubert Humphrey III had no doubts: "The tobacco bailout is dead. Now we have a chance to get it right." And the public health champions on the Hill, at least among the Democrats, joined in: "The President has moved the goal posts back where they belong," said Senator Dick Durbin of Illinois.

Senator Ted Kennedy, no advocate for the settlement, predicted: "Today will go down in history as the day President Clinton made the Marlboro Man blink." Congressman Henry Waxman called the president's position "pivotal." And he told me later, "At that moment, I concluded that the industry would have to pay a much bigger price than was in the settlement, and we would get legislation that would make real changes in the way cigarettes are marketed."

Even Stan Glantz was mollified. To his e-mail listservs he announced: "I believe that President Clinton's position represents a substantial step forward from the proposed deal. He has outlined a broad set of public health provisions that do not (explicitly, at least) require trading away immunity for the tobacco industry and which will not stop the ongoing litigation. He is also broadening the focus beyond only youth smoking and has raised international issues. . . . We are in much better shape than I expected to be."

David Kessler and C. Everett Koop took great pride in bringing all the elements of the public health community together under the banner of the Clinton principles—and not a little perverse pleasure that they had followed no one else's lead. Kessler told me that, as he and Koop stood together in the Oval Office surveying the surface harmony and knowing the underlying tensions and antipathies arrayed around the president, Koop said to him, "We must be doing something right. Everybody in this room is mad at us!"

Things Fall Apart—the Center Cannot Hold

Clinton's principles and the choreographed White House ceremony tiptoed silently around the gargantuan issue of liability concessions to the industry, allowing both anti-immunity firebrands and public health–firsters to read support for their position into the presidential vacuum. But Clinton was not quite silent. When he met with the press after the ceremony, a member of the White House Press Corps asked him this obvious question:

> Mr. President, you haven't said what you're willing to do for the tobacco industry. Are you willing to agree to immunity from future liability?
>
> The president: Well, I don't think they've asked for [immunity from] future liability. I think they've asked for immunity from liability for past suits. And the question there would be, what are they willing to agree to? They need to come and meet with us. We need to discuss it, and we need to see whether we can embody these five principles. These are the things I'm interested in.

That was apostasy enough for Stan Glantz. Within a week following the issuance of the Clinton principles, Glantz had returned to the warpath. He sent the following e-mail message: "When I wrote the note that I sent around immediately after Clinton's statement, I had not yet learned that the administration was willing to cave on liability."

Ralph Nader went on high alert even quicker. He immediately labeled Clinton's statement "a half-hearted attempt to fix a fundamentally flawed deal." Nader was certain Clinton was prepared to give the industry "effective" immunity if the industry agreed "to restore FDA authority and hike the penalties for company failure to reduce teen smoking." And this he dismissed scornfully: "The United States does not engage in horse trading with drug dealers, and it should not be cutting deals with the tobacco pushers."

But C. Everett Koop and David Kessler held their fire. Kessler had drawn Matt aside, standing out in front of the White House following the meeting with the president. He exhorted Matt that it was time to bring people together. Kessler felt strongly that to be effective, there needed to be a new coalition marching together under the banner of the Clinton principles. He told Matt he saw this as an opportunity for the two of them to join forces and work together again.

Matt readily agreed and told Kessler that a group of organizations had already been working informally together to support a strengthened settlement, and that he would take David's message to them.

The next day, the groups Matt had been working with convened and drafted a set of principles—mirroring the Clinton principles—around which they would organize the new coalition. They chose the name ENACT and prepared to announce that all the groups were rallying behind Clinton.

They focused, as did Clinton, on the public health issues, choosing, as did Clinton, to say nothing about liability. Matt explains the group's thinking on this:

> There were multiple reasons. The most simple was that the public health groups in the room agreed on the public health issues, but the liability issues were beyond many of the organizations' expertise. The different organizations were struggling with what was the right thing to do and didn't know the answer. Although none of the groups were absolutist on the issue of liability, there would have been different positions on where to draw the line. Some also wanted to try to avoid further fighting with Drs. Koop and Kessler. We all hoped that the decision not to make liability an issue in our statement of principles would reduce the potential for divisiveness. So if we were going to hold the coalition together, we needed to focus on that on which we agreed. And that's what we tried to say.
>
> Second, any liability statement we would have made probably would have been short of an absolute statement of "no concessions on liability."
>
> The settlement drew the lines wrong and was flawed, and we would oppose it as drafted, but we also needed to signal potential allies on the Hill that we understood that there would have to be hard decisions made for legislation to pass and we were prepared to be part of that debate. We wanted to push the envelope, but we also wanted to be realistic and communicate to potential leaders on the Hill that we would be reliable allies when it came time. We weren't going to draw a line from which we'd be forced to recede. That would have been a bad negotiating ploy.
>
> So we put a condition on membership in ENACT, at least informally. The coalition would be open to anyone who would at least be willing to

talk about variations on liability. No one had to sign on for any specific proposal, but they couldn't say absolutely and under no circumstance would they consider any type of liability resolution. They had to move past the rhetoric to understand that there might have to be some give. The coalition didn't decide what specific proposal we would accept, but agreed that we wouldn't rule out some concessions.

Matt placed a call to Kessler to report on the agreement to organize the new coalition the day after the White House meeting, but Kessler was traveling and didn't get back to him for three or four days, by which time the formation of ENACT was rapidly moving forward. Indeed, ENACT was planning a press conference at which Kessler could announce the new coalition. Matt reported to Kessler enthusiastically that the groups had done exactly what he had urged them to do, and they were eager to work with him. He expected Kessler to be pleased; he was wrong. Instead, Matt recalls, "He was furious, just furious."

Kessler was angry that the groups had gone ahead without his active leadership. He hated the name—it sounded too eager. And, although Kessler had publicly stated that he was flexible on the liability issues —and had earlier told Matt that he would help persuade others to focus on the public health provisions—he was angry that groups who refused under any circumstances to consider any such concessions were not welcome in the new coalition. He was not satisfied that ENACT would publicly take no position on the liability issues to help promote unity and avoid unnecessary concessions at that stage of the debate. He felt strongly that the new coalition needed to be all-inclusive.

Matt told Kessler they would postpone the press conference to look for ways to bridge the differences. The next day they spoke again. The more Kessler had reflected, the angrier he had become. He would have nothing to do with the new coalition. Matt urged him to come down to Washington and to speak with the groups to see if they could allay his concerns. He repeated their common desire to work together with him. Kessler refused. Matt found himself bewildered by Kessler:

> I'm normally pretty good at reading people, but here was somebody whom I misread time and time and time again. In retrospect, I realized that while David spoke in generalities, as he so often did, and about broad principles, he actually had a very specific vision that he did not disclose. And we didn't fit the vision. In our discussions he spoke about his opposition to any liability concessions, but that didn't ring true to me because I knew he

had taken a very different position on liability in private. He had even drafted a memo offering the tobacco companies near immunity for past wrongdoing, more than I was prepared to concede on the liability issue. The reality is I don't think David knew what his bottom line was in September 1997, and that made it impossible to predict what was necessary before he would support a proposal. It just kept changing. Thus, a crucial part of David's unspoken vision was his belief that the new coalition needed to be headed by him and Dr. Koop.

If Kessler was angry at the formation of ENACT, Koop was apoplectic.

Koop told me: "One of the things that separated the public health community was that, come hell or high water, we would never acquiesce to immunity for the tobacco industry, unless we came to the end and it was all over. And that's where I parted company with Matt. I said, 'Matt, if you go into Congress and you say, "If we have to, we'll compromise," then you've said you'll compromise.' He was really, as far as I was concerned, always on the opposite side of the fence from us."

On October 20, Koop wrote a letter to Stan Glantz, which Stan diligently fed to his e-mail network of raw-nerved activists: "ENACT has asked me to be their spokesman and I will have to tell them this week that I cannot be a spokesperson for a program that aims so low as far as public health goals are concerned. I also must say that when I am asked to take an important position as a spokesperson for an organization, I think I should have been asked a little bit about what I thought about its platform."

As Matt told John Schwartz of the *Washington Post,* he was mystified by Koop's position: "ENACT supports the strongest possible public health plan. Like Dr. Koop and Dr. Kessler, ENACT has endorsed President Clinton's proposals. . . . It's hard to imagine how we're shooting low." What Matt did *not* disclose to Schwartz was that Koop had earlier assured him in private that he was fully prepared to compromise on immunity, "when the time is right."

Shortly after Clinton's statement, an amalgam of dissident players and organizations, united by opposition to the settlement and antipathy to the leadership role assumed by Bill Novelli and Matt, John Seffrin of Cancer, and Dudley Hafner of Heart, formed a competing coalition, which came to call itself "SAVE LIVES, NOT TOBACCO, the Coalition for Accountability," or, as it would come to be called, "the

SAVE LIVES Coalition." The costs of organizing and staffing the SAVE LIVES coalition were underwritten by the Cerisi law firm, which represented Minnesota in its tobacco lawsuit. Michael Cerisi's overriding objective was to keep Congress from enacting the settlement—which would settle all the pending cases—at least until they had their day in court, now scheduled to begin early in 1998. Cerisi hired the lobbying firm Downey Chandler, headed by former Democratic congressman Tom Downey. Downey, an ally of Henry Waxman and close to Vice President Al Gore, had earlier been hired by Cerisi to lobby the White House against embracing the settlement.

The SAVE LIVES members were not as united in the outcome they sought as they were in their determination to undermine ENACT. Some key leaders of the coalition were, as we have seen from the bottom-line outline agreed to earlier by Waxman, Humphrey, and Kessler, not opposed to ENACT's goal of enacting legislation that met the Clinton principles, even with concessions on liability. Rather, they, like Koop, were queasy at what they saw as ENACT's premature readiness to compromise on liability. And they sought an organizing vehicle that would honor their own leadership roles.

By contrast, Rob Weissman, Nader's staff advocate on tobacco issues, and at least some of the grassroots activists involved in SAVE LIVES began and remained fundamentally committed to opposition to any liability relief for the tobacco companies—no matter how strong the public health provisions gained in exchange. For them, "justice" and the permanent undermining of the economic and political power of the tobacco industry, not public health, were the transcendent goals.

Julia Carol and Robin Hobart of Americans for Nonsmokers' Rights, who joined and were active in SAVE LIVES, and Glantz, who preferred to operate independently, had somewhat different objectives. Like Weissman, as Carol put it in a note to the other organizers, "Core value is—no immunity. (We may or may not choose to frame our issue that way—but that's our bottom line.)" Fundamentally, it was not so much their belief in the sanctity of the courts and the tort liability system that drove them, as it was their deeply held conviction that nothing worthwhile that would seriously impact tobacco use could emerge from Congress. They distrusted Clinton as well as the Congress. They were wary, with reason, that even their sometime champions—Waxman, Humphrey, Kessler, and Koop—might ultimately cut a deal that would undermine what they saw as the heart of tobacco control progress: the "bottom-up" progress in clean-indoor-air ordinances and other efforts at the local level.

Carol and Hobart, in particular, were also deeply committed to a true participatory movement decision-making process—in contrast with what they saw as the white male, elite, leader-dominated group led by Matt and the others at the core of ENACT.

SAVE LIVES also attracted those activists who seemed most energized not by fighting the tobacco industry, but by scourging the weak-kneed among their quondam allies. Chief among the scourges was Bill Godshall. While the Downey Chandler firm was paid to represent the interests of Minnesota by making sure the Minnesota case got to trial, for activist Bill Godshall, discrediting and blowing apart ENACT was a labor of love and he dedicated himself to that task. As a reward for such dedication, he soon emerged as communications central for SAVE LIVES, managing a new e-mail network that admitted no doubters.

Organizations with a manifest economic interest in stopping the settlement also gave SAVE LIVES their support, such as the American Trial Lawyers Association, representing the interests of lawyers not party to the settlement (or the settlement's fees), who feared the settlement's precedent of cutting off the claims of plaintiffs yet to be represented in cases yet to be brought.

Also joining were representatives of union health plans that had sued the industry (in vain it would turn out) for damages they claimed to have suffered paying for treatment of the tobacco-caused diseases of their members. Their animus was not that the settlement gave the industry immunity, but that *they* had been excluded as beneficiaries.

Despite the fear and dread of Congress expressed earlier by grassroots activists like Glantz and Carol, SAVE LIVES members argued in late 1997 that the political tides were running so strongly against the tobacco companies, strong legislation could now be enacted in Congress with no concessions whatsoever to the industry. Worse, in their view, the only impediment to such action by Congress was the lack of unity among the public health groups—and the timidity of ENACT.

Stan Glantz developed a multipronged attack on ENACT and all those leaders who remained open to even the most limited liability concessions. He proved at least as energetic and relentless as Godshall, driven by utter faith in the rightness of his own vision. No one understood better the emotive power of words and symbols deployed as weapons. The most evocative was the catchword "immunity." Glantz sought constantly to inflame Cancer Society and Heart Association volunteers and staff—especially those in California, who knew him well—to shame their national leaders, John Seffrin and Dudley Hafner and Cass Wheeler (Hafner's successor as CEO of Heart), and any who would follow them. He labeled them collectively "pro-immunity," a term that evoked the maddening image of a rogue tobacco industry triumphantly free of any accountability for its wrongdoing.

He would apply the pro-immunity label unrelentingly to Seffrin and Hafner, who now firmly opposed the settlement's liability concessions to the industry but would not foreclose lesser liability concessions in exchange for a full regulatory regime embodying all the Clinton principles.

Glantz also seized upon another symbolic weapon, "preemption." Preemption had rightly been a fighting word for tobacco control advocates for a dozen years. It applied to the stealthy effort by tobacco lobbyists in state legislatures to enact benignly entitled "Clean Indoor Air Laws" with weak and unenforceable standards for smoking in public places. The real objective of such laws was their fine-print preemption provisions, which barred cities and counties from enacting stronger local laws. Over many years, led by Julia Carol of Americans for Nonsmokers' Rights and the Lung Association's Fran Dumelle, activists in every state had been fully alerted to the insidious danger of such preemption provisions and mobilized effectively to oppose and even repeal the laws.

Bill Godshall first, then Stan Glantz, added preemption to the evils of the settlement. They did this through a rhetorical sleight of hand. The opportunity arose from a legal analysis prepared for the Cancer Society that noted that in order for the tobacco companies to be free of liability for their past fraud and deception once they had entered into the settlement of such claims, it would be necessary for Congress to make clear that such damage actions could not be brought either at common law, as many of the attorneys general cases and class actions had been brought, *or* under state consumer protection, anti-trust, or fraud laws. It would be necessary, the lawyers' memo noted, to *preempt* the use of such laws for such purposes.

It made no difference to Glantz or Godshall that the ENACT coalition *expressly opposed* any federal preemption of state or local *tobacco control* laws. Henceforth, those who were willing to consider any form of liability relief for the companies would be labeled pro-immunity/ preemption. Through these attacks, Glantz succeeded in at least distracting, if not unnerving, the leaders of these organizations—and making it harder for them to build an organizational consensus in support of comprehensive legislation that granted any concessions to the industry.

Dudley Hafner insists that hundreds of Heart Association staff and volunteers throughout the country went through a painstaking, deliberative process, reviewing the settlement and its strengths and shortcomings, and coming to a judgment generally supportive of a strengthened settlement with limited liability concessions. The only dissident voices he encountered in this process, he insists, were those subjected to Stan's rhetorical tour de force: "Stan Glantz stirred up our California folks so much that I'm still upset with him. Our staff and volunteers out there had no idea about what the issues were, but they kept mouthing Stan's words. We would have meetings and we would be flooded with faxes and phone calls from three, four, or five volunteers in California that Stan had convinced that we were getting ready to support the worst thing in the world. It was as though Stan was standing there cloned, trying to discredit Matt Myers."

The Heart Association's Washington lobbyist, Rich Hamburg, acknowledges the impact of Glantz's and Carol's campaigning: "It was a feeding frenzy. They clearly won the hearts and minds of our affiliates in places where there were strong activists—California, Missouri, Florida."

In a listserv message in early December, under the heading "Local Units of Voluntaries Must Speak Out Publicly," Glantz acknowledged that he had not achieved the broad uprising among Cancer and Heart Association volunteers that he had hoped to generate, but he did not see this as evidence of support for the leadership stance:

There is a real Catch-22 here. If the leadership thinks the troops are following, they will still think immunity/preemption is okay. My view of the people in leadership positions of both ACS and AHA nationally is that they are good people that want to do what is best for public health, but they are only hearing from (1) people who think that, under the right conditions it is worth giving the industry immunity/preemption; and (2) troublemakers like me. It would really help if they heard from their own internal constituencies.

In early December, Glantz and his allies achieved a major triumph: the adoption by the House of Delegates of the American Medical Association of a resolution—supported by a strong letter from Dr. Koop—that declared: "Resolved, that the AMA remains opposed to any form of civil immunity for the tobacco industry and remains opposed to giving the tobacco industry any other special legal advantages that would abridge the rights of individuals who have been harmed by this industry."

The adoption of this resolution was immediately followed by the activists' campaign to force the AMA leadership to resign from the ENACT coalition and join the SAVE LIVES coalition. The AMA leadership refused, insisting that the ENACT principles did not themselves contemplate any grant of immunity to the industry (true) and that the AMA leadership had always opposed any such grants of immunity and would continue to do so. This was only nominally true. The AMA leadership had been as supportive of the settlement—with liability concessions—as any health organization. Indeed, the AMA, chronically allergic to punitive damages in malpractice suits, had been in the forefront of the lobbies pressing for the broad elimination of *all* punitive damages in tort liability cases. Henceforward, however, while AMA continued to participate in ENACT, the revolt of its delegates significantly hardened AMA's stand against *any* such concessions.

In some ways, the SAVE LIVES coalition was a model for citizen mobilization. It reached out broadly, well beyond traditional tobacco control groups. At its core were deeply committed, passionate advocates, genuine grassroots activists. It had, thanks largely to Carol and Hobart, an open and truly participatory decision-making process. Michele Bloch, who single-handedly energized the American Women's Medical Association on tobacco issues, was a core activist with SAVE LIVES, and she recalls the exuberance of its creation: "States competed to see who could recruit the most number of groups to the coalition. In Maryland, which was also the backyard of the coalition, we probably had thirty-six groups, and every time another state would come up with another group, we would go look for another county coalition to sign on. So, things cooked along in that way."

But the passion came from negative energy—the passion to halt threatened apostasy among public health advocates, not to enact positive public health measures. While the daily SAVE LIVES battles raged against ENACT and other former allies such as the state attorneys general, little passion and energy was left for mobilization or lobbying for "unfettered" FDA authority or the other Kessler-Koop Committee objectives. By early January, one veteran state Cancer Society lobbyist, Eric Gally, expressed, in an e-mail note, his growing frustration:

> I'm getting sick and tired of people who talk about immunity as though it is the only important issue on the table. What bugs me most is that you never hear any of them talking about the public health parts of the legislation and how they could be strengthened. It's just, "No immunity, no immunity, no immunity." I'd rather be talking about raising the federal excise tax and pricing cigarettes beyond what has been proposed, strengthening the minors' access provisions and possibly going further on advertising and marketing. These are the things that will save lives and prevent suffering. These are the things I'm prepared to ruin the current deal and any legislation over. Instead, they just prattle on solely about immunity.

The ENACT coalition, by contrast, *was* focused on strengthening the public health provisions, but it was to prove only marginally more effective than SAVE LIVES in doing so. To begin with, ENACT was more bureaucratic, and by and large its membership lacked the zeal and passion of SAVE LIVES leaders. Its active members were midlevel staff from the member organizations, committed to tobacco control, to be sure, but not, for the most part, with the activists' passion.

Whatever energies were reflected in ENACT's staffing and committees were spent defending the coalition and its member organizations against the flank attacks from SAVE LIVES and Glantz. And, as a decision-making body, ENACT was hesitant to adopt any position that might call forth thunder from SAVE LIVES.

26

The Moving Kessler-Koop Line

As Matt looks back on these events, he marvels most at his inability to divine, at any moment, exactly where Koop or Kessler stood:

> Many of my lowest points personally relate to the interactions with Dr. Koop and Dr. Kessler. I admired them and valued their friendship, but they befuddled me. What Koop meant by "shooting higher" became a continually moving target, an amazing moving target. I wanted to address their substantive concerns as the best way to gain their support. When I met with Dr. Koop in April 1997, he said he would have no hesitation in trading strong public health protections that saved "future generations" for litigation that really only compensated those who had already been hurt. Every time I thought I was there, I'd discover it wasn't good enough, no matter what. And they kept reversing roles, from day to day; who was for compromise and who wasn't? You could break your neck watching them swivel around.

To be sure, neither Kessler nor Koop were ever comfortable with the settlement negotiations or the prospect of concessions leading to peace with the industry. Yet, each was initially focused on exacting the most formidable public health provisions possible while grudgingly accepting the necessity that some form of liability relief for the industry would ultimately be necessary for good public health legislation to be enacted.

Matt tells of meeting with Koop shortly after the negotiations had been leaked to the *Wall Street Journal*, and Koop had already publicly expressed his dismay. After meeting with Koop, Matt felt Koop "couldn't have been more clear . . . that he thought the trade-offs that were being talked about made perfectly good sense, that he didn't see litigation as a solution."

Indeed, Koop's initial frustration with the ENACT coalition was based not on his antipathy toward any liability relief for the industry as a part of a final legislative settlement, but on his perception that, by remaining silent on the issue of immunity, ENACT was, in effect, implicitly conceding to the industry its most powerful bargaining chip—opposition to immunity.

Later, Koop told me, "David and I said to each other we will compromise where it gets to the point where we cannot survive without compromising."

As he wrote Stan Glantz on October 20: "The avowed purpose of the new organization, ENACT is to see the President's proposals enacted into law. You and I know that when it comes to pass there will be all sorts of compromise and if the president's proposal is the goal, we'll end up with half of that. I can't understand why the public health people are not carrying the carrot out further in front of the horse. They should be setting up a gold standard so that when that is compromised, as it will be, it might not fall any lower than the President's proposal."

Even as late as December 23, Koop was telling the *Los Angeles Times* that he was still willing to negotiate, saying he might consider legal protections "if everything we want on public health" is in a final settlement. For now, though, he said, "I think the stance has to be: 'No Immunity.' "

Matt was fearful that Koop's—and Kessler's—vocal stance on immunity would scare off potential congressional champions: "I did not think it was inevitable that Congress would act. I had two fears. Good practical legislators would decide not to take a leadership role because they believed they would be attacked when they struck some inevitable compromise. Alternatively, there would be a perception that the public health community would only settle for what others considered pie-in-the-sky demands, and the congressional leadership and the tobacco industry would revert to their traditional position of active, intense opposition, thereby killing off any real legislative effort before it gained the needed momentum."

People appeared to have forgotten that as late as April 1997 there was absolutely no momentum for any serious tobacco legislation. It had been three years since many of the most explosive tobacco industry disclosures, yet nothing was happening in Congress before the settlement discussions. There hadn't even been a serious congressional hearing on tobacco in the two and a half years since the Democrats lost control of both houses of Congress. To say that legislation was inevitable under those circumstances—no matter how strong the tobacco industry's opposition—was totally unrealistic.

In mid-December, Kessler reached out to persuade Matt and EN-ACT to join with him and Koop and others in publicly opposing immunity—"at least for now." That "at least for now" condition was in keeping with Matt's own evolving strategy, so Matt welcomed the initiative. Indeed, it was timely, because Matt had been developing just such a statement for ENACT.

Bill Novelli was initially opposed to this attempt to once again find common ground. Novelli had decreasing tolerance for what he saw as Kessler and Koop's insatiable demands. In an e-mail to Matt on Christmas Eve, he urged sticking with support for the Clinton public health principles, and remaining silent on liability:

> Are we going to secretly say to our people that "although we don't 'support' granting protections, we will do so if it comes to that?"
>
> So, we are playing into Stan's hands; the other guys are the ones being devious. We should not be.
>
> I much prefer the Clinton approach. It is the most straightforward.

Matt argued with uncommon heat:

> I do not think we can publicly stay where we were and succeed. I do not think we can overstate the harm to ENACT and our ability to accomplish our goals if we continue to remain publicly with the Clinton position. It has gained us little or nothing although I believed that it is the most honest statement, given our priorities.
>
> The balance the statement needs to make is to assert our opposition to liability protections without being deceptive that, if we fail, it is not a drop dead issue under all circumstances. It is a delicate balance, but one we need to make if we are to have any chance of succeeding.

Bill was persuaded, and the statement appeared to meet Kessler's goal of putting ENACT on record against liability concessions—"at least for now."

David flew to Washington on December 29 to meet with Matt, who reported that night on the meeting and his impressions of Kessler's position by e-mail to Bill:

> As they say in diplomatic circles, there was a frank and candid discussion, often friendly, often quite animated. To synthesize his world outlook, I think it comes down to—"we don't know what works, we do know that the industry has had its way because of its power in Congress. Therefore, the key to long term change is to destabilize the industry financially in order to weaken its power in Congress."
>
> To what end or in support of what policies, he does not seem to know;

nor has he analyzed what is possible through litigation. His view is more a Machiavellian view of political power than a public health vision of where tobacco control should be going. Given our nation's past history with regard to tobacco, it cannot be dismissed out of hand.

His commitment to litigation is not based upon a moral view, nor is it based on a concern about victim's rights. He also does not have any overarching concern about the impact of tobacco on tort reform in general. He has not done a separate analysis of the potential of different types of litigation. His interest is straightforward—litigation is destabilizing and a big hit could weaken the industry. Anything that brings predictability to the process thus runs contrary to the goal of economically weakening the industry. He had not focused on the problems with how other mass torts, like asbestos, had been handled in the courts or the inequality in results they produced. . . .

In the end he seems resigned to accepting liability protections if Congress imposes them against his will, but he is unwilling to say he will willingly give in to them. He says, "No concessions," and repeats what he says in public that if we all pull together, we can force Congress to enact strong public health legislation without concessions, but then immediately acknowledges that the current makeup of Congress is terrible and unlikely to do so. He clearly understands that I (we) will evaluate any final package based on our view of whether it is the best way to reduce tobacco use and liability issues are only one factor we will consider.

We did accomplish a good deal by the discussions I believe. I think we both understand each other better. This is more important than I would have thought because he was under a number of serious misunderstandings.

He said he believed ENACT did not oppose liability protections for the industry even if a good law could be passed without making concessions on this point. He complained that ACS had endorsed the June 20 agreement, etc. and thought ACS endorsement of the June 20 agreement was outrageous. He believed that we (The National Center) were lobbying in favor of the June 20 agreement, etc. To be candid, I was taken aback by his perceptions. Either he had not been paying very close attention or hasn't been very open to anything that conflicted with his world view. I think it is a combination of both.

With a directness that I would never have done in any other forum and, frankly, without the deference I have often granted to him and his views, I addressed each of his concerns head on. If we didn't clear the record, it isn't because we weren't direct. We were. We also let him know that we were surprised by some of his views because the record was already so clear.

We ended up in a friendly tone with an agreement that it was in everyone's interest to minimize differences and to try to work together.

The reality is that we agree on almost all issues and don't disagree on liability related issues anywhere near as badly as it publicly seems. We pointed this out to David and explicitly said that the public perceptions of disagreement were as bad as they were because some had sought to take small disagreements and portray them as cavernous differences for their own propagandistic purposes and that, if those tactics continued, no effort at peacemaking was possible. . . .

We agreed to try to build on the meeting constructively in several ways. First, we agreed to jointly draft an editorial for JAMA [the *Journal of the American Medical Association*] that we and others would sign that reflected our areas of agreement.

The tricky part will be the liability section and I tried to steer him in the direction of the liability statement we have been privately working on. If we can get his agreement to something like that, we may be able to paper over our disagreement on how to measure any final bill.

Alas, papering over would not take place. Draft after draft passed back and forth among Matt, Kessler, Koop, their advisors, Tim Westmoreland (a former Waxman staffer), Jeff Nesbit, and a passionate anti-settlement dentist, Bob Mecklenberg, who had gained Koop's ear. Finally, Koop and Kessler, through Nesbit, confronted Matt with the take-it-or-leave-it demand that he and his colleagues immediately sign their latest version of the *JAMA* editorial, which unequivocally opposed "any concessions to the tobacco industry" no matter how strong the public health provisions of any settlement legislation. "With such a glaring difference between what is right and wrong for the public, Congress should have little difficulty in choosing a course that contains no deals and no trades." This, Matt could not sign.

The editorial, signed only by Kessler, Koop, and George Lundberg, the editor of *JAMA,* was published in late January. Kessler later talked to me about the dynamic of the relationship between him and Dr. Koop. Kessler acknowledged that his revulsion—and Koop's—toward any liability concessions had indeed progressively hardened. He attributed that hardening both to his evolving vision of the future and to the reinforcing effect Koop and he had on each other: "What shifted my attitude toward liability more than anything else may have been Matt's telling me of [industry negotiator] Herb Wachtell's comment in the negotiations that what the industry sought was 'peace now, and peace forever.' "

Kessler feared that the industry would use FDA authority over tobacco as a shield—indeed, a badge of safety. He foresaw that FDA would, under political constraints, issue only modest rules governing advertising and sales to youth—but the tobacco companies would be able to boast that cigarettes were a fully regulated product, and that they were law-abiding corporate citizens and should be left to market their lawful product freely. With the industry having proved time and again its ingenuity in circumventing regulations, Kessler foresaw, "under that scenario, the possibility that smoking would rise."

Once everything is resolved and everyone declares, "Peace now, peace forever," everyone goes home. We'll get a decrease for a period of time in the number of people who smoke. But if you study the industry over the last decade, they were trying to make this a legitimate product. We'll be under regulation; we'll pay for whatever sins we've committed over the last fifty years. And we will put all this controversy behind us the day after that settlement. If this happens, I think smoking ultimately increases.

I think that the companies, as they exist now, have to be substantially weakened. If you leave companies as strong as Philip Morris, even in their current situation, no legislation will work. They have to be substantially weakened corporate entities. They can't go around and simply buy politicians and votes. You have to undermine their political and economic power.

Kessler also believed that, ultimately, there would come a Congress that would control the tobacco companies without concessions:

I believe it will take multiple Congresses. But I'd rather wait for the right time and deal with it the right way. I know you can count the number of deaths until then, and I respect that. That's the hard part. But, once you do legislation, you do legislation for twenty years.

I could be proven wrong. It will certainly take a Congress where Trent Lott is not majority leader. It will take a Congress with the right people. Not today, not tomorrow, maybe not next year, maybe not the year after; but I can assure you, things come around. You'll have the liability cases; there will come a point in time when the votes are there. You will have leadership that will do the right thing. It's a matter of time before you have that leadership. It may not be for a decade until you have the Democrats recontrol the senate. But it will happen.

Until then, I'm not prepared to give the industry peace. I'm not willing to.

As the months passed following the convening of the Koop-Kessler Committee and the settlement, Koop and Kessler had formed a deep bond, and they reinforced each other's negativity toward any concessions to the industry. Kessler, again:

As things developed, we would talk between ourselves. These were complicated issues and we didn't always view them the same way at first. I would raise points, and Koop would raise points. For the first twenty-four or forty-eight hours, we might not be in sync immediately; but after that, in forty-eight hours or seventy-two hours, we were never in disagreement.

The relationship grew out of mutual respect, but also out of a sense that together we were stronger. That's obvious. What emerged was that Koop was at a stage of his life, in his career, at eighty-two, where he didn't have to negotiate. Whether "moral" is the right word or not, I don't know, but we believed we had to get this right.

It was probably after these conversations with Koop that I began to focus on the liability issues as well as the public health issues. It's interesting. At different times on different evenings, he was in one place one evening and I was in another place that evening on liability. Then, the next evening, we were exactly opposite. There was a point where he was considering supporting some kind of liability relief, and then I thought that maybe we should support it. But then we basically came together in opposing any concessions. Until we got there, there was a lot of soul searching, a lot of thinking. Our position hardened by the end of '97, even though it wasn't the most studied position.

Thus, the hard line in the Koop-Kessler *JAMA* editorial—which Matt and his colleagues could not sign. Still, the effort to reach common ground was not quite spent. Matt began talking more regularly with Koop to explore some bridging language that might be contained in a letter to the congressional leadership, signed by all the members of the Kessler-Koop Committee.

This round of calls and drafts produced a draft letter that was still so absolute in its condemnation of any trades or concessions that John Seffrin of the Cancer Society, Cass Wheeler of the Heart Association, and Bill and Matt for the Center decided that, while they would sign the letter for the sake of the cherished unity, they needed to write a separate letter to Koop and Kessler reserving the possibility that they might, in the end, support a bill with strong public health provisions—even if it contained some concession on liability.

To Matt's relief, Koop's final draft softened the immunity language sufficiently so that Matt, meeting with Seffrin and Wheeler and Novelli, argued that there was no longer a need to send the separate letter—that Koop's draft letter left room for its signers ultimately to accept some liability limitations without violating their word. His colleagues were not so easily persuaded, overrode Matt's counsel, and as a group determined to send the qualifying side letter anyway. It read:

It is possible that we may very well be confronted with legislation that meets our public health goals and the President's public health criteria, that includes provisions that the public health community agrees would save millions of lives by reducing tobacco use dramatically, but which also addresses the tobacco industry's liability in some limited way that does not grant the industry immunity or weaken the ability of the civil justice system to protect the public health or defend fundamental rights. Given that possibility and our commitment to the public health, we believe it would be wrong for us to take a position that would prevent us from fully evaluating such a proposal in its entirety at that time.

It is a little difficult at this distance to divine much significant space between the two letters. But the very existence of a separate letter rekindled the activists' rage, and this crack in the façade of unity was compounded by the provocative decision of the Center's communications staff to release the qualifying letter at the very press conference Koop and Kessler staged to announce and release the "unity letter." The ill feeling all around was ratcheted up by the indignant insistence by Koop and Kessler at the press conference that they had never been informed that there would be a qualifying letter—though, indeed, each had been so informed.

Stan Glantz immediately charged that the qualifications in the side letter "were the equivalent of saying, 'I won't go to bed with you—unless you tell me you love me.' "

Months later, activist Jack Cannon, wrote in a broadcast e-mail message, "Myers maliciously disrupted a press conference by Drs. C. Everett Koop and David Kessler in which Myers handed out his own release stating that he had absolutely no intention of abiding by his earlier promise and signed commitment to Drs. Koop and Kessler."

Matt, of course, did not hand out the release. Indeed, he had initially opposed the separate letter. And that letter did not repudiate his signing of the Koop-Kessler anti-immunity statement. But, by now, the well of trust among the advocates had become so poisoned that what had begun as a good-faith effort on both sides to reach movement unity only served to aggravate its disunity.

The All-Inclusive Anti-Immunity Club

> The principal test the President and Congress will face next year
> has nothing to do with the budget, taxes, Medicare, highways,
> trade—the normal stuff of legislative politics. It transcends all
> those in importance—it is literally a matter of life and death—and
> in the demands it will place on them. The demands are not just
> political, but moral. The question, in fact, is whether they can set
> aside normal politics long enough to pass decent, comprehensive
> tobacco legislation.
>
> —*Washington Post* editorial, January 1, 1998

In January 1998, as congressional leaders contemplated what exactly
to do about tobacco and the settlement, a surreal, bipartisan consensus emerged—not about *what* to do, but about what *not* to do: standing together (metaphorically) were Stan Glantz and Newt Gingrich
($113,500 in tobacco lobby contributions since 1991); Ted Kennedy
and Senator Don Nickles of Oklahoma (so rabid a corporate conservative that he was challenging Majority Leader Trent Lott as insufficiently
pro-business); Representative Henry Waxman and Majority Whip Tom
DeLay (the former bug exterminator and current regulation exterminator); Kessler and Koop and House Commerce Committee chair Tom
Bliley, from the tobacco constituency, Richmond, Virginia—all competing for the prize denunciator of Big Tobacco, the settlement, and,
above all, the abominable concept of immunity.

Newt Gingrich: "The more we have learned about tobacco's deliberate campaign about addicting children and the more we have learned
about their lying, the weaker their negotiating position has become."

House Republican conference secretary Deborah Pryce, representative from Ohio, newly designated by Speaker Gingrich to oversee
the House leadership's tobacco policy: "I don't know why anyone would
want to work with the industry. The tobacco industry becomes more

culpable every time you open the newspaper. We can't protect an industry that has damned itself to this extent and we won't."

Senate Republican Whip Don Nickles of Oklahoma, on giving the industry immunity: "There's not a lot of interest."

House Republican Whip Tom DeLay, on the settlement: "I think the whole thing stinks."

House Commerce Committee chair Thomas Bliley: "If the tobacco industry engaged in criminal or fraudulent activities, then Congress needs to know about these activities before we consider granting the industry unprecedented immunity from future lawsuits."

On January 27, the Associated Press reported, "In a House leadership meeting on Tuesday [January 27], no one argued to retain the lawsuit protection provision."

In February, the *Washington Post* reported that Geoffrey Bible, Philip Morris's CEO, went to Capitol Hill to lobby for the June settlement. When he got to Senate Majority Whip Don Nickles's office, he received a chilly response: "This isn't June. This is February 1998 and things aren't going well for you. You are not going to get what you are looking for here."

What was going on?

Well, for one thing, since the settlement, the wheel of fortune had not spun kindly for Big Tobacco.

In the closing weeks of the 1997 session, a torrent of public outrage, skillfully fueled and exploited by the Center's Anne Ford and others, had forced Congress, with near unanimity, to overturn a provision, stealthily inserted by Senate Majority Leader Trent Lott and House Speaker Newt Gingrich in July into the Senate-House conference report of a tax bill, that would have granted the tobacco companies a $50 billion tax credit to offset the $368 billion settlement payment the industry had agreed to. The odor hung in the air throughout the fall.

House Commerce Committee chairman Bliley had long been distinguished largely by his steadfast defense of the interests of his Richmond, Virginia, district's most prominent constituent, Philip Morris. But in early December, Bliley upended political Washington's sense of the eternal verities by issuing a subpoena demanding that the industry turn over to his committee 834 of their most secret documents.

Standing at Bliley's side was none other than Democrat Henry Waxman, tobacco's nemesis on the committee. To the natural skeptics who wondered about Bliley's instant conversion from tobacco industry defender to tobacco industry scourge, Waxman offered reassurance;

"I think he was genuinely determined to get these documents. I don't see an ulterior motive. . . . I think he is sincere and genuine."

By early January, Waxman was able to release a cache of eighty-one of the subpoenaed industry documents, revealing that the industry had closely monitored the smoking patterns of teenagers in order to develop advertising and marketing strategies for seducing young smokers.

In one 1974 document, R. J. Reynolds's vice president for marketing told the company's board of directors that "this young adult market, the 14–24 age group . . . represent[s] tomorrow's cigarette business."

And a 1981 strategic-planning document from Philip Morris coolly argued: "Today's teenager is tomorrow's potential smoker, and the overwhelming majority of smokers first begin to smoke while still in their teens. Because of our high share of the market among the youngest smokers, Philip Morris will suffer more than the other companies from the decline in the number of teenage smokers."

There was promise of much more, and worse, documentation to come. The Minnesota case against the companies, believed by many legal experts to be the strongest case now that Mississippi and Florida had settled, was soon coming to trial. And Minnesota attorney general Hubert Humphrey III had extracted from the industry defendants a warehouse full of more secret documents. Humphrey promised that when the documents were finally unveiled, "I think the public will be appalled to see the breadth of this deception and fraud."

By mid-January, the tobacco companies felt compelled to settle the Texas attorney general's case—a case they had once scorned as weak and had vowed to fight to the end—for $14.5 billion, the richest civil settlement in history and the third state settlement in six months.

Also lurking in the wings was an even more formidable threat to the tobacco industry's public standing: the five secret, but authoritatively rumored, criminal grand jury investigations into a wide range of tobacco industry wrongdoing as criminal behavior—from abetting smuggling to conspiracy to lie to Congress. On January 7, the Justice Department filed charges against DNA Plant Technology, accusing the company of criminally conspiring with Brown & Williamson Tobacco to develop a high-nicotine tobacco plant. And knowledgeable Justice Department observers were predicting that more significant cases reaching toward the top of the tobacco companies would follow—now

fueled by the hard evidence emerging from the release of the once secret industry documents.

The *Wall Street Journal*'s well-tempered political analyst Albert Hunt
characterized the tobacco lobby's condition as a "political freefall . . .
with revelations of one duplicitous and dastardly act after another."

So it was not entirely surprising that, as the *Journal* reported in mid-
January, congressional Republicans were in full retreat from their once
comfortable embrace with the tobacco lobby:

> Republicans privately admit that the politics are dicey for their party. The
> GOP has long been identified by its financial ties to Big Tobacco. . . . Some
> party strategists are arguing that that could leave GOP candidates in a vul-
> nerable position going into the 1998 elections. "I think Republicans should
> throw the industry overboard," said Rich Galen, a former aide to House
> Speaker Newt Gingrich.
>
> Meanwhile, signs of the anti-tobacco environment are everywhere. In
> California, publicly funded billboards mock the Marlboro Man as an em-
> physema victim. Conservative Tom Bordonaro, who won a special GOP
> congressional primary this month, joked, "If you're a smoker, you're not
> even a second class citizen." Even in conservative Nebraska, said Demo-
> cratic Sen. Robert Kerrey, there's been "a huge sea change" in public atti-
> tudes in the last several years: a consensus that "the tobacco industry has
> been misleading consumers."

The SAVE LIVES watchdogs could begin to breathe easier: just
about everybody was now anti-immunity. But what exactly was everybody *for?*

For the Democratic leadership, that was easy. They were for everything that Clinton, Kessler, and Koop wanted: comprehensive tobacco
legislation that cures all the flaws in the settlement—with no quarter
given to Big Tobacco.

So, on February 11, with two dozen other Senate Democrats and
with Vice President Al Gore alongside, Senator Kent Conrad of North
Dakota, who chaired the Senate Democrats' task force on tobacco,
unveiled the dream bill for all tobacco control advocates. It fulfilled all
the public health demands of the Koop-Kessler Committee and the
Clinton five principles. It conceded the tobacco industry nothing. It
would have imposed Kessler's prescribed $1.50 per pack excise tax.
And, among other tough provisions, the bill would have imposed look-
back penalties five time more stringent than those in the June 20, 1997,
settlement on individual companies that failed to reduce teenage smok-

ing by two-thirds within ten years—or forty cents a pack. It would have given the industry no liability relief except for the attorneys general cases themselves and any potential parallel case brought by the federal government (but allowing any state that thought it could do better in court to "opt out" and go it alone). Democratic congressman Marty Meehan, joined by Henry Waxman, introduced a similar Democratic bill in the House.

Conrad had no Republican cosponsors. And in the House, Meehan would ultimately attract only a hardy cadre of ten, led by Utah Republican James Hanson, himself a Mormon and representing a district with a heavily Mormon, anti-tobacco constituency.

Clinton and Gore endorsed the bill without reservation. As Gore told a gathering of tobacco control advocates and Democratic lawmakers as the bill was being introduced, "Let me leave no doubt . . . President Clinton strongly supports this bill and would gladly sign this bill if Congress puts it on his desk."

Of course, the Democrats were, mostly, sincere in seeking the health of kids—and adults—and genuinely committed to supporting the public health groups, which looked to them for leadership. But the politics of tobacco were simultaneously reinforcing their public health objectives. With the dramatic political shift in the 1980s and 1990s from a largely Democratic South to a predominantly Republican South, congressional Democrats were untied from the former embrace of their "Tobacco Boys" colleagues.

As for tobacco's seductive campaign contributions, the congressional Democratic Party had—at first, involuntarily—gone cold turkey. Once at least as lavish in their contributions to Democrats as Republicans, the companies had shifted their allegiance, and their dollars, almost exclusively to Republicans after the Republican takeover of the House and Senate in 1995. And there was little prospect that this would change, as tobacco lobbyists found increasingly congenial the Republican romance with corporate values and abhorrence of virtually all regulation that handicapped laissez-faire business practices. So the congressional Democrats were free, voluntarily or not, of the burden of indenture to this particular corporate interest.

But the Democrats did owe much to the nation's trial lawyers, who had become as sturdy a mainstay of campaign funding for Democrats as the tobacco companies had for Republicans. The American Trial Lawyers Association had been a charter member of the SAVE LIVES coalition, representing the interests of all trial lawyers (except for the fortunate few in line to be fed by the settlement) in holding out against any congressional breach in the judge-made law supporting corporate liability. This is not to suggest that the Democrats were pandering to the trial lawyers, but rather that standing in opposition to any weakening of the nation's tort liability laws was a most congenial position for Democrats to find themselves in.

Though all denied it publicly, there was also, among at least some congressional Democrats, Ted Kennedy included, a growing belief that tobacco could be good politics for the coming 1998 congressional elections even if no legislation emerged—so long as the Republicans could be blamed. The Lung Association's lobbyist/consultant Leon Billings, a veteran Democratic Senate staffer, now himself a state legislator in Maryland, skillfully—and successfully—persuaded Senate Democratic leaders that the failure of the Republican-led Congress to enact tobacco control legislation could be a strong issue for Democrats in the fall elections. In his efforts to sink the settlement, he encouraged the Democrats to set an uncompromising standard that Republicans could not possibly stomach.

What, then, were Republicans up to, in addition to being *against* immunity? They were not exactly consumed with a single-minded focus on saving lives from tobacco use; rather, they focused on saving Republican behinds. On March 29, the *Washington Post* reported that House Speaker Newt Gingrich warned a group of tobacco lobbyists— while catching a free ride on a U.S. Tobacco plane—"I will not let Bill Clinton get to the left of me on this!"

Publicly, the Republicans would continue to excoriate the tobacco companies. Privately, they would look for ways to protect vulnerable tobacco-state Republicans—and express tangibly their gratitude for tobacco's growing campaign-financing generosity.

In early March, *Roll Call* reported that Gingrich had met with and charged the House leadership's Tobacco Working Group

> to devise a plan to help bulletproof the GOP on the issue. Gingrich told several committee chairmen at the meeting to come up with a plan to punish tobacco companies and cripple the trial lawyers—who would benefit mightily from the tobacco settlement—without imperiling GOP candidates from tobacco growing states in the South. . . .
>
> Gingrich will focus less on enacting the $365 billion global settlement and more on winning a political war against the Clinton White House and the trial lawyers, who are among the Democrats' most generous campaign contributors, sources said.

What might a Gingrich bill look like? *Roll Call* speculated that "Gingrich . . . is leaning toward a hefty cigarette tax increase, spent on his priorities, and efforts to preclude trial lawyers from ever again profiting from a deal to punish a wealthy industry."

The *National Journal* reported that Gingrich had "broached the possibility of moving separately with a bill on teenage smoking and health issues." That made good political sense for Republicans. If they positioned themselves in steadfast opposition to the settlement and immunity, and foursquare behind a bill that funded an ostentatious national, Nancy Reagan–style "Just Say No" campaign targeted at teenagers, they could indeed effectively insulate themselves from portrayal as Big Tobacco's paid lackeys, without inflicting such serious harm on the tobacco companies as the unfettered FDA regulation demanded by Democrats.

On one crucial issue, Gingrich was crystal clear: if there was ever to be a coming together on comprehensive legislation building on the settlement, Clinton would have to extend to the Republicans a wide political umbrella on liability. Again, *Roll Call* cites its ubiquitous but anonymous Gingrich advisors. "Newt basically said that unless the President comes out and says he supports liability caps and does not disagree with how we allocate [the funds generated], [legislation based on the settlement] is not going to happen. . . . He said he told the White House just that."

And what was the White House saying on liability? Yes and no. In February, a Justice Department lawyer, testifying before Congress, told the committee that the administration would indeed be open to some liability limits if they were incorporated in a bill that met the president's public health goals. But Vice President Gore was simultaneously embracing the Conrad bill, which afforded the industry no liability relief.

With Democrats heading left, Republicans heading for cover, and the White House waffling, SAVE LIVES coalition members could indeed breathe easier—no relief for the industry from liability was in prospect. But the prospects for bipartisan agreement between Senate and House Democratic and Republican leadership on comprehensive public health legislation that would meet the Kessler-Koop-Clinton standards seemed equally dim.

McCain to the Rescue

For all the bipartisan rhetorical fist clenching and teeth gnashing at the perfidy of the tobacco industry, and for all the talk of irresistible momentum toward fierce, uncompromising legislation straitjacketing Big Tobacco, nothing was moving in the Congress. Matt's fears that his fellow advocates' uncompromising righteousness, congressional political positioning, and Clinton's refusal to espouse concrete legislative proposals would arrest movement toward serious legislating seemed well grounded. He was hardly encouraged, either, when, in early March 1998, Senate Majority Leader Trent Lott anointed Senate Commerce Committee chairman John McCain, from among the several competing committee chairs with jurisdictional claims on the legislation, to lead the Senate's response to the settlement and its warring constituencies. Lott was no friend of strong tobacco control legislation; and his anointment of McCain was no sign of Lott's blessing upon strong legislation.

This move was not exactly a surprise. In a bizarre private meeting in early March with John Seffrin, CEO of the Cancer Society, Lott had launched into an unprovoked tirade. He derided "Dr. Kook and Dr Crazy" and challenged Seffrin: "Just look at Kessler's eyes. They bulge out. He's a fanatic." Seffrin gamely defended Koop and Kessler, but Lott swept his protestations aside. "The tobacco companies are *wimps*," he fumed. "If you want a settlement, you can probably get one, because the tobacco industry are wimps. However," he admonished, shaking his finger at Seffrin, "if you ask for too much, you'll get nothing." And he told Seffrin that the Cancer Society should stick to research and leave the legislating to the Congress.

Lott's choice of McCain reflected his assessment that the Senate Commerce Committee was the *least* likely of the five committees that claimed and sought jurisdiction over at least part of the legislation to commit regulatory excess or offend the tobacco industry. Its Republicans were suitably conservative and high on the list of recipients of tobacco industry campaign contributions. And its two senior Democrats, Ernest "Fritz" Hollings and Wendell Ford, faithfully represented tobacco-growing South Carolina and Kentucky, respectively.

Before the settlement, Matt had no relationship with John McCain, and minimal expectations of him. Indeed, in September 1997, Matt had risked McCain's famed wrath by drafting a statement for the Center highly critical of McCain's decision to introduce, with the Commerce Committee's ranking Democrat, Hollings, legislation embodying the terms of the June 20 agreement. Matt:

> I had seen the bill that the industry was working on—and McCain's bill was essentially it. Our organization was very fast out of the block to criticize it very strongly.
>
> Our Republican consultants warned us, "Very big mistake! McCain won't forget. His intention wasn't bad. We were too quick to jump. This is going to make it harder to develop a really good relationship with him."
>
> But I felt then that we, uniquely, had a responsibility to prove that the settlement, without improvement, wouldn't be adequate, and that, therefore, it was vitally important for us to send that message to the Hill—as well as to our own community.

Earlier that summer, immediately following the June 20 settlement, Matt had asked former Republican congressman Vin Weber, a conservative highly respected by his former colleagues whom Matt had engaged as a contract lobbyist, to arrange a meeting with McCain. Wary, Matt nevertheless had found McCain engaged and open-minded.

> McCain was exceptionally supportive—not anything specific, but his interest in the issue seemed extraordinarily sincere. It was a general conversation, but a positive one.
>
> Still, I walked out of that meeting skeptical. McCain was better than I had expected him to be. But the committee as a whole was not. So my fear, in the fall of '97, was that the industry would maneuver the bill to the Commerce Committee. It was the place where we had the least hope.

But at least the meeting with McCain had given a hint that there was a sympathetic ear there. And during the ensuing months, Matt patiently set out to develop a working relationship with McCain's Commerce Committee staff member assigned to tobacco legislation, Lance Bultima:

Lance, who had been charged with responsibility, hadn't had any long-term contact with the public health community. He is a relatively conservative free-market Republican, no-nonsense sort of person. Frankly, at first he didn't seem to have a whole heck of a lot of respect for the public health community.

Within about a month of the introduction of the McCain bill, he and I had an initial, relatively long meeting. He had a myriad of questions about substance, about policy, about issues. And we had one of those brain-drain conversations, give and take about pros and cons and different approaches. Who would be favorable? Who would be opposed? What the policy implications were. Different options or ideas about ways to go that he had thought about.

As the rumors began circulating that Lott would anoint McCain and the Commerce Committee to take the lead, Matt also began meeting with John Raidt, McCain's Commerce Committee chief of staff and trusted alter ego: "I remember meeting with John Raidt and saying to him, 'Just let us know any way we can help you.' We were portraying ourselves as the people who were serious about legislating—the people you could come to and we'd give you honest answers, and we'd work with you to see if something could be done."

Then, on Friday, March 6, Matt received a call from Raidt asking if he would come to meet privately with McCain and his staff members:

That was the first really personal meeting, in part because McCain initiated it. He was engaged fully; he had a task; he wanted to get this done. The purpose of the meeting was for him to say, "We're going to take the lead. We're going to try to put something together that the public health community will like."

But he warned us, "Before I venture down this road, I want to know if you're still willing to make some of the basic compromises that would be necessary to get this legislation out. Otherwise it's not going to happen. To get this through my committee, there are going to have to be some compromises made, because it's fundamentally conservative."

It was clear he had already had lengthy conversations with Hollings and Ford.

"I can't tell you where exactly the line is," I told him, "but we're prepared to work with you. We're not out there on the fringe. For us this isn't rhetoric. This isn't politics. We want a bill."

He also asked about where Koop and Kessler would stand. And I replied that I would be the last one in the world to be able to predict.

McCain ordered his chief of staff, John Raidt, to put the legislation on an intimidating fast track—a bill drafted, hearings held, and committee action (the "mark-up") within two to three weeks. This was "mind-boggling to all of us," says Matt.

Mind-boggling or not, the next three weeks consumed Matt and others in a series of negotiating sessions—not unlike the earlier settlement negotiations in their day-into-night intensity and the constant threat of derailing. The most salient and benign contrast, however, was that McCain had banished the industry lawyers and lobbyists from the table. Matt: "McCain was adamant that the industry would not be represented. He wasn't going to be tied to having kowtowed to the industry. He wanted to be able to say with honesty and sincerity that this bill represented the best he could do and that he had not fashioned it to satisfy the tobacco industry."

With the aid of his dog-eared appointment book, Matt reconstructs that time:

> I had another meeting with McCain on Monday afternoon. Same players at that meeting. McCain says, "Okay, we've taken several additional steps. Here's our core game plan. We're working on a bill. We're going to hold a series of hearings first. And we're going to be drafting. Lance is going to take the lead in drafting the bill. Please work with Lance on that. Do you have advice on the hearings? These are the people who we're getting."
>
> There was a hearing the next day; then there were more hearings two days later. I testified. My calendar shows hearings that week on Tuesday, Wednesday, and Thursday—two of them on Thursday—and a host of meetings with White House people and the Hill folks through the end of the week.
>
> Then I had a one-week vacation scheduled, I think we were to leave Saturday the twenty-first to go to Florida. My recollection was I didn't get out on Saturday with the family, but I did go down the next day and got in late Sunday night. The twenty-second. And on Monday, I had two or three conversations with John Raidt. He said to me they were moving ahead; they were doing more serious drafting.
>
> Tuesday morning I had a conference call with JR and a few other folks. And at that point they said to me, "I think you need to come back."
>
> And I said, "Is there no other way that I can do this?" And he said no.
>
> Tim Westmoreland was there, not through all of it but through much of it, for Koop, and on rare occasions, Jeff Nesbit appeared on behalf of Kessler.
>
> We went through the settlement bill section by section and renegotiated the whole thing.

With the industry lawyers and lobbyists excluded, and with support even from such unlikely sources as Senator Hollings's staff—despite his South Carolina tobacco-growing constituents—the negotiators made good progress in strengthening the bill's public health provisions.

There were struggles, of course. Ironically, some of the committee senators who were most supportive of public health shied away from the settlement's tough smoke-free workplace standards. "That wasn't just the bad guys," says Matt. "It was the good guys, who were saying, 'I'm not going to tell my state to do *that!*' " There were side battles, such as those between the White House staff and Oregon Democratic senator Ron Wyden, a strong public health advocate, who pushed hard—ultimately successfully—for a series of provisions designed to provide support for international tobacco control efforts.

Day-by-day, draft-by-draft, the public health provisions grew stronger. At least, that was true during the daytime sessions. On FDA authority, for Matt a central public health issue, the sessions went late into the night—and the path proved rocky, even treacherous. Matt:

> The FDA provisions were very difficult, because early in the discussions, McCain had felt it important to try to reach an agreement with the chairmen of the other key committees who shared jurisdiction over parts of the legislation—Jim Jeffords of Vermont, chair of the Health, Education, and Labor Committee, and Orrin Hatch of Utah, chair of the Judiciary. Each had crafted their own FDA provisions, which were weaker, dangerously ambiguous, and reflected fundamental disagreements with the positions taken by the FDA team.
>
> McCain was in and out of the meetings, and I told him of our frustrations with the Hatch and Jeffords drafts. The Hatch and Jeffords people would participate, then they'd go back, do redrafting, and they would come back with something that they'd profess was much closer to what we had wanted but still reflected the same basic disagreements that we had had from the very beginning.
>
> There came a point, late one night that week, where McCain threw up his hands at the process. He became convinced that no agreement would be reached with the Hatch and Jeffords staff in the room. And he contacted [Tennessee senator] Bill Frist and asked him to take the initiative.

McCain convened a rump meeting in the committee office with his staff, Matt, people from the White House and FDA, a small group of the negotiators, and Senator Frist—but not the Jeffords or Hatch staff members. Matt recalls:

McCain said to Frist, in what was extraordinary for me, "I know you sit on the Health Committee [which Jeffords chaired]. I know this is difficult, because you have relationships with Senators Hatch and Jeffords, but if you're going to take up this responsibility you can't defer to them. I am now convinced we will never reach a compromise if they are part of the negotiations. So, while that's a heavy burden, that's the responsibility [and] I'm asking if you're willing to take it up." And Frist said yes, he would do that; he would take on the responsibility for crafting an FDA proposal acceptable to all.

Frist, though the Senate's only physician—a cardiac surgeon—had been no friend of tobacco control legislation. But, like McCain, he took his new charge seriously. Still, he had only two days to come up with a highly technical section of the legislation, with Hatch and Jeffords staffers still pressing for adoption of their language.

Both ENACT and FDA had insisted that FDA should treat tobacco under its "drug" and "drug delivery device" authority. Hatch and Jeffords, echoing the industry, demanded that tobacco should be treated in a separate chapter for tobacco only. ENACT's and FDA's fear was that if a separate chapter was created for tobacco, it would be weaker and inadequate. Nonetheless, Senator Frist made it clear that he sided with Senators Hatch and Jeffords on this issue, even though he also said his goal was not to weaken the authority of FDA over tobacco. The problem was that FDA had previously resisted all requests to draft a separate chapter of the Food and Drug Act for tobacco, and there was growing risk that Frist would adopt Hatch's and Jeffords's language if there was not an alternative.

Matt urged the White House to have FDA at least attempt such a draft to see if writing one was possible. Matt was convinced that the only way to get Frist to agree to a level of FDA authority for tobacco that met ENACT's criteria was in a separate chapter, and the only way to guarantee a good separate chapter was for FDA to draft it. In a mad dash against the deadline set by Senator McCain, an FDA team led by Bill Schultz did just that. And their draft became the framework for the final proposal negotiated by Senator Frist and everyone else working on the legislation. FDA would have full authority to radically transform both tobacco marketing and advertising and the fundamental nature of tobacco products sold in the country—the "unfettered" authority Matt had sought and Kessler and Koop had demanded.

29

A Cliffhanger on Liability

What was not okay with Matt in the draft bill were the liability provisions, which still included much of what the public health community had found so obnoxious in the settlement itself. As late as Monday, March 30, the *Wall Street Journal* was reporting that Chairman McCain had met the demands of "conservative committee members, who had insisted that the compromise provide cigarette makers with extensive protection from lawsuits."

Matt did not object to what he considered the one acceptable concession on liability: an overall cap on how many additional billions the industry would be required to pay out to smokers in total damages each year—with no overall limit on the total damages they could be forced to pay. The draft bill set such a cap at $6.5 billion a year. Under its provisions, the companies would remain fully liable to all private claimants for all court judgments, in any form that the ingenuity of the trial lawyers could maintain in court—to say nothing of the ten to twenty *billion* they would pay each year in indemnity for their wrongs in settlement of the attorneys general suits. All that the caps would achieve would be to allow the companies to spread out their additional payments over several years in the highly unlikely event that combined jury awards in any single year totaled more than the cap. As an added prod to the companies, the draft bill provided that the companies would be protected by the cap only if they met the bill's stringent targets for reducing teenage smoking.

Indeed, even the secret bottom-line outline that Kessler, Waxman, and Humphrey had agreed on among themselves the previous fall included: "Industry granted immunity for past actions, with a cap on financial obligations." Kessler and Koop's key strategist, Jeff Nesbit, told me, "I didn't mind the cap. I thought it was a way to get out from under that problem."

But the McCain compromise would also have freed the companies from exposure to potentially huge punitive damages in lawsuits based upon their past wrongdoing. And, like the settlement, it would also have immunized the companies from all class actions based on past misconduct. This, Matt resisted fiercely.

Matt's intransigence triggered an explosive response from the attorneys general lawyers Joe Rice and Dick Scruggs, which surged beyond the boundaries of the negotiations into print. The *Journal* closed its story by reporting "an angry outburst from plaintiffs' lawyer, Richard Scruggs. Messrs. Scruggs and Myers helped craft the proposed settlement with the industry, and Mr. Scruggs pointed out that Mr. Myers had endorsed its generous legal protections."

Jeff Nesbit, who witnessed this outburst, is somewhat more graphic in capturing Rice's apoplexy: "Joe was at one the end of the table, and Matt at the other end arguing the public health position—and winning the day. Then Joe gets up from the table and storms around to Matt and yells, I just can't believe you—you signed the fucking deal!' "

"Dick was more controlled," says Matt, "but just as angry."

Right or wrong, through his intransigence, Matt forfeited his seat at the negotiation table: "I had negotiated my way out. I had been pushing so hard on the liability issues that I was on the edge. The attorneys general no longer wanted to deal with me. I was no longer a team player, no longer capable of satisfying them. And we had no support from the White House." But Matt had one remaining recourse: two staunch public health allies with whom he had built a strong working relationship, committee Democrats John Kerry, from Massachusetts—the senior non-tobacco-state member on the committee—and Oregon senator Ron Wyden. Earlier in that week, Kerry's staff member Greg Rothschild had told Matt that Kerry considered the immunity issue "overblown; that the litigation was not a solution to the tobacco problem; that there was a deal to be made here and now; and that Kerry was determined to find a middle ground to get there."

So Kerry and his staff accepted the broad concessions on liability that McCain's staff was proposing. Matt: "I remember one night talking with Kerry's staff guys, David Kass and Greg Rothschild, saying to them, 'I just have to warn you that all the good intentions in the world are just going to get you into a firestorm. There's no way the public health community will accept what you are currently discussing.' "

Throughout the week, Matt continued to warn both Kerry's staff and Ron Wyden of the abuse they would take if they accepted the liability provisions then in the bill. He reminded them of what he himself had been through over the past six months—and how painful that had been. It was not an experience, he assured them, they wanted to replicate.

McCain, Kerry, and Wyden all desperately wanted Kessler's and Koop's blessing—or at least their acquiescence. On Wednesday of that last week, David Kessler flew down from New Haven for an early evening briefing from McCain's staff and a meeting with McCain. He also had a brief conversation with Matt. They each recall that Kessler was satisfied with the public health provisions. Indeed, Kessler told me that he had braved Henry Waxman's wrath even by talking to McCain, and that the final FDA provisions justified his doing so. But he could not stomach the liability concessions.

Kerry and Wyden were jolted into action. They shared with McCain their concern about Kessler's and Koop's threatened opposition. And McCain listened.

Meanwhile, Matt had kept pressing Bruce Reed, Clinton's domestic policy advisor, for White House support. Finally, Reed assured McCain that Matt spoke for the administration in opposing the liability provisions.

McCain had set a press conference for late Monday, March 30, to announce the terms of the bill he would present to the Commerce Committee for approval. Shortly after midday Monday, Matt received a call from Mike Moore, still negotiating in the committee chambers. Moore asked whether Matt could support the bill if all of the liability protections were removed, leaving only the caps. Without making a commitment, Matt assured Moore that it would be far easier to gain the support of ENACT with only the caps than with the existing provisions.

A few minutes later, a call came from Greg Rothschild of Kerry's staff. McCain had told Kerry that he would agree to eliminate all of the liability protections in the bill other than the caps if Koop and Kessler would endorse the bill. Rothschild asked Matt for Koop's and Kessler's phone numbers so that Kerry could call them, tell them of McCain's agreement to strip all the liability concessions other than the caps from the bill, and seek their endorsement. Matt suggested that Kerry call Koop first. As soon as he hung up from Rothschild's call, Matt called Koop and, finding him out, left a message for Koop to call him back before taking Kerry's call.

Koop called. He was still not happy with a $1.10 price per pack increase (the Koop-Kessler Committee had called for a $1.50 per pack increase) or *any* caps on liability. But Matt reminded him of the good things in the bill, not pressuring him, soft-spoken, respectful. There was no argument.

Earlier that day, Matt had commented that as he and Kessler and Koop had together fought the liability relief provisions in the emerging McCain bill, "My relationship with both has never been better than in the last few days."

At 3:00 P.M. Matt heard from Moore again. McCain had not waited for word from Koop and Kessler. "We have done this," Moore told Matt. "Will you come to McCain's press conference on the bill at 5:00 P.M. this afternoon?"

The McCain bill was done. By any measure it was a substantial strengthening of the settlement. It met the Kessler-Koop demand that FDA be given full authority over tobacco, and it eliminated all liability protections except for the annual cap on damage payments. It would virtually double the three-year price increase forced on the industry, from the settlement's estimated $0.63 a pack to $1.10 a pack. Of course, the bill was not perfect. Its environmental tobacco smoke provisions could have been interpreted to make federal nonsmoking rules pre-empt even stronger state and local regulations; the caps could have been higher; the bill did not mandate that funds paid by the companies must be spent on tobacco control programs; and the headlong rush to produce a bill inevitably left ambiguities that could prove troublesome.

Would Matt *now* join in the press conference?

30

Not Good Enough

Mike Moore had said, "We have done this [accepted the elimination of the liability protections except the caps—exactly as Matt had demanded]. Will you come to McCain's press conference?" Matt hadn't answered his question.

Matt's sense of obligation as a lobbyist was clear and strong: When you make demands upon a legislator, he or she knows that you are prepared to attack if those demands are not met. But if your demands *are* met, then you need also to be prepared to stand up in support. It was a similar sense of obligation that earlier kept Matt from walking away from the settlement talks when most of his public health demands had been met—and from abandoning colleagues like Washington attorney general Chris Gregoire who had worked so hard with him to meet those public health objectives.

But Matt was not free to follow his own instincts. He was the spokesman for ENACT, and he knew that many ENACT members would be reluctant to stand up with McCain—unless Kessler and Koop led the way. And Matt could not be sure whether McCain's last-minute concession on immunity was enough to gain Kessler's and Koop's seal of approval.

Monday afternoon, I stopped by to learn what was happening. Gathered in Matt's office for an unrelated ENACT committee meeting were several of the senior representatives of ENACT members, as well as Matt's own staff members. Matt asked each whether he should appear at McCain's press conference.

Susan Polan of the American Cancer Society quickly responded, "You have to go!" But all the others counseled caution. Elaine Holland of the American Academy of Pediatrics was full of worries: "There are bad parts of this bill; if we endorse it now, will we lose our leverage to cure its flaws?" Anne Ford, Matt's deputy, was equally cautious. "What will you say? If you can call the bill a good foundation, but it needs improvement on ETS and caps on penalties, okay. Otherwise, it will seem like an endorsement—and the Democrats will be furious." Bill Novelli counseled, "Go with Koop, either way." Diane Canova, from the Heart Association, was skeptical: "Can you trust Koop? Look how slippery he has been."

And Matt answered, "You can trust Koop to keep his word."

Canova cautioned Matt against speaking for ENACT unless and until the ENACT coalition had formally deliberated and come to judgment on its position.

Linda Crawford, Polan's superior at the Cancer Society, called in, remanding Polan's support for Matt's attendance at the press conference. Crawford insisted that no support for McCain be given unless and until *both* Koop and Kessler supported the bill.

Matt listened. "I don't have to appear formally on behalf of EN-ACT," he concluded. "But if I do go, only to be attacked by other EN-ACT leaders, I'll risk destroying the trust that we've so painstakingly built up." Matt called Koop. Koop remained unmoved by the McCain agreement to drop all the liability protections save the caps. He was, said Matt, "quick and adamant. He would oppose the bill." Matt mused that Koop was like a great ocean liner: once he was bearing on a particular course, it was difficult for him to turn back. Matt:

> I called back and told Mike I couldn't participate in the press conference. But I went down and actually succeeded in finding McCain and having a conversation with him before the conference, saying to him that I hoped he wasn't disheartened by the failure of our group to line up behind him after all that he had done. I said we did, in fact, appreciate it; we did, in fact, believe he had done a fantastic job. But we had to work out Dr. Koop's strong opposition, and it would be harmful to him and to us for us to stand up there and endorse the bill before we could do that.
>
> McCain was incredibly gracious, as he so often was in dealing with us during this time. He understood our reasons, and he didn't hold it against us. Of course, he was disappointed, because he thought that he had done everything that we and Kessler and Koop had asked of him.

Among the ironies of the press conference was that Matt found himself "standing on the sidelines" with Gale Norton. Like Matt, Norton, the conservative attorney general of Colorado, could not bring herself to join her colleagues at the podium—for the opposite reason. She had favored broader liability protection for the companies. She said to Matt, "You know, when you got your way, they lost my support."

The decision to forego the press conference and not endorse the McCain bill left Matt acutely unhappy, even if it proved prudent, for Koop not only didn't endorse McCain's bill, he attacked it with even more venomous invective than he had unleashed on the June 20, 1997, settlement—as did Henry Waxman, who assailed it as unacceptably weak. On March 31, 1998, the AP quoted Koop as labeling the McCain bill "a sellout." "They're teaching kids just how to manage to spend a few cents a year to get their fix. . . . That just won't do it. It must be more than a kid's allowance can afford."

It took the ENACT coalition many hours of strenuous navel gazing to come up with a kind word for John McCain and his bill—and that kind word was buried in a sea of reservations. In the shadow of Koop's rage, this was the best that Matt could eke out of them. The letter was sent and signed by the ENACT coalition members to Senator McCain on Wednesday, April 1, the day of the committee mark-up and votes. It read, in part:

> We commend you and your staff for your tremendous work over the last few weeks to draft comprehensive tobacco legislation. Your ability to unite political parties, interest groups and branches of government is admirable.
>
> The bill you are marking up today represents a constructive step forward and contains many improvements over the Agreement reached by the State Attorneys General last June, particularly with regard to the authority of the Food and Drug Administration, although we would still prefer tobacco to be treated as a drug and device.
>
> While we have had only a brief opportunity to review the bill which was made available for the first time yesterday, based upon our first impressions, it provides an opportunity for fundamental change and builds momentum towards the passage of historic tobacco legislation this year. We believe this bill will enable a solid foundation to be in place after Wednesday's mark up by the Commerce Committee but urge that a number of concerns of the public health community be addressed.

The letter called for the following changes: a price increase of $1.50 rather than $1.10; tougher penalties for companies that do not meet smoking reduction goals among youth; stronger environmental tobacco smoke provisions; and assured funding for tobacco control programs. The letter also pointed out the need "to address the . . . questions raised by the liability cap." There was little appreciation expressed for the giant steps McCain had taken to meet the public health communities' demands—including the elimination of all immunity provisions save the cap.

Matt deeply regrets his and ENACT's failure to support McCain unequivocally and publicly.

> I felt strongly that I should have been there; that we should have been there, standing with McCain. That was the biggest mistake we made. In retrospect, I've always wished that McCain could have given us twenty-four hours to have had a shot at bringing Koop around—at least trying! To this day, I regret the decision not to support McCain's bill the day it was introduced. We acted out of a desire to maintain unity, but John McCain did everything we asked and he deserved our support.
>
> I have often looked back on that day and wondered what would have happened if we stood up there with McCain and said, This is a good bill and it is time we all unite to make it happen. I know we would have been criticized, but eventually our unwillingness to unite behind a vehicle that could be passed allowed our opposition to bury the bill during the amendment process. If we had all united in early April, we might have pushed the bill to the floor before the tobacco industry could mount its opposition.

Despite Koop's invective and ENACT's tepid response, McCain achieved at least a minor miracle that Wednesday, April 1, reporting his bill, intact, out of the Senate Commerce Committee by the remarkable vote of 19–1. The *New York Times* reported:

> Sweeping aside challenges favorable and unfavorable to cigarette manufacturers, the Senate Commerce Committee gave a strong bipartisan vote of approval today to legislation that would raise the price of cigarettes and stiffen regulations on tobacco.
>
> No other measure before Congress this year could lead to such fundamental changes in society. If the sponsors are right, it could reduce the number of teen-agers who smoke by as much as 40 percent and prevent millions of early deaths from smoking-related illness.

But the *New York Times*'s David Rosenbaum added a cautionary note: "The ease with which the bill cleared the committee without substantive change belied the extent of the opposition and the many obstacles that lie ahead."

The *Wall Street Journal*'s columnist Al Hunt—the *Journal*'s lone moderate and a consistent supporter of comprehensive tobacco control legislation—offered McCain the praise that ENACT withheld:

John McCain may not have found the precise fault line for optimal to-bacco legislation, but he's close.

The Arizona Republican achieved two important objectives: Politically, he moves closer to the public health-oriented alternative offered by Senate Democrats than to the settlement that the tobacco industry negotiated with the states' attorneys general last summer. Also, he realized the legislation's principal objective should be to curb youth smoking; other issues will take care of themselves. . . .

Chairman McCain, delicately trying to get a measure that would be effective and win sufficient support, opted Monday to give the industry only minimal liability protection from a public health standpoint. There are clear improvements that can be made in the McCain bill. Most important, the lookback penalties are too mild. But overall, congressional liberals and their outside allies would make a mistake by going too far. The best course is a deal in which tobacco reluctantly participates.

Hunt had interviewed Kessler, who had spoken warmly of McCain's "courage."

There are lots of good provisions in the McCain bill; Dr. Kessler, for one, is basically pleased with the expanded authority over tobacco given to the FDA.

After working with and watching the process through last weekend, Dr. Kessler . . . says: "It was John McCain's courage that made it happen. . . ."

There are still some problems that must be fixed but the Republican Chairman of the Senate Commerce Committee has said to the tobacco industry, "You don't own us."

But Kessler's relatively warm remarks were shadowed by Koop's harsh words. Matt feared that Kessler would not separate himself from Koop for long.

Matt was not prepared to celebrate the Commerce Committee action:

That, ironically, was one of the worst days. We had this unbelievably good bill, despite its flaws—a 19–1 vote—and there wasn't a single representative from the public health community who was enthused.

That night the Hollings staff and the McCain staff went out for drinks with the attorneys general—and they invited me along. I debated—and initially said no, because it was so clear that this would upset some in my community. But, eventually, I decided it was wrong not to go, and so I did.

And Chris Gregoire—who was so upset at our attitude—said to me, "Come on, Matt. You *have* to be pleased by what happened!"

I started to give her the standard answer of the groups—but she suddenly cut me off, saying, "I don't care *what* Koop's telling you; tell me what you, personally, think. That's what I want to know."

And I told her that I had been pushed in so many directions I no longer could tell what I felt personally. For me, that was a horribly low moment, because deep down, I know I agreed with Chris and hated not being able to build the consensus needed to make it happen.

Worse Than Nothing!

However tepid ENACT's praise for McCain might have been, Stan Glantz once again broadcast his displeasure to all within reach on the Internet:

> ENACT does not list the preemption and immunity provisions in the bill as a problem, so one can only conclude that they accept those provisions.
> ENACT has also backed off "full authority for the FDA" by accepting McCain's compromise position. ENACT would "prefer" it to be different, but seems willing to go along with a law that will create a new industry [excuse for] suing the FDA.

On March 30, Ralph Nader wrote a letter to the president decrying any legislative "liability limits"—not just broad "immunity"—as part of a deal:

> A deal on liability limits as part of a "comprehensive" package will decompress the political climate, create a sense in which tobacco seems a "finished" issue and remove the litigation spur to media, public, legislative and regulatory focus on tobacco. The result will be to foreclose, or at least slow, future public policy health innovations.
> The history of efforts to tame Big Tobacco makes it clear that this approach should be avoided at all costs.

And to make sure no one missed the message, Nader's Public Citizen issued a broadside to all SAVE LIVES members, with the headline: "A CAP ON LIABILITY = IMMUNITY FOR BIG TOBACCO. Rob Weissman and Russell Mokhiber wrote an article for the Nader-sponsored *Multinational Monitor*, delineating the many "reasons why the industry loves the McCain bill." "Outstanding," wrote Stan Glantz in admiration. "The McCain bill is indeed the 'briar patch' that the industry wants to be tossed into!" Reading the Weissman-Mokhiber critique, Matt noted wryly, "It's interesting that none of the criticisms actually relate to reducing tobacco use or preserving the rights of individuals."

Who was paying attention to this ferocious but insular group of activists, none of whom but Glantz had access to the mainstream media? Certainly Dr. Koop, who was constantly reinforced in his growing militancy by Glantz and by others who were both resonating with the negative chorus and counseling its members, like Dr. Robert Mecklenburg. Kessler, in turn, was resonating to Koop's negativism, and the mainstream media paid attention to Koop and Kessler.

By April 20, when he appeared before the full Senate Democratic caucus, Dr. Koop had developed a full head of denunciatory steam. He dwelled at length and with passion on every large and small shortcoming in the bill, and then he came to the liability provisions:

> The liability portion of S1415 is the most egregious to the public health community. Indeed if there were one segment which I think might have been written by the tobacco industry, it is this one.
>
> In short, S 1415 is a windfall for the tobacco industry.

Just in case anyone was confused, Koop assured the Democratic caucus: "Let nothing that is said today nor anything that has been quoted in the press—sometimes out of context—as said separately by Dr. Kessler or me indicate that Dr. Kessler and I are not of one solid mind on the issue of tobacco control."

Matt and Bill Novelli did manage to publish an op-ed article in the *Washington Post*, on April 24—under their own names as president and executive vice president of the Center, not on behalf of ENACT— in which they were able to pay modest tribute to McCain and his committee for an action that "threw off decades of influence by the tobacco industry" and a bill that offers "the best opportunity yet to reduce tobacco use by young people." They then proceeded to urge the Senate to adopt a series of needed improvements.

Both temperate and intemperate assaults on the McCain bill framed the broader media response. The editorial boards of the newspapers that Washington heeds, the *Washington Post* and the *New York Times,* as well as others that had supported strong legislation, took up the negative trend: "Rough Draft on Tobacco," headlined the *Post;* "Make the Tobacco Bill Tougher," said the *Times;* and "Snuff Out Poor Tobacco

Deal" cried *USA Today*. The McCain bill was reported out of the Commerce Committee on April 1. It would not reach the floor of the Senate until May 18. Once again, as it had with the chorus of critiques against the June 20, 1997, settlement, the unorchestrated combination of Koop, Kessler, and the activists' "outside" hullabaloo and Matt's "inside" lobbying forced strengthening changes.

On May 16, the White House and Senator McCain announced that they had reached agreement in principle on amendments sufficient for the president to fully endorse the bill and pledge to sign it into law. Among other concessions, McCain agreed to offer "manager's amendments" to his own bill:

- Raising the annual liability caps from $6.5 billion to $8 billion
- Imposing higher penalties—from $3.5 to $4 billion annually if the industry failed to reduce youth smoking by 30 percent in five years, and 60 percent in ten years—and the fees would be assessed company by company, based upon each firm's share of the youth market
- Preventing states from opting out of federal standards for smoke-free workplaces unless they could demonstrate that state rules were at least equally effective
- Narrowing protections the original bill would have given the tobacco companies from antitrust and civil liability laws

Enough? Nope. The *Post* reported:

David Kessler . . . was cautious, "There's still a substantial way to go." Former Surgeon General C. Everett Koop called the changes "an improvement, but let's go further."

Sen. Kent Conrad who has led a Democratic task force on tobacco agreed, adding, "But is it the end of the process? No."

No, indeed.

32

Guess Who's Not Coming to Dinner

The accusation of Nader's colleagues, Rob Weissman and Russell Mokhiber, that "the industry loves the McCain bill" proved dead wrong. The aversion to the bill of Koop and his kindred spirits in the tobacco control movement was mirrored by the industry leaders who had accepted the June 20 settlement. So, too, by their Wall Street investors, who abandoned ship, driving share prices down again; by conservative Republicans; and by a large segment of the American public, once the tobacco propagandists had, on their terms, "engaged in a public policy debate."

In the very AP story on March 31 that greeted the coming out of the bill, in which Koop labeled it "a sellout," one industry spokesman called it "an act of vengeance." And, in a uniquely inept turn of phrase for an industry whose product shortens lives, another spokesman moaned, "We are fighting for our life."

Even before McCain abandoned the full panoply of liability protections in his early drafts, Al Hunt of the *Wall Street Journal* was reporting that RJR's leaders were ready to "walk away from any deal, to try to sabotage it in Congress, and then take its chances in court."

Then, on April 8, in a melodramatic appearance at the National Press Club, RJR's CEO, Steven Goldstone, cast a plague on all of Washington's houses. He pronounced the June 20 settlement dead, Congress beyond redemption, the White House devoid of nerve and leadership, and the public health community abandoning what "should have been a public health advocate's dream come true." Goldstone: "The extraordinary settlement reached on June 20 last year that could have set the nation on a dramatically new and constructive direction is dead, and there is no process which is even remotely likely to lead to an acceptable comprehensive solution this year."

As testament to the strength of the settlement—and to Matt Myers's rue—he cited one of Matt's more exuberant press comments on June

20: "Now a leading public health advocate, Matt Myers of the National Center for Tobacco-Free Kids, said, quote, 'This plan offers the best hope for protecting our children.' He called it, quote, 'The single most fundamental change in the history of tobacco control in the history of the world.' "

Then Goldstone offered his account of "what's happened since June 20:"

> Washington has rushed to collect more tobacco revenues while playing the politics of punishment.
>
> The comprehensive settlement failed because the administration, while publicly praising the concept, privately dismantled it piece by piece. This resolution cried out for strong, bold political leadership; precious little was forthcoming. The settlement was, instead, subjected by the administration to partisan positioning. The comprehensive resolution also failed because some leading public health advocates who, seeing the realization of all the programs they had ever fought for, for years, to obtain—and some others they had never even dreamed of asking for—added a new cry: a demand for retribution.

And Goldstone clearly signaled the industry's plan to sink the McCain bill:

> We are going to speak out and engage in a public policy debate on the issues that affect our industries and our customers. . . .
>
> . . . The primary issue is taxation. Is it fair to increase the taxes on cigarettes by huge amounts to pay for new federal spending programs or to provide tax cuts for wealthy Americans?
>
> . . . We will discuss the questions openly in towns across this country. And I have no doubt that when the debate occurs, the American people will bring wisdom and common sense back to these issues.

The decision to "talk to the people" reflected a highly fortuitous— and fateful—discovery the industry's public relations consultants had made: the public indeed loathed the tobacco companies, but not enough to reject messages from them that resonated with people's feelings and suspicions.

Until this moment, tobacco executives had believed, as the public health advocates believed, that nothing tobacco companies could possibly say in their own names would be credible to most Americans. Back in December, the industry was contemplating an advertising blitz to support the settlement, but Peter Stone in the *National Journal* reported that even the industry's own lobbyists "fear that the industry's credibility is so low that a lavish PR effort could backfire."

But the industry found a pied piper in the unlikely person of Carter Eskew, a former Democratic campaign consultant, a diet and exercise advocate, and a close confidant of Vice President Al Gore—later called in to doctor Gore's faltering presidential primary race. Eskew treated the industry's credibility as a "researchable question," convened a series of focus groups with a cross-section of ordinary citizens, and found that they would respond to a "simple, straightforward message"—even one signed by the tobacco companies themselves. These "simple, straightforward messages" tapped suspicion of politicians at least as deeply embedded in most Americans' breasts as their distrust of tobacco companies. So one of Eskew's ads displayed a tinkling Christmas tree in front of the Capitol, with a resonant voice-over telling viewers, "It's the season of giving in Washington, but remember, it's your taxes they're giving away." Another ad—obligingly run by the U.S. Chamber of Commerce—presented a televised image that Melinda Hennenberger of the *New York Times* characterized as "a harried, sweaty waitress with earrings the size of onion rings who leans into the camera and sighs: 'I'm no millionaire. I work hard. Why single me out?' "

One series of television commercials featured man-on-the-street interviews with working people angered by the bill. Another displayed an exploding cuckoo clock as the announcer shares the news that "Washington has gone cuckoo again. Washington wants to raise the price of cigarettes so high there'll be a black market in cigarettes with an unregulated access to kids. "

And a print ad was headlined "Big Taxes, Big Government. There they go again."

The companies also rolled out all the standard techniques of technologically fertilized grassroots protest: petitions to Congress displayed at truck stops, convenience stores, and other congregating places of what the behavioral researchers call "confirmed smokers"—those roughly 25 percent of smokers who are not constantly trying to quit and identify with the defiant rhetoric beloved by the tobacco companies.

By mid-May, the *Times*'s Hennenberger reported that the companies' advertising, lobbying, and grass roots-mobilizing campaign "has been remarkably successful in turning what tobacco opponents view as a bill that would discourage teen-age smoking into a tax issue and an assault on working stiffs who cannot afford to pay more for cigarettes."

And on June 19, 1998, the *Post*'s Howard Kurtz chronicled Eskew's triumph: "Eskew is the first to admit that 'the other side has a powerful argument: that this is about kids versus big tobacco, about saving lives.' His challenge was to change the terms of the debate, and he did it by drawing on his political experience and what he called a 'tried and true theme.' Blame Washington."

At the end of Goldstone's and his allies' exercise in participatory democracy, his "public policy debate," his "talking to the people," his "open discussion," Kathleen Hall Jamison, director of the Annenberg Public Policy Center, released a study that analyzed the ads and found that "a regular consumer of news-like programming, who believed the broadcast ads . . . would be seriously misled by the industry ads."

Between them, the Center for Tobacco-Free Kids and the Cancer Society reached deep into their limited treasuries and came up with about $2 million for ads, some featuring support for McCain ("Senator McCain is STANDING FOR AMERICA'S KIDS and AGAINST BIG TOBACCO"), who had come under special attack from the tobacco companies in ads run in the presidential primary states of Iowa and New Hampshire. This was an unprecedented advocacy ad budget for nonprofit groups. It was dwarfed by the companies' media blitz.

Saundra Torry and Helen Dewar in the June 17, 1998, *Washington Post:* "This much is clear; the industry's effort to defeat the bill has been enormous. Now in its ninth week, the ad blitz has far surpassed other campaigns to defeat congressional action, including the well-known 'Harry and Louise' campaign that helped kill the Clinton Health plan in 1994 and cost the Health Insurance Association of America about $14 million. Sources familiar with the tobacco industry's strategy confirmed the $40 million figure."

And *that* was on top of the industry's record-breaking lobbying expenditures that then totaled about $67 million since January 1996.

Did this ad campaign work? The ad blitz began in early April. It was how most Americans learned about the McCain bill. On April 23, the *Wall Street Journal* reported that:

A new *Wall Street Journal/NBC News* poll suggests the public's appetite to make increasing demands on tobacco companies is limited. The public is evenly split on whether Congress should pass the McCain bill, with 47 percent favoring passage and 46 percent opposing it. . . . When Americans are asked whether the proposed Senate legislation is too hard or too easy on tobacco companies, they are more inclined to say it's too hard. Two in 10 call the legislation "too lenient," while 37 percent call it "too tough." Moreover, the vast majority of Americans question the motivation for the legislation. Asked whether the tobacco bill's sponsors are more interested in cutting teen smoking by raising prices or getting additional revenue for government spending, 70 percent say the main motivation is to get the extra tax revenue.

Of most political salience was the news on the political significance of the poll: "Perhaps most heartening for Mr. Gingrich and others who harbor doubts about Mr. McCain's bill are findings that suggest most voters will not be heavily influenced by the fate of tobacco legislation. Two in 10 say they would be less likely to vote for a member of Congress who opposed tobacco legislation, but 63 percent say it would make little difference."

By early June, when Saundra Torry of the *Washington Post* made a foray to St. Louis, Missouri, to see what Middle America was thinking and feeling about the McCain bill, she brought back two unsettling answers to public health advocates: (1) not much, and (2) what the tobacco juggernaut wanted people to think. She found little interest among politically active people, certainly no groundswell of support. She wrote on June 5: "The tobacco bill that has obsessed Washington, roiled Congress and lighted a multimillion-dollar lobbying war has caused barely a ripple here in Missouri. Many people haven't even heard of it. And those who have often express views that sound much like sound bites from the tobacco industry's ubiquitous radio-and-TV campaign to kill the measure."

While the tobacco lobby was building a firewall against the McCain bill, and the Center, the Cancer Society, and the Heart Association were vainly trying to shore up support for it, the SAVE LIVES activists saw a diabolical scheme. In the May 12 issue of *Mother Jones* magazine, Russell Mokhiber and Ron Weissman, Nader allies, warned progressives:

In the month since they announced they are walking away from the negotiations over tobacco legislation, the tobacco companies have taken an unprecedented pounding. The Clinton administration, members of Congress from both parties, and the media have lined up to take potshots at the tobacco industry's shocking display of arrogance—after all, under the constitution, corporate CEO's do not have a vote in Congress, nor do they share the president's veto power.

It has been the best month Big Tobacco has enjoyed in a long time.

By denouncing the legislation introduced by Sen. John McCain as an extremist, "Big government" approach that is likely to bankrupt the industry, the tobacco merchants have succeeded in luring many to a defense of the McCain bill.

That is exactly what the industry hoped to accomplish. Big Tobacco cannot help but be happy with the McCain bill, which grants the industry a wide array of concessions and protections. But it knows the best way to generate support for the bill is to pretend to oppose it—a tobacco industry endorsement would be the kiss of death on Capitol Hill.

Well, maybe. But, also, just maybe, the industry's $40 million campaign might have been the "kiss of death" for the McCain bill itself. As one Republican tobacco lobbyist had told the *Washington Post*'s John Schwartz, on April 9, 1998, speaking on background the day Goldstone declared war on McCain: "Now we have to mobilize and try to stop the bill. This changes the nature of the assignment." He said he would rather be part of a drive to win approval of a comprehensive settlement, agreed to by all the principals, but he acknowledged that "killing the pending legislation may well be an easier task than trying to pass a comprehensive solution."

33

The Window of Opportunity Slams Shut

On April 27, Ceci Connolly in the *Washington Post* quoted an anonymous tobacco lobbyist: "If the vote were held today, it would be 80–
20 for McCain. But we're hoping in the next few weeks House leaders
will be able to turn things around for us."

House leaders? What had happened to House Speaker Newt Gingrich, who only three months earlier had vowed, "No one is going to get
to the left of me on tobacco?" What had diverted the House Speaker
who, earlier in the year, came upon Dr. Koop in the House chambers
and greeted him warmly: "Just give me a bill, and we'll pass it." The
congressional Republicans had been liberated by the industry's success in reframing the issue from the protection of children from Big
Tobacco to the protection of working people from the grasping hand
of Big Government—liberated to indulge their aversion to regulation
and taxation, and to redeem their huge debt to tobacco. Linda DiVall,
a Republican pollster, assured their congressional leaders that Congress's failure to act to control tobacco would have no resonance—
and no consequences in the upcoming elections.

Gingrich, on April 21, appearing on CNBC's *Tim Russert Show,*
trashed the McCain bill: "I think that bill is a very liberal, big government, big bureaucracy bill. And those people that say that's not a Republican bill; they're right." House Whip Tom DeLay scorned the bill
in an op-ed article: "Limousine Liberals, by forcing their vision of a
healthy lifestyle on American workers, will cost them billions of dollars." House Majority Leader Dick Armey told his weekly press conference that he did not consider the McCain bill "the appropriate bill."
Asked if he could explain his opposition, he answered, petulantly, "No,
I can't." Pressed as to why not, he grumbled, "Because I don't want
to."

And who was it that the "House leaders" had to turn around to keep from being embarrassed and pressed by the McCain bill being sent over from the Senate with an intimidating 80–20 vote? None other than Senate Majority Leader Trent Lott, who had been uttering increasingly ugly noises about the McCain bill or anything close to it, seeking only to avoid the political risk of appearing to be doing the industry's dirty work.

In this concern, Lott had been reassured by his visit home to Mississippi for Congress's April recess. Tobacco legislation was not exactly at the top of his constituents' passionately held priorities. Returning to Washington, he told his first press conference that *no one* had even raised the issue of tobacco while he was home. "I'm not trying to diminish it, but that's not number one, two, three, four, or five on the list of things that people ask about." And as for the Clinton administration's support for the legislation, "All they have seen in the tobacco settlement," quipped Lott, "is a cookie jar for them to get money." But Lott had to find a way to kill the bill without being easily labeled a tool of the tobacco lobby. Burying a bill that had surged out of the Senate Commerce Committee by a 19–1 vote required the subtlest legislative legerdemain.

Lott and his colleagues found a way.

First, Lott bulldozed the otherwise sturdy McCain by insisting that a tobacco farm amendment authored by Agriculture Committee chair, Senator Richard Lugar, be substituted for the farm provisions of the Commerce Committee bill. The original provisions had been worked out with the Commerce Committee's senior tobacco-state Democrats— Hollings of South Carolina and Ford of Kentucky—and were far more favorable to the tobacco farmers. This little-noticed maneuver, as the Senate began its debate, left Hollings, Ford, and Virginia's Chuck Robb feeling abandoned by McCain and lost their hard-won support for the McCain bill.

Next, Lott took cynical advantage of the determination of the SAVE LIVES coalition and its allies in the Senate (and the grudging support of ENACT) to eliminate the $8 billion annual cap on industry liability payments—the last vestige of any concession to the tobacco industry remaining in the McCain bill. By striking the caps, the Gregg amendment—cosponsored by conservative Republican Judd Gregg of New Hampshire and liberal Democrat Pat Leahy of Vermont—would provide conservative Republicans who were prepared to vote against the McCain bill an opportunity to cast a "no immunity" vote that would inoculate them against later charges that they were doing the tobacco industry's bidding.

Moreover, by opening the bill to all amendments, no matter how much time they took to consider, before reaching the necessary cloture vote (to close off debate to allow the Senate to vote on final passage of the bill itself), Lott would give the industry's public relations campaign ample time to turn the public against the McCain bill.

On May 18, Koop and Kessler joined Senators Gregg and Leahy in a press conference calling for passage of the anticap amendment. On May 21, the motion to table the Gregg amendment failed by a 61–37 vote—over the cautionary opposition of the White House, McCain, and McCain's Democratic ally on the bill, John Kerry. The amendment later carried by voice vote.

Koop takes great pride in his role on this vote:

> Senator Conrad has a little hideaway in the basement of the Capitol and it looks right down the Mall at the Washington Monument. So I was down there calling. Then, I did two things that you're not supposed to do: I went past that place where the Senators lunch and their caucuses, with a sign that says, "Members of Congress only." But I can get away with a lot of things because a lot of people like waiters know me. So the maitre d' of the dining room came out and introduced me to the sergeant at arms and we had a long chat. Then I was able to corner about twelve Republicans and twelve Democrats as they came in for lunch. And when that was finished, I went around, and I got about ten coming out of the Republican caucus.
>
> Then I went down to the basement and I telephoned all of the people that I hadn't spoken to or shaken hands with, not knowing that at the same time the president was in the Oval Office, calling the same senators telling them to vote against the amendment.
>
> This is one of my greatest political triumphs because the president and I were on opposite sides of the fence and he was calling the same people, and we won, 61–37.

Rich Hamburg, the Heart Association's veteran congressional lobbyist, concludes otherwise: "That was a dead bill once that liability language came out."

Of the sixty-one votes supporting the Gregg amendment, thirteen came from Republicans who, according to the Center's vote charts, voted "pro-tobacco," not "pro-kid," on all eight of the other key votes—including the final cloture vote. Another sixteen came from Republicans who voted pro-tobacco on most of the nine votes, and all would later vote to sustain the filibuster to kill the McCain bill. That's twenty-nine strange bedfellows for Dr. Koop and SAVE LIVES.

During the floor debate on the McCain bill, ENACT established a "boiler room," funded by the American Cancer Society, in the Holiday Inn near Capitol Hill, and it hummed with Cancer Society, Heart Association, and other volunteers taking assignments, dropping briefing papers, button-holing Congress members, and taking intelligence reports on a bank of ringing phones. The action began at eight each morning, when Tom Sheridan, an ENACT strategic legislative consultant, Matt, and others would provide the latest briefing; it lasted until well into each night. There was a sense of exhilaration, of possibility. The lobbying team was proving highly professional—and effective. As the Center's Anne Ford recalls: "A lot of times when there was an amendment on the floor, I could see that a member was holding an ENACT piece of paper in their hand, reading off it. That's pretty good." Cass Wheeler, the American Heart Association's new CEO, showed up on several days and took his assignments along with all the volunteers. AHA's lobbyist Rich Hamburg recalls:

> At any given time, we had dozens of Heart people there, from all over the place—from New York, Iowa, Kansas. When the call went out, our affiliates responded. The New York people coordinated a phone bank. We devoted the home page of our web site to the fight; we did telemarketing; we got individual passes for our volunteers to Capitol Hill; we did ads.
>
> We had staff and volunteers calling and demonstrating in town squares in Des Moines so effectively that Senator Grassley's staff came out and said, "Stop making calls to our office. We've heard you." We had a hundred people in New York City out in front of Senator Demato's office, protesting.
>
> This was a level of involvement we had never reached before—it's hard, frankly, to get people to do this. It was a war room atmosphere, and it was terrific!

And there was relief that the public health community was united, its members no longer fighting each other. Even Stan Glantz volunteered, when coming to D.C., to take lobbying assignments from Matt—only now, of course, that the $8 billion liability caps had been lifted.

But all this spirited effort would be in vain. Although the McCain bill gained Glantz's support with the passage of the Gregg amendment, which removed the liability caps, Matt says he and the Center

> reluctantly supported the Gregg amendment to maintain unity, but I believed then and still believe that its passage doomed the bill. Secretly, I hoped it would fail. I feared that its passage would in the long run cost us the swing votes the bill would need for final passage. Unfortunately, this turned out to be right.
>
> I don't know what would have happened if we joined with President Clinton in opposing the Gregg amendment. The criticism we would have received could have destroyed the public health coalition completely. On the other hand, passage of the amendment doomed the bill, I think. It was an excruciating choice. And, frankly, I don't think we did the right thing.

The boiler-room operation had some major lobbying successes, such as the Durbin-Dewine amendment, which further shifted the bite of the look-back penalties from industrywide to company-specific penalties, a change hard fought by the company lobbyists—and, of course, the Gregg amendment.

But Matt viewed these victories with even greater foreboding, as he saw time slipping by, new hostile amendments piling up, and Lott's public utterances on the bill growing darker and darker. Matt remembers seeing the political reality clearly: "It became clear early on that the opponents of the bill were seeking to bury it with amendments to upset the carefully constructed senatorial coalition supporting it. With each new amendment, the bill looked less like a disciplined effort to reduce the harm of tobacco and gained more opponents."

ENACT supported the Kennedy amendment, which would have forced the price increase for each cigarette package from $1.10 to $1.50, but Matt was privately relieved by its failure. He feared that this amendment would only have added fuel to the industry's claims that the bill was not about health at all, but a liberal-Democrat Trojan horse for a massive tax increase to be shouldered by largely working-class smokers.

Koop, at the other extreme, excoriated the White House for "cowardice" in refusing to lobby for the Kennedy amendment.

After the Gregg and Durbin-Dewine amendments passed, Lott's distaste for the bill grew. He growled, "This is a bad bill." The substance of these strengthening amendments played into the Lott strategy of encouraging a free-for-all on amendments from all sides and on all issues, whether or not germane to the bill. As the Democrats pressed their amendments to ratchet up the payments and penalties in the bill and strip it of the last vestiges of liability caps, Lott's Republican colleagues offered a dizzying array of pet schemes—such as Texas senator Phil Gramm's amendment ending the so-called income tax marriage penalty, which forced some married taxpayers earning dual incomes to pay more in taxes than they would if single. Gramm would have paid for the lost revenues by grabbing a huge portion of the funds generated by the tobacco industry's payments—thereby happily alienating liberals who had other plans for the money, but also enraging the state governors and legislators who had otherwise stood to gain half of the payments as the states' share for settling *their* cases. The Gramm amendment passed.

Consider again Nancy Kaufman's cynical but shrewd assessment of the intended role of the Kessler-Koop Committee: "If you are really against something but want to look like you're really for it, what you do is to take a Christmas tree and overweight it with as many ornaments as you can to satisfy all possible constituents that would have an interest in it. But your endgame is that the ornaments will overshadow the tree, and you won't be able to get the tree through the house anymore."

As the debate continued over the next month, Lott's open-door policy to these wide-ranging amendments assured that the focus on youth and tobacco use became increasingly blurred. The Senate Republicans shifted the focus from tobacco to illicit drugs by offering, debating, and adding an amendment strengthening conventional drug control programs. Next they succeeded in spotlighting the political Achilles' heel of both the settlement and the Democrats: the billions in fees that a small group of trial lawyers—as much the Democrats' fiscal patrons as Big Tobacco was the Republicans'—stood to gain from passage of the law. They adopted an amendment capping attorneys' fees for the lawyers who had brought the state cases.

As the debate and the string of votes and amendments lingered into its fourth week, the pressure of time and other business began to be felt. It was time to invoke cloture—the sixty-vote super-majority required to close off the debate and schedule a vote on final passage. On June 17, Lott convened the closed-door Senate Republican caucus and, over McCain's impassioned pleas, called upon his colleagues to vote against cutting off debate—thereby killing the bill, but without a recorded vote against the bill.

Later that afternoon, with sixty votes needed to close the debate, the cloture vote failed, 57–42. The McCain bill was dead. The settlement was dead. The "window of opportunity" had closed.

The next day's *New York Times* editorial (June 18) got it mostly right:

> During four weeks of debate Republicans demanded one amendment after another, threatening to kill the bill at every turn. The Senate majority leader, Trent Lott, asserted repeatedly that without those concessions there would be no bill. Yet yesterday he criticized the bill for having grown like Topsy, completely ignoring the fact that Republican amendments contributed to the situation he was deploring. In a final bit of chicanery, he orchestrated procedural votes that effectively killed the bill even though a majority favored it. The Republicans refused to vote on the legislation's merits because they fear that the voters want tough tobacco controls. Instead they hope to hide their allegiance to the tobacco industry by shelving the bill on technical grounds.

The *Times* missed only one critical piece of Lott chicanery: his switching of tobacco farm provisions. That drove away two votes that could have brought cloture closer—Kentucky's Ford and Virginia's Robb.

And the *Times* was wrong in its prediction of the political price Lott and his colleagues would pay. "Their craven performance . . . will not be forgotten by voters in the election season." It *was* forgotten. Though a few Democratic challengers tried to hang Big Tobacco around their opponents' necks, it didn't work. The voters were preoccupied with the House's clamorous impeachment proceedings and other fresh issues. The outcome of not one congressional race in 1998 was said to have been determined, or even influenced, by the issue of tobacco votes, tobacco money, or tobacco regulation. The public either forgot or didn't care. Just to be safe, the tobacco companies kept running their ads well into the summer and fall, long after the McCain bill was dead. This, Kentucky Republican senator Mitch McConnell assured his Republican caucus colleagues (before the vote to kill the bill!), was to make certain that no Republican was harmed by his or her vote to kill tobacco control legislation.

Looking back, Dr. Koop concludes that the loss was probably inevitable: "The reason I left Washington was because of my disappointment in all this. I just figured that if someone with my credibility and my access to the Senate and to the White House, which was unlimited, couldn't pull it off, with the kind of record I had, and the support of the people I had around me like David Kessler, you probably couldn't do it. We were up against insurmountable odds, when it came to someone so lacking in ethics as Lott."

Senator McCain himself shared Koop's disdain for Lott, but in a June 14 op-ed postmortem in the *Washington Post*, he spread the net of accountability for the bill's loss wider than Koop did: "Among the most serious obstacles supporters of the McCain bill encountered was the marriage of convenience between some conservatives and liberals who joined in opposition to any protections for the industry."

And John Raidt, McCain's chief of staff, added in an interview: "It didn't matter if you were going to raise the price to $1.10 . . . it didn't matter if you gave FDA unprecedented authority, the strongest possible authority they could ask for. None of that seemed to matter as much as 'Are you giving these people liability protection?' That was very frustrating, and it hurt our chances to be able to win."

Part IV

Lessons from the Settlement
and Its Aftermath

What Was Gained?
What Was Lost?

No Harm Done?

What was lost when the June 20, 1997, settlement and the McCain bill died? Not much, judged Julia Carol, Stan Glantz, Ralph Nader, and John Garrison, among others. Indeed, its death was a "victory" for tobacco control, wrote Carol; a "Pyrrhic victory for Big Tobacco," wrote Nader. As for Drs. Koop and Kessler, they were outraged at the congressional perfidy but confident that the future would bring even better laws than the McCain bill.

A few days before the final vote, Carol wrote to the SAVE LIVES e-mail listserv: "If I had my druthers, being I'm not much of a gambler, I'd rather they called off the game and we were left with no harm done—that would still feel like victory to me."

When the McCain bill died, Glantz explained to *his* listserv why there was nothing to lament in its loss: "The bald effort of Lott and the Republicans to kill the McCain bill was a testament to how far we have come. . . . It is important to recognize that even with the Republican effort to kill the McCain bill, all it did is throw the tobacco industry back into court against a much stronger public health opposition, armed with a series of victories in court and (thanks to Skip Humphrey) a ton of documents."

Later, Glantz drew this optimistic scenario for the still unsettled state attorneys general cases:

> The proper strategy . . . is simply to take these [the attorneys general] cases one at a time, and either take them to trial or settle. If they settle, include a most-favored nation clause and go around the country slowly ratcheting

up the ante, with each AG told to get one thing more than the one before. The other benefit of this strategy is that it enables you an opportunity to learn from your mistakes. One of the problems with the national deal is that it was a one-shot blowout. To the extent anybody got outsmarted by the cigarette companies or made a mistake in the agreement—and there were a whole lot of loopholes and technicalities in there that were very problematic—when you are doing it one state at a time, there is an opportunity to look at the settlement and think about it, and see what people did right and wrong, and to move forward incrementally. I am still hoping that is what happens.

Glantz concluded: "Public health has emerged from this battle in better shape in the long run than the tobacco companies and their Republican friends have. . . . Let's get back to work at the state and local level, where it is easier to win."

Nader issued a press release: "This is a Pyrrhic victory for Big Tobacco. Their desire to end uncertainty has boomeranged. Moreover, even if no bill is passed, the drug-dealing tobacco industry will remain on the defensive, as state and private litigation continues and registers increasing success, researchers cull through internal industry documents to further demonstrate the industry's calculated strategy to addict the young, deceive and prevaricate, and states and localities enact tough tobacco control regulations."

John Garrison of the American Lung Association took comfort in momentum: "The tobacco industry is celebrating tonight, but its happiness will be short lived. Momentum is still very much against the industry."

Koop vowed: "This is not over. I am determined that we will win this bill this year." Kessler, equally unbowed, had a longer timetable:

In some ways, [the loss of the McCain bill] was the best thing that could have happened. If it had passed the Senate and gone to the House and died, that would have given me great pause. That Lott was so blatant in the way he killed it, in some ways sets it up: not for today, not tomorrow, maybe not next year, maybe not the year after. But I can assure you, things come around.

It will take years; it doesn't happen overnight. There will come a point in time when we will have leadership that will do the right thing. It may not be for a decade until the Democrats re-control the Senate. But it will happen.

What Was Gained

Hindsight is the enviable, if loaded, weapon of the critic who bides his time. Hindsight now suggests that the most optimistic of these predictions were hardly surefooted. From the vantage point of summer 2001—more than three years after the events chronicled in this book took place, very few of the benefits that the defeat of the McCain bill was said to unleash have been, or are likely to be, realized. The state attorneys general, frustrated in their efforts to craft a broad settlement with significant federal public health laws embodied in federal legislation, declined to follow the Glantz prescription that they should proceed single file, state by state, ratcheting up incrementally each jury victory or advantageous settlement. Most of them, guided by anxious counsel, feared losing their cases if they actually went to trial. In November 1998, they all, even the boldest among them, entered into a multistate settlement (the master settlement agreement, or MSA) that public health advocates—ironically, fully united in defeat—promptly labeled at best weak, at worst a "sellout."

That settlement has accomplished some good. Joe Camel and other giant tobacco billboards are, indeed, history. The companies agreed to end billboard advertising, though the Marlboro Man still lurks in the pages of popular magazines, beckoning to young romantics, and on smaller billboards on the outside walls of cigarette retailers. But the settlement did not bring about a fundamental change in the industry's market. In the year after the settlement, tobacco industry marketing expenditures actually rose 22.5 percent.

The American Legacy Foundation, funded by the settlement, is broadcasting and publishing—in each of the five years beginning in the year 2000—$145 million worth of aggressive, national, state-of-the-art paid counter-advertising, targeted at young people. It has also generously funded innovative activities especially designed to broaden the reach of the tobacco control movement to youth and minority communities. It may not, under the terms of the multistate agreement, directly attack the tobacco companies, but it has aggressively pressed the limits of its mandate, for instance, by shifting focus and unmasking the tobacco industry's massive new target marketing of college-age smokers and potential smokers.

Still, the MSA provided for a board to oversee the Legacy Foundation, with substantial membership drawn from state attorneys general and governors, which raises the future specter of a politics-driven rather

than a public health–driven agenda. The payments required of the tobacco companies under the multistate settlement—$206 billion over
twenty-five years—have resulted in an average price per pack increase
of approximately forty-five cents. There is, to be sure, much money
going toward tobacco control in this country today—however unevenly.
Rough estimates place the total at around $1 billion being spent annu-
ally on tobacco control by federal, state, and local public health authorities and private nonprofit foundations.

Perhaps most important, tobacco control advocates in about a third
of the states have fought hard and well in their state legislatures—aided
energetically by the Center for Tobacco-Free Kids, the national health
voluntaries, and the Centers for Disease Control—for the allocation of
major funding from their state's share of the settlement payments to
comprehensive state tobacco control programs. However, as of this
writing, only six states have met or come close to the Centers for Disease Control guidelines for a minimally adequate state program, and
only fifteen states have allocated more than half of what CDC has set
as the minimum. Some state programs, pricked and spurred by vigorous nongovernment advocates, are well designed and effectively led.
These same advocates continue to make progress, especially in the
vanguard states, guided by Julia Carol's Americans for Nonsmokers'
Rights, in gaining more and stronger local clean-indoor-air laws.
Other state advocates, such as Maryland's advocacy pied piper Vinny
DeMarco, have succeeded in enacting steep cigarette excise-tax increases through nonpartisan, election-focused issue campaigns.

But many state advocates lack the energy, will, or resources. Many
state programs have yet to demonstrate vigor or effectiveness, and most
are subject to both recurring political raids to divert the funds, and to
continuing political hamstrings. The country has thus been cleaved into
tobacco control–rich states and tobacco control–poor states.

What Was Lost?

Much of the hope for a major federal role in curtailing tobacco use and
reining in the tobacco companies was prompted by the Food and Drug
Administration's 1996 legal assertion that FDA possessed, under existing law, the authority to regulate tobacco products, and the landmark rules Kessler issued curtailing tobacco advertising, marketing,

and sales to children. Despite the confident predictions of tobacco control advocates, the Supreme Court, on March 21, 2000, held that FDA had been wrong in asserting authority to regulate tobacco products. Congress, the Court declared, had made clear its intent that FDA *not* have such authority, and only a deliberative act of Congress could now grant such power to FDA. With the Supreme Court's decision, David Kessler's brilliant work to empower FDA was nullified, leaving a gaping hole that the November 1998 multistate settlement did not fill. For example, it did nothing to reduce illegal sales to kids, and it did far less than the FDA rules to curtail marketing to kids.

The McCain bill would not only have affirmed FDA's full powers to regulate every aspect of cigarette manufacture and marketing, it would have done so with a politically legitimatizing congressional mandate. It is reasonable to assume that, by now, FDA would have in place a nationwide and consistent effort to reduce marketing and sales to kids— enforced by regulatory teeth lacking in the multistate agreement. The FDA rules had already started to prove effective before the Supreme Court halted them. FDA would also by now have convened independent expert panels to lay the groundwork for scientifically sound regulations to reduce the addictive power of tobacco products and reduce the harm caused by them. FDA would have had the power to mandate safety testing, to force the tobacco companies to disclose anything in their research that might have a bearing on the health impact of their products, to force the tobacco industry to change their products, and *then* to control what the companies said about those products so their marketing no longer seduced old or new smokers.

Under the McCain law's authority, FDA would be well on the road to mandating new, far more bold and chilling, health warnings—more vivid and visible—with the residual power to revise them as FDA came to learn what warnings were truly effective, in contrast to today's fifteen-year-old tired warnings, for which an unlikely new act of Congress is required to change a syllable. Further, the FDA would also have had $225 million each year of guaranteed funding from tobacco company payments to develop and enforce its regulatory schemes, funding that would not depend on the congressional appropriations process. We do not know, of course, just how vigorously or effectively the McCain bill's grant to FDA of power over tobacco, if enacted, would have been enforced in the Bush administration. Matt's vision—the vision that drove him to the negotiating table despite the risks—was of a

fully empowered *and* politically unintimidated FDA commanded by a
future David Kessler, which would drive toward the elimination of
carcinogens or nicotine in tobacco products in a decade or so.

To be sure, others, especially Ralph Nader, never considered FDA
authority worth the risks of restricting liability in any way; Nader was
convinced that no future president or FDA chief would ever have the
political nerve to impose such radical regulation. Still, other, parallel
federal schemes of regulation survived even Nixon and Reagan, to be
mated, over time, with determined regulatory champions—they have
transformed markets and corporate behavior. Not the least of these have
been federal automobile safety standards, initiated and prodded by
Ralph Nader himself, which have now saved tens of thousands of lives.

Certainly, Philip Morris's negotiators believed FDA regulation under the terms of the settlement would dramatically alter the nature of
the cigarette industry within the United States. When one of them con-
fided to Matt that they intended to develop state-of-the-art, competi-
tive nicotine delivery devices under FDA regulation, which could wrest
that market from the drug companies, they were contemplating an
American marketplace free of addictive, lethal cigarettes as we now
know them.

Americans also lost a battery of yet unrealized, major new policy
and funding initiatives:

- The companies would be facing the looming threat of up to $4
  billion a year penalties against them for their failures to reduce
  teenage smoking by stringent percentage goals.
- By now, we would have seen a $1.10 per pack price increase that
  would have resulted from the McCain bill's mandated payment
  of $506 billion over twenty-five years, rather than the multistate
  agreements payments of only $206 billion, or a per-pack rise of
  $0.45.
- A nonprofit organization similar to the American Legacy Foundation, but with a board made up entirely of public health advocates, would have had $500 million a year to spend on counter-
  advertising without Legacy's constraints against directly attacking
  tobacco companies' practices. And this campaign would have
  continued indefinitely—rather than for the five years funded for
  the Legacy Foundation.
- Comprehensive tobacco control programs, independent of local

politics, would have been established and federally funded in every state. Unlike those funded by the MSA, these programs would not have been subject to the political whims of every governor and state legislature looking for nontax dollars for pet projects that have nothing to do with tobacco or public health.

- These programs would also be providing at least $680 million a year to fund cessation programs and nicotine-replacement drugs for those addicted to tobacco.
- Every state and community—whether in Kentucky or Montana— would be bound by nationwide minimum standards to protect people from secondhand smoke in all workplaces.
- The tobacco industry's lawsuit against the Environmental Protection Agency, challenging EPA's landmark classification of environmental tobacco smoke as a "Class A carcinogen" would have been terminated.

Also lost were provisions skillfully introduced into the bill through the educational efforts of a cadre of advocates for minority communities, led by Jeanette Noltenius and Charyn Sutton. Noltenius, heading the Latin-America Council on Alcohol and Tobacco, and Sutton, of the National Association of African-Americans for Positive Imagery, despaired of serious attention from *either* the ENACT or SAVE LIVES coalitions and set out to educate and energize a powerful—and unique—coalition of *all* the congressional minority caucuses to demand McCain bill provisions that met the unique needs of their communities.

With the help of Commerce Committee member Ron Wyden, who supported and worked closely with McCain in developing the final bill, Noltenius and Sutton made certain that language was added to virtually every provision of the bill to assure that all public health programs funded by the bill included components specifically designed to meet the needs of minority communities. For it has been these communities that have notoriously been targeted by the most aggressive tobacco industry marketing and the cynical "philanthropy" that had become a lifeline for many important minority community institutions and events. Such funding continues to buy community credibility and the silence of community leaders who otherwise have every reason to be up in arms about the companies' target marketing of the most vulnerable among them.

What Might the Future Hold?

Some form of FDA legislation may be enacted by the current Congress. But as of this writing, there is a good chance that it will have been crafted more by Philip Morris's lawyers than by public health advocates—and will serve Philip Morris's economic interests.

Even David Kessler was beguiled by Philip Morris's change of strategic direction in the fall of 1999, when it issued a public statement admitting that smoking caused cancer and that nicotine was indeed addictive. Kessler told the *New York Times*: "It is a profound change. It really sets a new stage for regulation and legislation." He was soon contacted by Philip Morris's Steve Parrish, who met with him and told him that Philip Morris now believed that the FDA should be given the authority to regulate tobacco. Kessler was intrigued, but " 'No deals,' I said, thinking back to the settlement offer with the state attorneys general that I had opposed. 'No immunity.' " Parrish readily agreed, telling Kessler that they did not seek immunity, only regulation.

The question was, what kind of regulation did they seek? In the fall of 2000, following the Supreme Court decision striking down Kessler's effort, Senator Bill Frist reintroduced—or *appeared* to have reintroduced—the FDA portion of the McCain bill, which he had overseen under McCain's direction. But subtly inserted in the nooks and crannies of the bill was the evident handiwork of the Philip Morris lawyers—language that would effectively handcuff any efforts by FDA to impose serious regulations, such as the mandated reduction of nicotine yields or other modifications in the design of cigarettes that could reduce the health risks. At the onset of the Bush administration, in January 2001, Frist reintroduced this bill.

Good FDA legislation faces formidable hurdles. The bill, dealing now only with FDA matters, was referred not to the Commerce Committee, which McCain chairs, but to the Senate Health and Human Services Committee. Even in the spring of 1998, with the public demanding strong tobacco control legislation, that committee had seriously entertained an industry-friendly FDA bill. Worse, the Republican leadership of both houses still rests in the hands of tobacco-friendly and FDA-hostile Republican conservatives, who will have ample opportunity to riddle the bill with Philip Morris's fine print as it moves through the tortuous stages of the legislative process.

Even worse, any bill must satisfy and be signed by a president who demonstrated, in Texas, little taste for regulating tobacco, and who remains within earshot of his former campaign manager, Karl Rove, now a senior White House advisor, formerly a strategic consultant to Philip Morris. The face and voice of FDA and the Bush administration on FDA legislation will be that of Health and Human Services secretary Tommy Thompson, former Wisconsin governor. One might not think of Wisconsin as a tobacco state, but it is surely a Philip Morris state—with Philip Morris subsidiaries Miller beer and Oscar Meyer meat products among its largest employers. So close was Thompson to Philip Morris that he not only received more than $70,000 in campaign contributions from the company but enjoyed its surreptitious funding of three overseas junkets.

There remains one sharp arrow in the government's quiver that could be used to prod Philip Morris and the other companies to concede McCain-strength FDA authority: the Clinton-initiated Justice Department "racketeering" lawsuit that charges the companies with a conspiracy to deceive the American public, including the government, as to the risks of tobacco use. That conspiracy, the Justice Department lawyers argue, resulted in billions of dollars in excess Medicare costs incurred in treating tobacco's misled victims, borne by American taxpayers—billions that the government now seeks to recover.

The lawsuit's outcome is uncertain. Its legal theory is novel, though it has passed initial industry challenges before an exemplary federal district court judge in Washington. The case does, once again, expose the companies to the risk, however remote, of a multibillion dollar jury award, and hence an incentive to settle. It is certainly conceivable that part of the Justice Department's price for such a settlement might be the companies' agreement to support McCain-bill FDA authority. But not under Attorney General John Ashcroft. On April 30, 1998, when Senator McCain achieved the high-water mark for his bill (the 19–1 supporting vote of the Senate Commerce Committee), the one No vote was then-senator John Ashcroft of Missouri. And Ashcroft, as soon as the Justice Department suit was filed, promptly labeled it "unwise." By the time this book is published, there is every likelihood that Ashcroft will have found ample, if transparent, excuses to terminate the case!

So the Bush–Philip Morris forces are once again likely to prevail over John McCain. And the public is likely to be saddled with the illusion of FDA oversight of a domesticated cigarette industry.

In his fine book *A Question of Intent,* David Kessler narrates the dramatic and truly inspiring story of his successful battle as FDA commissioner, struggling up through the rungs of the Clinton administration through the White House to assert FDA regulatory power over cigarettes—and the disheartening climax of the Supreme Court's decision denying the existence of that power. Kessler acknowledges that the only jury award on the horizon with the potential for forcing the companies into bankruptcy, the Engle case, the Florida class action case in which the trial court jury voted to impose a $144.8 billion punitive damage award, is not likely to stand on review. Most legal scholars agree. Among other hurdles that award must overcome is the Florida law expressly invalidating punitive-damage awards that would drive the punished companies into bankruptcy.

Wall Street—Glantz's trusted gauge of Big Tobacco's health—is no longer running scared. By February 2001, Philip Morris shares had risen from a fifty-two-week low of $19 a share to $46.

Nonetheless, Kessler is convinced that litigation remains "the strongest tool to chip away at the power of the industry. Without [immunity] legislation, liability attaches to everything owned by the parent companies of the tobacco companies." He concedes that even successful product liability cases will not end the continuing marketing aggression of the companies, but he believes that the liability risks to the parent companies will eventually force them to protect themselves by transferring their tobacco assets to a new entity. At that point, he proposes "some sort of government buy-out. . . . I want to give them an incentive to walk away from the cigarette business."

> Congress should charter a tightly regulated corporation, one from which no one profits, to take over marketing and sales. . . . The entity would supply tobacco products to those who want them, but with no economic incentive for sales. Promotion in any form should be banned. No more Marlboro Man, no successors to Joe Camel, no more colorful packaging. Ultimately, cigarettes should be sold in brown paper wrappers, with only a brand name and a warning label. Distribution should be tightly controlled to prevent access by children and adolescents. Sales revenues should be used only to underwrite manufacturing and distribution costs, with the remainder going into a fund created to pay liability claims and fund medical research and programs to counter youth smoking. It would be the end of the industry as we know it.

As Kessler readily concedes, "Dismantling the industry will not happen easily." This is doubly true because, to a distressing degree, the industry has been achieving the very "peace" that Kessler most feared—

not through legislative liability relief but through such strategies as embracing FDA regulation. However weak a congressionally blessed and Bush-signed FDA law turns out, it will still bring a measure of Kessler's dreaded peace to the industry, even if no immunity is granted. It will not be peace from continuing litigation, whose threat will wane as the industry's more egregious misdeeds recede in time, but peace from the now slumbering public clamor for more action against the industry. Moreover, the state attorneys general's widely heralded November 1998 master settlement, with the companies paying billions in reparations for their past misdeeds, may have been assailed as a sell-out by a handful of activists, but it plainly left many in the general public satisfied that the companies have paid for their sins.

And the industry, led by a $100 million Philip Morris public relations campaign, has sought skillfully to reposition itself in the public mind as a chastened, reformed sinner. The essence of their message: "Oh, that was then; this is now. Those were bad guys that ran the companies back then; we're reformers. We've paid our debt to society. And now, we *really* don't want kids to smoke, and we're funding programs— approved by public health authorities—to help keep them from smoking." Polls and focus groups continue to place tobacco companies on the lower rungs of citizen regard, but this antipathy is reflected neither in the priority that those polled put on holding the companies newly accountable, nor in any broad or energetic demand for such dramatic action as nationalization. Indeed, even while those polled scorned the tobacco companies, the percentage who gave the companies a strong rating for supporting "good causes" leapt from 10 percent in 1999 to 40 percent in 2000.

Finally, despite the continued energetic mining of the secret industry documents—in February 2001, Glantz and his colleagues received a $15 million grant from the Legacy Foundation to organize, scour, and preserve the documents—there seems little likelihood that damning secret industry documents remain hidden that are sufficient to rekindle public outrage. Former Minnesota attorney general Hubert Humphrey's "smoking howitzers" have just about run out of new explosive charges.

So perhaps the most serious of all that was lost in the spring of 1998 was the combined public *outrage* and *attention* on the national public policy agenda that tobacco control legislation briefly enjoyed. Glance back at chapter 27 and savor the rhetorical high dudgeon and voiced determination by the leadership of both parties to enact legislation holding the tobacco industry accountable. Yet, as soon thereafter as June 1998, as the McCain bill sank out of sight with little broad public outcry, Dr. Koop was forced to ask, achingly, "Where's the outrage?"

In the end, what now appears irretrievably lost in the rejection of the June 1997 settlement, and in the April 1998 McCain bill built on its foundation? Matt Myers, for once, abandons lawyerly restraint:

> What we lost was staggering. For those (like Kessler and Koop) who believe price increases are the most effective way to reduce tobacco use, we lost the largest mandatory price increase ever seriously made possible. For those who are convinced restrictions on where people smoke should be a top priority, we lost the single biggest legally mandated expansion of smoke-free areas ever contemplated. For those who believe marketing, especially advertising, creates or sustains a tobacco use norm and that counter-marketing is critical to demoralizing tobacco use in society, we lost heavily on both counts.
>
> For those who say that the most important tobacco reduction efforts focus on helping people quit, we lost a massive funded national cessation program.
>
> For those who say the tobacco industry always finds a way around every regulation and that we will always fail until we hold them accountable for their actual sales to kids, we lost out on the first serious effort to hold the tobacco companies directly financially accountable for how many kids get addicted to smoking.
>
> And for those who believe that we have to change the product if we are going to make a dramatic change in the number of people who die from tobacco, we failed to give the FDA broad authority at a time we had a government not only willing, but *eager* to be bold.
>
> And we failed at all of these things at once.
>
> Under normal circumstances—and *today*—we would have celebrated if we had achieved any of these high public health goals. In one instance, we had an opportunity to accomplish more of our agenda by far than we had accomplished in the previous thirty years.
>
> The June 1997 settlement, as improved by Senator McCain, wouldn't have solved the problem. But it would have made a great difference. If we believed our own rhetoric over the years, this legislation could have saved tens of thousands of lives—beginning nearly five years ago.

35

And the Rest of the Globe?

In grandiose style, Dick Scruggs, the lawyer-architect of the the attorneys general's cases, had christened their negotiations in the spring of 1997 the pursuit of "a global settlement." In the U.S. context, of course, it was indeed global—it encompassed all the state and private lawsuits and set the menu for comprehensive congressional tobacco control legislation. But for many tobacco control advocates around the world, the adoption of the word "global" was a global provocation! Surely, a global solution to the ravages of tobacco use is sorely needed.

By 2000, more than 70 percent of the world's tobacco consumption was in developing countries. This means that by 2020, 70 percent of the projected 8.4 million annual deaths caused by smoking will also be in developing countries. Meanwhile, the wonders of globalization have brought Philip Morris and BAT (British-American Tobacco), with their full kit of marketing tricks targeted at the "developing" markets of women and children—now at least dampened in the developed countries—to those same developing countries.

Soon after the settlement negotiations became public, on May 23, 1997, Ralph Nader and Rob Weissman warned:

> The tobacco industry talks about "global peace," yet it steadfastly refuses even to discuss its practices abroad. The Fifth Commandment does not say, "Thou shalt not kill *Americans*." No acceptable deal can discriminate between American and non-American victims, or fail to afford at least equivalent protections and guarantees to other countries' citizens in terms of marketing limitations, labeling requirements, nicotine and ingredient regulation, requirements for reduction of new child smokers and other provisions. In the absence of such protections, the potential American public gains from any deal with the tobacco companies will be out weighed by the tobacco companies' efforts to hook youngsters in other countries.

Weissman and Stan Glantz took full advantage of the lively international tobacco control Internet exchange, "Globalink," run by the International Union Against Cancer (UICC) to mobilize overseas outrage and opposition to the settlement. They speedily alarmed and recruited an array of the globe's most prominent tobacco control advocates as signatories to a statement denouncing talks "aimed at achieving a 'global settlement' " for excluding "consideration of the public health consequences of U.S. tobacco exports and the U.S. tobacco litigation which does not include measures to control the use of U.S. tobacco products outside of the United States."

The statement maintained that "to avoid doing public health harm, a settlement must set a worldwide floor on U.S. tobacco company practices, and a series of specific demands both for comprehensive regulation of U.S. owned tobacco company practices abroad, full compensation by the companies to foreign governments for the medical costs sustained in treating tobacco's victims, full liability exposure of the U.S. companies for damages caused their foreign victims, and $10 billion annual reparations from the U.S. companies to the World Health Organization." Glantz cut the argument succinctly: "Even if fewer Americans die as a result of this deal, it will be at the price of more deaths overseas."

These demands were not likely to resonate for the state attorneys general, beholden only to the state citizens on whose behalf they were employed, and for whose benefit they had sued. Nor were they likely to be taken seriously among senators and members of Congress chronically resistant to taking any serious measures to indemnify or protect *American* children from the domestic U.S. companies, let alone *foreigners.* There are also constitutional constraints on the ability of Congress to regulate the activities of overseas subsidiaries of U.S. companies, and the U.S.-based companies had the ability to divest themselves of their overseas subsidiaries—as R. J. Reynolds subsequently did, selling its subsidiaries to Japan Tobacco and rendering them unreachable by U.S. laws and regulations.

Still, the public health negotiators of the settlement, principally Matt, Christine Gregoire, Lonnie Bristow, and Tom Green, had not neglected the outrages committed by U.S. tobacco companies overseas. Indeed, the settlement included $1 million a year in industry payments to the Department of Health and Human Services, earmarked to fund international government and nongovernment tobacco control efforts. This was a huge sum compared to the less than $1 million a year then allocated by the World Health Organization for all *global* tobacco control efforts, which in turn was far more than was spent by the fiscally malnourished UICC and all other international nongovernmental advocacy organizations combined.

Then, as the McCain bill took shape, Democratic senator Ron Wyden of Oregon, a strong tobacco control advocate, took the lead in crafting a set of international tobacco control provisions, which McCain tentatively accepted. They provided for the creation and funding of an International Trust Fund financed directly from tobacco company license fees, from which $150 million a year would go directly to a newly chartered American Center on Global Health and Tobacco, directed by nongovernment public health leaders and charged with the unrestricted funding of a truly global nongovernmental tobacco control media education and advocacy movement. In addition, the Department of Health and Human Services would be authorized to tap the trust fund to support the tobacco control activities of foreign governments as well as national and international nongovernment organizations fighting tobacco use.

These provisions were lost as the McCain bill went down, and even the minimal interest Congress had in providing such support for international tobacco control evaporated. But that by no means is all that was lost to the citizens of other nations seeking to curb their own epidemic tobacco use and the transnational marketing aggression of the U.S., Japanese, British, and German tobacco giants.

Michael Daube, an early campaigner and leading tobacco control strategist in Great Britain and then in Western Australia, and now, globally, the chair of the bold new International Union for Cancer Control initiative, wrote to me of the lost opportunity:

> For overseas observers, there were three depressing outcomes from the McCain bill episode:
>
> First, we saw our close friends and colleagues in the U.S.—people we have come to admire enormously over the years—attacking each other instead of the industry, and doing so in public. There are few enough of us in this battle, and we simply cannot afford splits like this.
>
> Second, various benefits the opponents of the bill thought might later accrue have not materialized.
>
> Third, those working for international tobacco control were worried about the use of terms such as "global" when, like the "World Series," the bill ran the risk of ignoring countries outside the U.S. But the settlement— and the subsequent McCain Bill—held the promise that the U.S. could

show the way in defeating the companies that inflict their lethal products on the rest of the world. We need them to show the way by controlling the companies and the way they operate. And we need them to show the way by forcing these companies to change their products. From the outside looking in, the U.S. now has less to offer by way of controls and example than seemed to be achievable then.

One of the signatories to the international statement of demands, Dr. Witold Zatonski, the moving force behind Poland's uniquely strong and comprehensive tobacco control laws, now reflects eloquently on his own reactions to the settlement and its subsequent loss:

When I first learned about the settlement negotiations, I thought, well, this was very good news from America. This came at a time when I had begun to think that the tobacco control movement was sinking.

Ten years ago the international tobacco control movement had many good people, with many new ideas, and good achievements, as well. But in the last ten years, many of the best people were leaving the movement; there was no more active thinking, no new strategies.

We had, in effect, two models. One is the Scandinavian model; a good example is Finland. They started at a very high level, with a very comprehensive program—led by government and government officials. Tobacco consumption in Finland went down very quickly and the health of the population improved. But then, in the last fifteen years, nothing happened. This was a government-led model, with the private community, including the medical profession, involved only superficially.

Then you have America as a second model, and what you see there is a fantastic achievement at the community level, how well organized the nongovernmental organizations have been, how people with passion are working to go forward.

But from the point of view of federal regulation, even compared with Poland nowadays, you are a very, very undeveloped country.

The Finns, with only government, were not able to win this battle; and the Americans, only using local communities, are not able to win. If you compare Finland and the U.S. you are both at the same level. You are able to some extent to come up to the governmental model and to some extent with nongovernmental organizations, but then you must put them both together.

Then came this beautiful news from America that people were coming together. They developed this very nice tactic to use children, which, from the politicians' viewpoint, especially, gives you many new possibilities. And I was really excited. I was really excited, as we were getting more and more information about what was going on in America, how things are going to develop.

And I was thinking, really now probably we are able to win this war, and there will be tremendous progress. In Europe, there were many skeptics. As usual, the French people were the most skeptical. I was naively saying this shows that in the U.S. they have spirit. They will be showing us the way, and they will be helping us to resolve this problem globally.

Every day, I was learning how strong this settlement will be, how strong tobacco control will be in the United States.

I was really thinking something extraordinary was happening, and then I was asked to come to Washington to lobby for the good international provisions that were in the McCain bill. Meetings were organized; there was a press conference with journalists and meetings with politicians. I was in the Senate speaking with people.

After this visit I was one hundred percent sure that things were going in the right direction. At first, I did not understand, because I was not in everyday contact with people in America, that in the tobacco control society, there was a big fight. But then I recognized that this fight created danger for these policies, because if people are fighting—not for establishing the settlement—but fighting one another, that was dangerous.

Speaking as a European, I could not understand why Stan Glantz was using such strong words. He seemed to be talking about some old history, and forgetting what the goal was, and fighting one another.

And I was a little surprised that some big organizations in America were setting unrealistic goals.

I began to think that what they wanted to achieve, in one step, was to finish off the tobacco industry.

To me, this was silly; it was not possible to do, and maybe not useful to do. And this is what was worrying me. But never in my wildest dreams did I think this would result in nothing happening, going backwards. I could not believe this.

The settlement was not just good for the U.S. It was good for Poland, for Eastern Europe, for other developing countries, because we are not able to stop tobacco aggression without success in the United States. We understand very well that we are U.S. dependent, whether you like this world order or not. Most important, I was thinking, look, this is so powerful an industry, but we will be able to show all people in the world what the United States has done to control them

In Europe, news of this settlement was pressing quite strongly on the European Union. One of the reasons the European Union was moving toward a total ban on tobacco advertising was the settlement. If there had been no settlement, it's certain that the 100 percent total ban in Europe will be not in the air.

The news of the settlement helped me in Poland, as well. I was using the settlement argument all the time, in Poland, and so were many others. It was easy because it was big news in the mass media—nearly every week, on the front pages of Polish newspapers. That helped a lot.

It seems that it will take a long time before we will come once again to the same level. Maybe never.

36

Thirteen Ways to Lead
a Movement Backward

Thus far, I have largely withheld my own explicit judgments on the dysfunctional behavior of too many of the key leaders and activists upon whom this narrative has focused. That reticence ends with this chapter. As for Matt Myers, I devote the whole of Chapter 38 to his scorecard.

As I reflect on the shortfalls of the public health leadership during the settlement and its congressional aftermath, I draw from them a set of ironic cautions. Taken together, they offer a surefire guide, comprised of thirteen battle-tested rules, for the aspiring leaders of any comparable citizen movement similarly determined to stumble on the threshold of large opportunities to which their successes have brought them:

1. Fight! Fight! Fight! Fight! or Talk! Talk! Talk! Talk!
2. Take no risks.
3. Keep doing what you have been doing no matter how the world is changing.
4. Lose track of your fundamental goals.
5. Never set priorities.
6. Let your strategic thinking be captive to mind-numbing metaphors.
7. Beguile yourself with the illusion of an endless summer of momentum.
8. Resolve good-faith strategic differences with your allies by plugging your ears and shouting them down.
9. Neglect to convince your grassroots followers that your vision of victory is not their nightmare of defeat.
10. Be united—even in folly.

11. Follow your followers over the cliff.
12. Never learn from looking back.
13. Let your outsize ego be your guide.

Let me elaborate.

1. Fight! Fight! Fight! Fight! or Talk! Talk! Talk! Talk!

Great movement leaders, from Gandhi to Mandela (not to mention Mao), have practiced the strategy that has been encapsulated as "Fight! Fight! Talk! Talk!" This acknowledges that, in any long-distance struggle, there is a time for warfare and a time for negotiation—and that both are essential to ultimate success.

It is never easy, however, for warriors to transform themselves into peacemakers, to shift from the comfort of combating a securely demonized enemy to the moral ambiguity involved in acknowledging an enemy as simultaneously a bargaining partner. Thus, Nelson Mandela, in his autobiography, confesses that he kept his negotiations with the apartheid regime secret because he knew that his colleagues were not yet emotionally ready for negotiating with the hated enemy.

To Stan Glantz, there was only fighting: "The fundamental reality of tobacco is that the way to beat them is to beat them, not to make a deal with them." For three decades that had been a sound strategy—and an important shield against those who might take seriously the tobacco industry's sham professions of readiness to accept significant restraints.

But the accumulating pressures on the industry in 1997—especially from its own investors—created an opportunity different in kind and dimension from anything that had come before. Yet neither Glantz nor many others were capable of stepping back and asking themselves whether a time had indeed come to suspend the fighting—not end it forever—and negotiate.

The *Los Angeles Times*'s Myron Levin, long a clear-eyed and sympathetic commentator on the tobacco wars, got it exactly right. In his analysis of the failure of the McCain bill, he wrote:

> The bill lumped in one big package many cherished goals that the anti-smoking movement had perennially sought but never gained. . . . Moreover, health groups themselves would be involved in running the anti-smoking programs.

But in a sense the war culture and psychology of the anti-smoking movement worked against those incentives.

As it turned out . . . the traditional story line at least superficially held up. Big Tobacco didn't like what Congress was up to, and rose up to swat away the threat. The forces of darkness prevail, the plucky insurgents continue their uphill fight, and so the world makes sense. How comfortable and familiar it is.

The habit of war, and the gut abhorrence of negotiations with the treacherous industry, led Glantz and others to rationalize their resistance by indulging in rosy fantasies about the ultimate rewards of continued conflict, such as Glantz's predictions not only that litigation would drive the industry into bankruptcy, but that bankruptcy would in turn result in the nationalization of the companies and thence a permanent end to their greed-driven marketing abuses.

Jim Tierney, the former Maine attorney general and counselor to the attorneys general during the settlement negotiations, observed: "I know that I should not be this harsh when dealing with addicts, but I believe the fight against the tobacco industry is as addictive as nicotine itself. The very best of public advocates, often in deep personal pain from the loss of a loved one to the deadly cancer marketed so callously by the tobacco industry, were addicted to the fight."

At the other extreme, there were those who can be faulted for the premature cessation of hostilities, for a tendency to abandon "fight" for "talk, talk, talk, talk."

Bill Novelli, Mike Moore, and Chris Gregoire resisted the effort by the Kessler-Koop Committee to demand *any* fixes to the June 20 settlement, for fear such demands might drive the industry to opposition and sink the prospects for legislation. If that counsel had been heeded, we would not have seen the significant strengthening improvements— spurred by the fighters—that in the end graced the McCain bill. At least some of these improvements could well have survived the congressional obstacle course.

2. Take no risks.

Julia Carol exhorted her colleagues gathered in November 1996 to "have the courage" to resist any compromise with the tobacco industry. But for the leaders of moral crusades, compromise often requires more courage than does relentless combat.

That exchange led Elaine Holland of the National Academy of Pediatrics, who had been one of the silent participants in the meeting, to reflect upon the recently released film *Michael Collins,* the story of the great Irish independence leader.

Eamon De Valera, the titular head of the rebellion but nevertheless a rival of Collins, had designated Collins, a hero of the rebellion, to represent the forces of independence in peace negotiations in London. De Valera knew that the only sane course of action at that time was to accept the partition of Ireland. He also knew that such a compromise would enrage the most militant of his followers, and he didn't want his own fingerprints on the settlement. Collins negotiated partition. De Valera distanced himself from the settlement. On his return, those compatriots who had earlier followed and adored Collins assassinated him. De Valera went on to serve for decades as the revered president of the New Republic of Ireland. Which was the profile in courage, Holland asked?

John Seffrin acknowledges the "lack of institutional courage to do the right thing, to step forward at the right time, to say the tough thing:" "It was a mistake for us to capitulate and fall in line on the Gregg Amendment [stripping the liability caps from the bill]. The ENACT coalition should have opposed the Gregg amendment aggressively, recognizing openly that once there were no concessions to the industry left, the bill was dead on arrival. Instead, we went along with the anti-immunity purists, and helped sink the whole bill. I would think long and hard before I fall into line again just because it's the popular thing to do in the tobacco control community."

Jim Tierney argues: "In 1994, Mississippi Atty. Gen. Mike Moore, Minnesota Atty. Gen. Hubert H. Humphrey, III, Florida Atty. Gen. Bob Butterworth took the plunge and threw up the 'Hail Mary' anti-tobacco lawsuits. Each man took a huge risk and staked their careers on these cases. With the exception of Matt Myers, I never saw a single public health official or advocate take any risk. To the contrary, they took the safe approach and hid from making hard decisions at virtually every step."

3. Keep doing what you have been doing no matter how the world is changing.

Most of us are uncomfortable changing our accustomed ways of look-ing at the world or going about our daily work. State and local advo-cates had developed successful—and comfortable—strategies for pur-suing ordinances and fighting industry stealth campaigns to preempt local efforts through the statehouses. The American Lung Association had often led among the national organizations in supporting state and local action. The state coalitions and public health officers supported by the National Cancer Institute and The Robert Wood Johnson Foun-dation all had painstakingly developed both short- and long-term state action plans. None had contemplated the possibility that Congress might enact comprehensive legislation that would turn this relatively com-fortable world upside down.

And few would. With the exception of the November 1996 meeting that Matt and Dick Daynard convened, there were no organized efforts prior to the March 1997 negotiations to explore in a crisis-free atmo-sphere the kinds of questions that later erupted in crossfire.

Even as late as September 1997, Julia Carol quite rightly lamented that no talks or sessions were scheduled to provide a serious forum for considering the issues raised by the settlement, such as the viability of litigation-caused bankruptcy as an effective corrective to wrongful in-dustry marketing practices and political influence. Carol and Glantz had long been concentrating their efforts at the local level—and view-ing congressional intervention as a threat, not an opportunity. But they would not acknowledge that local efforts had limits or that tobacco use had leveled off at unacceptably high rates or was climbing among teen-agers even in places with model local tobacco control policies.

Only Congress could give FDA the power and political impetus to regulate cigarettes themselves, and to reduce the addictive power or the harm caused by cigarettes. Yet so discomforted were Carol and Glantz at the prospect of the locus of action shifting to Congress, that they were unwilling, or unable, to confront the potential contribution to be made by FDA product regulation. Ken Warner expressed both the potential for such regulation and his fears for the rigidity of move-ment activists: "How might the public health community be enticed to buy into a harm-reduction strategy, if indeed that's what the experts end up recommending? There is a distinctly puritanical streak within the public health community that would rebel against any notion that there should be any alternatives to 'Just say no' when it comes to nicotine—and especially any alternative that might involve the tobacco industry as participant in the solution, as opposed to just being the problem."

Glantz's response to the potential of FDA-regulated competition toward less hazardous and less addictive cigarettes? "I just think it's silly. You could basically eliminate tobacco use in ten years. Why screw around with the cigarette?"

And, with enlightened California as the site of their abundant successes, they could not acknowledge that only Congress had the power to authorize the *national* counter-advertising and smoke-free workplace and other broad tobacco control policies that could help those citizens whose state and local governments were more benighted than those of California and Massachusetts—and not just in tobacco-growing states.

They could not entertain the prospect of complementing federal and local strategies. So they clung to the time-tested local strategies, successful but limited.

4. Lose track of your fundamental goals.

I never thought I would find myself in agreement with a tobacco company executive on any issue, much less an analysis of tobacco control strategy. But Steven Goldstone, R. J. Reynolds's CEO, got one thing right. In addition to other daggers in the heart, Goldstone argued, in his April 8, 1998, National Press Club speech: "The comprehensive resolution also failed because leading health care advocates who, seeing the realization of all the programs they had ever fought for, for years, to obtain—and some others they had never even dreamed of asking for—added a new cry: a demand for retribution. The comprehensive agreement which should have been a public health advocate's dream come true was left behind in favor of a surprising new public agenda: the need to promote litigation and punitive damages against this industry."

Far more comforting than finding common ground with RJR is finding support from historian Richard Kluger. He, too, chastised the public health leadership for misplaced priorities. "They should have understood," he wrote in the *New York Times*, "that regulating tobacco, not punishing the industry, was the primary goal."

When the Koop-Kessler Committee first listed its priorities for model tobacco control policy, it kept its focus on public health, relegating opposition to liability relief for the industry to a sentence in a task force report. But having achieved virtually all of their public health objectives in the McCain bill, Koop and Kessler raised liability concessions to industry to the top rank of priorities.

To be sure, as Bill Novelli laments: "We didn't have a common purpose. Some people had as their purpose to destroy the tobacco industry. Some people had as their purpose social justice for all. Some people had as their purpose . . . reaching a national agreement to bring resources to bear on driving down tobacco use in their kids."

Thus, in fairness, Ralph Nader and his associate Rob Weissman did not identify themselves as tobacco control advocates, but as broader public interest advocates. Accountability for the industry *was,* all along, their priority objective. Unlike Glantz, both acknowledged the possibility that public health goals might well suffer if settlement-based legislation was doomed—and they were prepared to accept the consequences. For Nader, the preservation of the integrity of the tort liability system was of overriding importance. But others, especially Koop, Kessler, Congressman Henry Waxman, and Senator Ted Kennedy, began with their sights squarely focused on the public health, and ended, as Goldstone charges, with "a demand for retribution"—and not just retribution, but full retribution.

Richard Hamburg, the Heart Association's veteran lobbyist in Washington, summed it up:

> I have said on a number of occasions, regarding the opposition to the McCain bill because of its liability caps, that from time to time, running a government relations program, you need to take out your mission statement and figure out if you are advancing the mission. The opportunity to save millions and millions of lives appears in the American Heart Association's mission statement. Addressing liability law, who can sue and who can't sue, is not in the mission statement.
>
> Clearly, litigation is a tool. What the bill's opponents always said was, "This is a tool you can't take away from us!" Okay, but the tool unto itself doesn't particularly do anything. It was a tool for leveraging negotiations on broader public health legislation. At some point, the opponents lost sight of what it was leveraged for!
>
> Did the original settlement give away too much to the liability side? I think clearly so. Were the liability concessions of the McCain legislation reasonable? I think they were clearly reasonable, as a quid pro quo for the public health provisions in that bill.

But the people in the SAVE LIVES coalition were willing to let it die—
they actually saw it as a victory that the bill ended up dying. To us, it was
a tearful, incredible lost opportunity to save tens of millions of lives. That
was the big difference.

5. Never set priorities.

Matt tried to set priorities in November 1996; Stan Glantz and Julia
Carol ambushed the effort. David Kessler tried in the last minutes of
the Koop-Kessler Committee's deliberations; ASH's John Banzhaf
protested indignantly. Kessler abandoned the effort.

In September 1997, Waxman, Humphrey, Kessler, and Kessler counselor Jeff Nesbit met secretly and outlined a common bottom line for
acceptable tobacco control legislation. They never shared it with their
fellow advocates or sought to build a consensus around it.

When the McCain bill went down in June 1998, Russ Sciandra wrote:
"There was never consensus among us on what was really important,
and therefore no ability to prioritize the issues and know what, in the
end, to give up, in order to get a bill. Consequently, we were boxed
into demanding everything, a position that we could not back up politically. As a result, we got nothing."

6. Let your strategic thinking be captive
to mind-numbing metaphors.

The cognitive linguistics scholar George Lakoff teaches us that most
people arrive at their positions on issues of public policy not by rational analysis in the context of a coherent liberal or conservative political philosophy, but by largely unconscious association of the issues
with dominant metaphors that evoke strong feelings.

The *Washington Post* "Outlook" section headlined a cautionary article I wrote in late April 1997 on the risks and potential benefits of a
settlement with the tobacco companies "Dealing with the Devil," and
accompanied the article with a cartoon of a leering Mephistophelian
caricature.

I have spent the better part of a working life demonizing the
tobacco companies, a characterization they have justly merited. That
demonic image served the movement well as an extraordinarily

powerful organizing tool—in which every tobacco control advocate could be assured of the absolute virtue of his or her advocacy. We were, after all, on the side of the angels. So it was no surprise that the same advocates felt betrayed upon learning that some among them would consider shaking hands, breaking bread, sitting at a table, and even seeking common ground with the devil.

Yet reifying the transnational tobacco companies—their complex of executives, past and present, their investors, their intra-industry rivalries, the market forces acting upon them, their motives simply as Big Tobacco—as the devil, without deconstructing that metaphor, proved a severe impediment to essential strategic analysis.

The civil rights movement gained much of its success by a determined effort on the part of nonviolence leaders like Dr. Martin Luther King Jr. and now Congressman John Lewis to bear in mind the common humanity—not just the brutality—of their adversaries. The tobacco movement has done just the opposite—obliterated the humanity of those who work in the tobacco industry, substituting the image of the fictional person of the corporation, and imbuing that fiction with diabolical qualities.

Matt Myers and his colleagues began to be open to the possibility that these negotiations could produce fundamental change by recognizing that Philip Morris's Geoffrey Bible and R. J. Reynolds's Steven Goldstone were neither saintly nor diabolically motivated but driven by their large institutional investors. These very human, if not admirable, actors saw the value of their share holdings depressed by billions of dollars as the threat, however distant and unlikely, of litigation-wrought bankruptcy loomed. Matt and those who sat with him came to recognize that these investors' horizons were short term. A settlement that allowed the value of their holdings to rise *immediately,* swept upward in the current boom market, was a sufficiently strong impetus that they would be willing to accept long-term controls and lost revenues *later*—even FDA regulation that could lead to the eventual elimination of nicotine from tobacco-burning products and the substantial long-term decline of tobacco use, at least in the United States.

To be sure, there were, and are, serious rational arguments for not giving the tobacco companies peace through a settlement. A settlement in which the public sees the companies as abandoning their old ways and adopting a new course of corporate responsibility would greatly restore their political credibility and influence. Indeed, as happened in Florida following the settlement of that state's case, politicians who had come to shun Big Tobacco's campaign contributions might well feel free to start taking them again from a "reformed" industry.

If, instead, litigation were given free rein, it might come about that the companies, financially weighted down by a series of punitive-damages awards, would be far less capable of wielding political and economic influence.

But it was also possible, with a negotiated settlement, that a new generation of tobacco industry executives would find it in their economic interest (to say nothing of their social rehabilitation) to shed their horns, and to conform to the spirit of the settlement—and the oversight of the strongly empowered regulatory agencies—and cease at least the most offensive of their marketing and political activities. In any event, when David Kessler continuously shied away from granting peace to the industry on the grounds that "peace is what they want," he was captured at least in part by the specter of granting peace to those who are intrinsically evil.

"Bankruptcy" was another technical term that took on metaphorical life. This is best seen by the recurring rapture with which Stan Glantz and others visualized the companies "driven to their knees" by bankruptcy. The unstated dramatic tableau they contemplate is of the lying, mendacious corporate chieftains on their knees, in chains, brought to deserving penury before the bar of justice.

But wait a minute. The worst offenders—those notorious seven executives who lied to Henry Waxman under oath—have all since died or retired in comfort, no doubt having rapidly diversified their bulging investment portfolios. The survivors will be disinterestedly watching the bankruptcy proceedings from their projection TVs on their retirement yachts. To be sure, the portfolio values of large investors, including worker pension plans, would be significantly diminished. But the current tobacco company executives would only continue, with full pay and corporate perks, to manage the enterprise under the bankruptcy courts' mandate to *maximize* sales and profits for the benefit of creditors.

This is precisely why the *New York Times* reported, in December 2000, on the growing appeal of voluntary bankruptcy proceedings as a safe haven for corporate CEOs discomforted by the hot breath of product liability litigation.

Russ Sciandra, the veteran New York State tobacco control advocate, was one of the few not caught up in the metaphor of Big Tobacco as the devil incarnate, or of bankruptcy as the weapon for bringing the devil to his knees: "I was never convinced that bankruptcy would do anything to solve the problem of smoking and health. What exactly does bankruptcy mean? Who is being punished? People seem to forget that tobacco companies don't actually exist in the physical world; you can't put a tobacco company in jail. If you cut them, they don't bleed. You can put their executives in jail, and we still could. The settlement wouldn't have done anything about that. But who exactly was going to be punished by bankruptcy?"

We have also seen Stan Glantz, as propagandist, effectively wield the term "immunity" as a powerful metaphor. "Immunity" evokes for us the image of a criminal miscreant freed of accountability for past crimes and free to continue a life of criminal acts. But who and what would have been granted "immunity" by the settlement? Not those past or present executives who may have committed crimes, for the attorneys general rejected at the outset the industry negotiators' plea for immunity from criminal prosecution. Immunity for past civil wrongs? Not exactly, since the industry was agreeing to pay the largest civil fines in history in reparations for its civil wrongs. The only true immunity embodied in the settlement lay in its provision barring punitive damages and class actions for future wrongdoing by the companies— a provision that was eliminated in the McCain bill.

The liability caps in the McCain bill, which would have set a limit of $8 billion on the amounts that the companies would be required to pay out in any single year, would not have immunized them from any civil suits but merely stretched out their damage payments. This was a provision that at least some objective observers saw as insolvency protection for tobacco's *victims*, a means of assuring that the companies remain sufficiently solvent over time to be able to pay the damages awarded to all successful claimants. Still Glantz and Co. continued to wield the image of "immunity" as a rhetorical whip to churn the blood of those who might otherwise have weighed more coolly the costs and benefits of the trade-offs proposed.

For Matt and other settlement advocates, one potent metaphor that blurred their strategic thinking was "window of opportunity." "Slamming shut" was always the negative pregnant in the open-window metaphor, and the fear of the window slamming shut led at least some of the settlement advocates to exaggerated fears that even modest and limited efforts to lobby the White House or the Congress to rectify flaws in the settlement would jar the open window and bring it crashing down.

7. Beguile yourself with the illusion of an endless summer of momentum.

The winter of 1997–1998 was a heady time for tobacco control advocates. Too heady. Momentum—"Big Mo"—was on the movement's side. The litigation was driving company stock prices down and investors toward abject settlement. The Republicans were falling into line, with Gingrich vowing not to let Clinton "get to the left" of him. The tobacco lobby appeared prostrate; polls showed the public revolted by the continuing stream of industry revelations flowing from the publication of the industry's own secret documents. The Justice Department's simmering criminal grand jury investigations seemed certain to return criminal indictments of high-ranking tobacco executives. And if strong legislation wasn't enacted, the Republicans were sure to be punished by aroused voters in the coming fall elections. These were good times for tobacco control; they could only get better. Though it was winter in Washington, the movement basked in the warmth of an endless summer for tobacco control.

There was, there is, no endless summer. A few voices—especially experienced trial lawyers—offered cautionary notes: litigation, as a public health remedy, was all thumbs, no fingers. Most state attorneys general were petrified at the prospect of actually trying their cases. They would settle their cases anyway, and their settlement would prove far more anemic in public health protections.

Criminal indictments proved a vain hope. The public and the press were nearing surfeit with secret industry documents; there would be a diminishing return on public outrage. The public's distaste for the tobacco companies never translated into strong public volition for steep tax increases or drastic regulatory remedies such as nicotine removal from all tobacco-burning products. And the unprecedented media and public attention waned, as it always does. By election time, other issues preoccupied the electorate.

The Washington veterans knew this. The Heart Association's Rich Hamburg: "Sure, it's very frustrating to think, how did the American public and the U.S. Congress make this the number one health issue in the country—a world-level issue—and then it disappears? The professionals, good people or bad, know how Washington works, knew that you have only one shot at it. It is an odd duck, the U.S. Congress. You have a piece of legislation everyone agrees on; everyone knows something is going to happen on it. Then you miss the opportunity, and it is deader than a doornail."

Looking back, Ralph Nader ruefully acknowledges the truth of this. He himself lost his battle in the late 1970s for a national consumer agency to act as an advocate on behalf of all consumers before other government agencies—though the bill had majority support for a while in both houses of Congress:

> The problem is that whenever there is a real resurgence of public opinion and grassroot organizing against some corporate abuse, you always like to think that it is just the beginning. And that it has got a momentum that is going to continue. And then someone puts a bill in Congress, and we say, "Well, we can get a lot better bill six months from now." But when the [McCain] bill failed, it took the steam out of the grassroot movement because there is a tendency in grassroot movements not to bounce back.
>
> What Glantz conveyed was, "We're just starting to fight. And we're getting new recruits and new supporters by the day." The real phenomenon we are talking about is the degree to which popular movements have momentum and stamina at critical junctures. One critical juncture is a bizarre one, which is that when an imperfect bill fails, they don't seem to have a second-strike capability.

8. Resolve good-faith strategic differences with your allies by plugging your ears and shouting them down.

From the first moments that news leaked of the negotiations, before Matt had a chance to explain what he was free to explain, a cadre of angry activists moved directly into combat mode, and each succeeding meeting was treated as a battlefield. Apostates were scorned and shunned; tentatively open but closeted minds were outed. Constituents were propagandized and sent into battle to prevent the leadership of organizations like the American Cancer Society, the American Heart Association, and the American Medical Association from approaching the settlement and Congress with any degree of openness.

Waxman's indignation at Matt's temerity in usurping Waxman's rightful role as negotiator; the Nader troops' picketing and distributing fugitive-style "WANTED" posters, framing Matt Myers and Bill

Novelli as brigands; John Banzhaf's habitual sneer at anyone who would consider less than utopian demands; Stan Glantz's awesome armory of dismissive rhetoric against any "fool" who happened to view the world through a different prism; Bill Godshall's inability to comment on events without challenging the integrity, commitment, insufficiently scratchy hair shirt, bureaucratic timidity, "political correctness," government freeloading, elitism, and unmerited government-subsidized salaries of those who might disagree with him; Michael Siegel's excommunication as a movement Judas of anyone who would entertain any diminution of any tobacco victim's (largely theoretical) day in court—all poisoned what might otherwise have become a reasoned intramovement debate.

Among the low blows struck by foes of the settlement, in lieu of serious debate, were those that accused Bill Novelli and the Center for Tobacco-Free Kids of supporting the settlement so they could reap the financial jackpot of settlement funds. There was never any truth to this, and the Center issued a statement as soon as the issue was raised, unequivocally forswearing any funds from the settlement. But Bill Godshall and others kept these accusations alive, both in their e-mail blasts and by word of mouth.

There were, indeed, conflicts of interest, emotional as well as economic, that might well have influenced almost all of those who either supported or opposed the settlement, though the more subtle conflicts might have remained largely unconscious and unacknowledged. Julia Carol insists she asked herself "every day" whether ANR's fierce opposition to settlement-generated federal legislation was motivated, even in part, by ANR's economic and emotional stake in continuing its highly satisfying advocacy for local and state laws. I can't judge how well she succeeded in looking objectively at ANR's threatened signature work—leading local clean-indoor-air battles—which the settlement might have ended by decreeing all workplaces in the nation smoke free. But at least she made a conscious effort to do so.

Many of us have earned a respectable living for decades fighting Big Tobacco. Might the McCain bill not have undermined our appeal to the concerned citizens who contribute to our cause, or the philanthropies that respond to the urgency of our proposals? And what of the subtle threat to those who have enjoyed their long day in the media spotlight? Could that prospect have dampened their enthusiasm for a solution that might return them to obscurity?

Matt and Bill Novelli and John Seffrin and the Heart Association's

Dudley Hafner also had emotional conflicts of interest: their roles as architects of historic tobacco control legislation would have greatly burnished their renown as leaders and added heavy weight to their biographies. The point, of course, is not to cast a plague on all houses equally for remote as well as notorious conflicts of interest, but to caution each of us to examine constantly, as Julia Carol at least tried to do, wherein our own conflicts may dwell, and to what extent such conflicts may indeed be polluting our judgment. Such self-examination may stretch the bounds of our capacity to view our own motives without self-delusion, but, in any event, it might at least restrain the impulse to cast "conflict of interest" charges recklessly.

When activists with impeccable grassroots credentials like Russ Sciandra challenged the prevailing line that the settlement was a sellout, they were scorned. Sciandra: "Immediately, anybody who was for the settlement became one with the tobacco industry. I stopped reading the listservs. Frankly, there are a lot of people whom I will never again hold in esteem because of the way they've behaved the past few months. Not because of their opinions, but because their opinions have been formed without thought and expressed with the moral righteousness of dime-store evangelists."

In the settlement struggle, the incivility was largely confined to opponents of the negotiations. This was partly the result of the strategic decision made by Bill Novelli and others *barely to respond* to the attacks, in the mistaken belief—or prayer—that, however nasty, these were voices in the wilderness who would not be heard in Washington. Novelli was also convinced, not without reason, that if the Center sought to actively promote its view of the settlement, the effort would only evoke new barrages of invective.

The most debilitating consequences of this nastiness was that all but a handful of those who disagreed with the invective hurlers were intimidated into a silence that could be taken for acquiescence.

Matt's lieutenant, Mike Kirshenbaum, tallies the costs to the movement of such alienation but also holds the Center at least partly accountable: "There was a great 'silent middle' of the tobacco control field who just became turned off. Stan is dead wrong when he claims that 'the field' was against federal legislation. Most of the field was sick and tired of the carping by Stan and the lack of communication from—and the arrogance of—the Center."

9. Neglect to convince your grassroots followers that your vision of victory is not their nightmare of defeat.

The national headquarters and Washington-based lobbies of the tobacco control movement are enthusiastic about building grassroots support for lobbying campaigns. They are less inclined to invite grassroots participation in the decision-making process that sets the objectives of such campaigns.

To the first flurries of anxiety at news of settlement negotiations, Bill Novelli's message to the national government relations staffs of the health voluntaries, and to their state and staff and volunteers was, essentially: "We are working with your leaders. Trust us." They didn't.

Rich Hamburg, a senior staff lobbyist in D.C. for the Heart Association, supported his organization's leadership and understood the need for closely held secrecy and why he had to learn about the negotiations when the news media called him to comment on the breaking story. But he's convinced his and the other organizations paid a price in losing the opportunity for stronger, more cohesive organizational support: "We didn't engage everybody as early as we should—so we didn't get the buy-in we needed. We were simply told, 'This is the greatest thing since sliced bread—that's our line; stick with it.' "

Karla Sneegas, among the most balanced and open-minded community leaders, is convinced that an early, vigorous, and genuine outreach effort by Matt and the Center to state tobacco control leaders could have substantially mitigated the pervasive distrust and sense of betrayal.

Not all of the unrest among Cancer Society volunteers, especially the Californians, was fomented by Stan Glantz and Julia Carol. ACS chief executive John Seffrin's admirable fortitude in seizing upon the negotiations as a historic opportunity and resisting Glantz's relentless pressure to abandon Matt and the settlement was undermined by his limiting his early consultations to national ACS elected officers, not the rank-and-file staff and volunteers in the field. While constitutionally appropriate, this limited consultation left many staff and volunteers alienated, feeling insufficiently consulted or respected. Seffrin did organize a series of teleconference briefings of regional staff and volunteers in late April and May of 1997. But built-up resentment at what was seen as corporate man-on-a-white-horse decision making still simmered months later. He acknowledges, "I can see now that others felt left out." As a consequence, ACS was less able to mobilize grass-roots activity when it was sorely needed. "We should have been able to generate more heat, more mail, marches, demonstrations, and we didn't," acknowledges Seffrin.

Matt recognizes that he left not only the grassroots behind, but most of his colleagues at the Center itself:

> We were not only too far out in front of the field, but we were too far out in front of the Center. We didn't do a good job of bringing our staff along on this. . . . You can't take people into a fight unless you're all there, and you can't ask people to fight a fight of that intensity unless they believe in it.
>
> One of the things we did differently from what had been done before by the tobacco control movement was systematically build relations with the White House, with senior policy people on the Hill, with attorneys general—whoever the people were who were most likely to be in the position to cause opportunity to occur. That was strength and a weakness. It was strength because it was the right thing to do. It meant for the first time that when these decision makers wanted to strike an agreement, someone from public health was given an opportunity to be part of the process. It was a weakness because we were seen in the field as too top-heavy, too arrogant, too connected, and not tied closely enough to the grassroots, with the heartbeat and soul of the movement.

And Novelli adds: "If we go off by ourselves . . . if we try to exert leadership that's not consensus leadership, we're going to be two guys in a forty-person organization marching up the hill, and we're not going to have any parade or any troops behind us."

10. Be united—even in folly.

Most of those who chose scapegoating over self-reflection honed in on the lack of movement "unity," and for them, the lack of unity meant the failure of Matt, ACS, and others to drop any hint of openness to any form of liability limits. On June 30, 1998, Stan Glantz wrote: "ENACT's refusal to move on the immunity issue and the resulting diversion of effort on the part of Koop, Kessler, and the rest of us doing damage control as well as the loss of effectiveness of the public health community because of the divisions is why we failed to get the McCain bill (before it was wrecked) out of the Senate. Had we had everyone working together from the beginning (as they were de facto at the end) together with ACS and ENACT's resources, we could have prevailed."

Koop later chastened Mohammed Akhter, the president of the American Public Health Association, for co-signing an article in the *American Journal of Public Health* with Novelli, Myers, Seffrin, and Heart Association CEO, Cass Wheeler, that rather mildly suggested that the unyielding resistance of those, like Koop, to *any* form of liability relief did contribute to the failure to achieve good legislation. In an angry letter, Koop demurred: "I do believe your co-signers are primarily responsible for the division in the public health community because of their dichotomous position, and therefore for, in part, the dismal failure of the legislative process to bring forth a bill that would advance public health. This includes standing with the public health community in a press conference on February 17, 1998, and then passing out letters at the door, retracting their position."

So far as I have determined, no seasoned observer of Congress has given any credence whatsoever to the notion that if all the public health groups had just held out together against any concessions, then John McCain and his committee, the White House, the Lott-led Senate, and the Gingrich-led House would have embraced the model blueprint produced by the Koop-Kessler Committee with no liability relief for the industry whatsoever.

John Seffrin prefers the word "solidarity" to "unity." What was lacking, he argues, was not lock-step unity on concessions—indeed, even the leaders of the SAVE LIVES coalition were not always unified in opposition to liability caps—but the "solidarity that comes with being able to stand together on certain issues and not undermine one another where there are differences on other issues."

11. Follow your followers over the cliff.

In the one-page secret outline embodying their September 1997 consensus on the bottom line they would fight for, Kessler, Waxman, and Humphrey signified their willingness to accept not only caps on past industry liability, precisely as embodied in the McCain bill, but also substantial concessions on future civil liability, which were *not* granted by the McCain bill.

So it was not surprising that, as Koop and Kessler assumed the leadership of all the dissident voices, with Koop embraced by and embracing the SAVE LIVES coalition, Julia Carol and her more militant colleagues expressed well-grounded fears that, as the legislative process progressed, their "leaders" could not be trusted to hold the line on immunity. They sought various subtle and not so subtle means to keep Koop from wavering. Glantz, for example, kept up a flow of flattering messages hailing Koop's leadership on the immunity issue. Koop and Kessler's desire to maintain overall leadership boxed them in. As the McCain bill began to emerge from the Senate Commerce Committee, meeting virtually all Koop and Kessler's public health demands and yielding only caps on liability relief, Koop, then Kessler, then Koop again grew increasingly strident in condemning the inadequacy of the bill.

As Russ Sciandra observed wryly of Kessler and Koop, "They weren't leading so much as just sort of being carried along by these people that were hoisting them up on their shoulders and taking them over the cliff."

Others who might have galvanized support for a bill like the McCain bill, which strengthened the settlement in ways critical to the public health community with just such modest liability relief, simply failed to lead. As Bill Novelli lamented, following the death of the McCain bill: "If Clinton had been a better leader . . . if Shalala had been a better leader . . . if Gore had been a better leader . . . perhaps they could have brought the community together instead of what they essentially did, which is to let the community go its way."

Bill is right. And Matt is right when he assails Clinton for failing to lead on the crucial issues:

When the June 20, 1997, settlement was announced, the White House dropped the ball. They prompted the negotiations with promises of leadership and support. They were part of every major decision. . . . It was unfair to those who negotiated the settlement, made worse by the fact that some of the worst provisions in the agreement were things that were explicitly endorsed by the White House—such as the liability provisions, and the FDA provision, indirectly. Indirectly, because at critical junctures I asked the White House to look at the FDA provisions and to get FDA to look at them, and to tell us if there were flaws in them that were sufficiently troublesome to cause a real problem. And the White House's response was that the FDA had decided not to help.

Then, Secretary Shalala and her people spent the whole summer of 1997 picking apart the settlement agreement instead of saying, "I don't like it, but what an opportunity. Let's fix it. Let's make it better."

And when the McCain bill emerged, Clinton could have called Kessler and Koop in and said, "This is all we can get."

Among the members of Congress with a just claim to trust as consistent public health leaders, only Ron Wyden of Oregon and John Kerry of Massachusetts demonstrated constructive leadership. Within the Commerce Committee, they fought for stronger FDA international, minority, and other health provisions, and they held out for limiting liability relief to caps. And when McCain acceded to these demands, they stood foursquare with him in support of the committee bill. But they could not rally the public health community around the bill because other congressional health leaders, especially Kennedy and Waxman, hewed to the absolutist demands of the SAVE LIVES coalition.

The monument to Stan Glantz's leadership in the settlement struggles was his genius in flogging a hostile internal movement environment that inhibited other movement leaders who knew better from supporting the McCain bill essentially as it emerged from the Senate Commerce Committee. He's proud of that achievement. They shouldn't be.

12. Never learn from looking back.

In the interviews of movement leaders I conducted for this book, I asked each interviewee if, looking back, he or she would have done anything differently. Most came up with minor tactical lessons. For example, Nader's colleague Rob Weissman regretted his failure to mobilize what became SAVE LIVES earlier. Dr. Koop said he would have been more "political" in cultivating relationships with members of Congress. Of those who opposed even the strengthened McCain bill, only Ralph Nader acknowledged that there were important lessons for him and for citizen movements generally to be learned from its loss. He remains troubled by the caps in the McCain bill and is still not certain that he should or would have supported the bill, but he acknowledges frankly his own and others' fatal failure to recognize that the momentum toward strong tobacco control legislation would not last. He admits, "This is what we should know but we didn't know."

Another notable exception was economist and teacher Ken Warner, long among the most thoughtful and reflective movement leaders. Warner had struggled throughout the process with the right course of action, sometimes open, sometimes fiercely resistant. He had early challenged Matt—with civility—as willing to settle for too little. But in the fall of 1998, after the death of the McCain bill, Ken wrote a characteristically reflective e-mail note:

> The lessons of the past year deserve a sharp eye. The tobacco control community may have blown it—gone for the gold ring, when the brass one would have represented a great prize. I continue to believe that the June 20th proposed settlement was not a good deal for public health. But the ramped up versions in Congress might have been very good. If only "we" hadn't been so unbending on the liability issue. Once the limits were raised high enough (e.g., $8 billion), I think we would have gotten everything the court system could have delivered to us and obviously, more in the form of the non-monetary features of the legislation.

In the days following the death of McCain's bill, the e-mail exchanges were buzzing with indignation at published criticisms of the movement by such hard-to-dismiss observers as Richard Kluger and Myron Levin.

Dick Daynard, an apostle of the glories and rewards of litigation throughout the process, nevertheless called for a pause to reflect:

> Many commentators have put part, much, or most of the blame for the fall of McCain on our part of the public health (anti-smoking, tobacco control) community. I don't feel bad about the role that any of us played, and I could come up with lots of other folks to blame if blame needs to be distributed. But when Myron Levin of the *L.A. Times* writes a piece suggesting that we were too stuck in a fighting mode, I need to think about it more. Myron has been writing incisively and sympathetically about tobacco issues for a dozen years or more; his judgment is worth something.
>
> I'm really not saying we were wrong, or should have done anything differently. But I am a great believer in the importance of reflection, and listening, and constructive self-criticism, and I worry that in responding quickly and firmly to our critics (which we should keep doing), we may be missing an opportunity to learn something ourselves.

One veteran northern California activist, Rick Kropp, wrote to another e-mail discussion group: "While many activists are no doubt perturbed at this faultfinding and criticism, these articles and commentary can also serve as a catalyst for accomplishing a worthwhile purpose. That could stimulate a healthy critical self-examination and soul-searching of our tobacco control policy and programmatic goals, methods, and differences. A reasoned dialogue and respectful exchange of views could be a very cleansing and clarifying process."

Even this small window of self-reflection slammed shut. Daynard, having ventured out into self-reflection, was quick to retreat and circle the wagons against nameless conspirators: "The more I read about how Koop and Kessler are starry-eyed idealists, and especially the more comments I see trashing our position from 'realists' in the tobacco control community, the less I am able to sustain that self-critical detachment I urged in an earlier e-mail. With so many people making the same unfair judgments about us, I begin to suspect a coordinated attack. The b———s seem to be closing in for the kill. I think we can fend them off, but we may have to defer our reflective moments until later."

It is now later, but to this day, with the unlikely exception of Ralph Nader, neither Glantz, nor Koop, nor Kessler, nor Waxman, nor most of those who failed to support McCain and the McCain bill at the critical hour have expressed any cause to question their strategic thinking or behavior.

13. Let your outsize ego be your guide.

Evaluating the role of ego in leadership is tricky business. A strong ego is an absolute predicate to effective leadership. Dr. Koop's heightened sense of his role as surgeon general, his undaunted confrontation with the tobacco industry, and his defiance of pressures from the Reagan administration to cool it were each manifestations of an uncommonly strong sense of his own importance—of a man not uncomfortable referring to himself as "an icon."

Kessler would be the only FDA commissioner to assert jurisdiction over tobacco, knowing that such action would rouse fearsome counterattack from the tobacco lobby—and from threatened tobacco-state politicians. Again, his well-developed sense of his own rightness fueled his determination. But he was also shrewdly tactical in both his focus on tobacco as "a pediatric disease" and his finely calibrated, modest regulatory initiative.

Stan Glantz shrank neither from pinching the tail of a tobacco industry that had the infamous capacity to bite back through PR calumny as well as abuse of the legal system, nor from goading established public health leaders and organizations out of their torpor. Only a strong ego could propel him and sustain him in such confrontation.

And those like Bill Novelli, John Seffrin, Dudley Hafner, Russ Sciandra, Nancy Kaufman, and others who took a stand in support of Matt and the settlement and compromise, in the face of ferocious opposition from the movement's Furies, were distinguished from the silent ones, and the waffling ones, by their healthy confidence in their own judgment. So I criticize a show of ego in leaders gingerly.

In the preceding narrative, I have tried to let the key leaders speak for themselves of the thinking that led them to the positions and actions they took—so that readers could draw their own conclusions on the leaders' decision-making processes.

But it is hard for me to escape the conclusion that the unremitting enmity of at least some leaders toward Matt, Bill Novelli, John Seffrin, the June 20 settlement, ENACT, or the McCain bill was subtly shaped by resentment, conscious or unconscious, at having been unjustly bypassed or neglected, and by a concomitant envy of Matt's role on center stage. This seems especially true of those who viewed themselves as preeminent movement leaders.

Nancy Kaufman, of The Robert Wood Johnson Foundation, had been a close observer of all the events. She was briefed early by Matt and counseled him and Bill Novelli throughout the negotiations and the ensuing fractures. She observes, looking back:

We have a number of "Mullahs" in this field who want to lead the Jihad, and each sees himself as *the* leader. We had a Jihad going on here, and we had all these clerics—and it would drive them crazy if Matt were the only one at the table.

I've worked in public health now for thirty years, and I've worked with a lot of egos, especially among the physicians. We are an ego-driven field, and tobacco control is one of the most ego-driven fields within public health. I've often tried to figure out why this field, in particular, has developed leaders who had a passionate love of what they were doing, but who were, in some ways, so driven that the movement had become for them a Jihad, a holy war. And I've often asked myself—and others—why this is so.

First, you have to have a strong ego when you're working in politics—and tobacco control is among the most political of public health issues.

But there is also something about this group of people—maybe it was being oppressed for so long; maybe it was being seen as loners or weirdos; maybe it was being told that tobacco was just not that important, in essence. Maybe such an environment shaped these leaders, or maybe it attracted them in the first place.

But we certainly have a number of Mullahs now, and sometimes they are in conflict with one another. They want to lead the Jihad, and each sees himself as *the* leader.

David Kessler is a good example of this. I have a lot of respect for David. I think he's brilliant. I also think he has a tremendous ego. He's a media hog; he has to be in the newspapers as the linchpin in every deal. This became for him his cause célèbre, which was good because he made a lot of good things happen.

But at some point, he went over the edge. He became seduced by being so enraptured in this effort—and being the spokesperson that was always quoted on the Sunday morning talk shows—that perhaps he lost perspective.

Then, there was Koop; there was Henry Waxman. They contributed so much—but they were all fighting to be the top guy, to go down in history as the person who made this happen.

Stan Glantz never let a hint of doubt disturb his conviction that he alone held all the keys to wisdom. Fran Dumelle of the Lung Association's relentless antipathy toward the settlement was fueled by Lung's resentment at its diminished role "at the foot of the table" headed by the Center and the Cancer Society. Henry Waxman, who saw himself, with reason, as Congress's leading health legislator, not only raged at Matt's effrontery in undertaking a negotiating role, which Waxman believed should be reserved only to him, but excoriated even his close colleague David Kessler for usurping what Waxman saw as *his* own rightful role in negotiating with McCain. Dr. Koop never forgave Matt for his resistance to Koop's 1996 offer to lead a new national campaign to end tobacco use in this century. And both Koop and Kessler were enraged at the creation by Matt and his ACS and AHA colleagues of the ENACT coalition without first consulting them and allowing them to be the founding and central leaders.

Jeff Koplan, the director of the Centers for Disease Control during the settlement-related events, looks at the leadership of the tobacco control movement in the broader context of successful public health campaigns and finds it wanting: "Most great successes in public health have involved diverse partners subsuming their egos and differences to achieve a difficult grand goal—smallpox eradication, fluoridated water, the sanitation movement, auto safety, etc. While the anti-tobacco advocacy community has both been very effective and made great gains, the end result seems to be diminished by self-righteousness, rigidity, and confusing its allies with its enemies."

Richard Kluger had the first words in this book about the potential of settlement. He deserves the last word on the role of inflated ego in its failure. He wrote me:

> In the course of researching the anti-tobacco movement, I was struck by two characteristics of its leadership that seemed to foreshadow—perhaps even to insure—the disastrous overreach when it at last cornered the cigarette industry and then egregiously failed to deliver the knockout punch. First, these fiercest foes of the tobacco companies were a charismatic bunch, as full of themselves as they were of passion dedicated to doing in the devil. In their righteousness, they saw as few others did the enormity of the industry's calculated, greatly enriching deceit and were appalled that most of the rest of American society viewed with such indifference the immense toll that smoking exacted on the U.S. public health. Egos invested to the hilt in the uphill fight, they looked at the combat as a validating effort, the core mission of their lives.
>
> Yet, even while they raged volubly against the satanic host, this heroic stance of theirs deluded them into believing that they would triumph in the end because they were on the side of the angels and did not have to rein in their fervor or their personas. The antismoking leaders, estimable in so many ways, never managed to submerge their individual priorities and psychic needs for the good of their cause and to thrash out intramurally a coherent, plausible battle plan. Their dream became unconditional surrender by the enemy, with huge reparations—or nothing. It was a case of retributive justice run amuck. And, irony of ironies, the cunning, monolithic enemy was able to claim itself victimized by a cadre of unforgiving control freaks and health fascists.
>
> The truest kind of hero is selfless and disinterested. The anti-tobacco stalwarts, for all their good works, fell well short of that standard. As a result, the cigarette remains a largely uncontrolled killer-at-large because its well-intentioned stalkers fell before their own friendly fire.

The Wrong Leaders for the Right Moment

At the close of this gloomy tale, it may seem odd that the tobacco control movement remains the envy of advocates in sister social change movements, from gun control to universal health care. After all, if one looks at cigarette-smoking rates and trends in 1965 and then in the year 2000, some fifty million Americans who do not now smoke would likely be smoking today if it were not for this movement. The legal environment for smoking has been transformed—thirty-five years ago, smokers unselfconsciously occupied virtually all public spaces; today, in most American cities, they must extinguish or be banished. And, in many communities, especially among better-educated Americans, the cultural environment for smoking has been equally transformed: fewer and fewer smokers dare to light up in the presence of their children— or their social arbiters.

Of course, the social history of tobacco use in the latter part of this century is complex and fascinating, although not fascinating enough to justify digressing from our central focus in this book at this late point, except to acknowledge the contribution of what is surely a unique cadre of leaders who emerged at the right time and in the right combination of roles to move this movement forward. And none have contributed more than those whom I have just finished chastising.

In the last twenty years, especially, the tobacco movement has been blessed with the right leadership at the right time. In the early 1980s, the best top-down, science-led public education efforts to reduce the deadly harm of smoking had been undermined and deflected by the tobacco industry's disinformation strategies, while the worst and brightest of the nation's lobbyists stealthily squashed modest public health initiatives in Congress and the state legislatures.

It was then that Stan Glantz, the scientist-advocate, emerged to help build the scientific case that secondhand smoke sickened and killed bystanders at a rate that dwarfed far more notorious environmental hazards; Stan Glantz, the movement "spark plug," emerged to sound the call for "bottom-up" grassroots political warfare against the tobacco industry, waged community by community; and Stan Glantz, the strategic communicator, emerged to model aggressive, bite-sharp media advocacy that focused public attention on tobacco industry corruption and exploitation of smokers, and away from the culpability of "weak-willed" smokers themselves.

In the mid-1980s came Dr. Koop, Ronald Reagan's and Jesse Helms's unwitting gift to the movement. Koop was the authoritative presence and voice of science and moral authority. He was the medical statesman who engaged the broad public in a combined scientific and moral crusade against villainous tobacco. And, as superb a communicator as Glantz, he also reframed tobacco use from an issue of personal choice to both an environmental public health issue, and a drug addiction issue. ("Yes, more addictive than heroin and cocaine!")

By the early 1990s Julia Carol had become the movement builder and organizer to complement Stan. Along with Fran Dumelle of the American Lung Association, Carol helped build and sustain a nationwide network of trained advocates who would effectively challenge the industry's lobbyists in the state legislatures they had formerly dominated.

In Congress, Henry Waxman had demonstrated great legislating skill in forging consensus on key mature health issues, from pesticide regulation to food and drug regulation. But in 1994, Waxman made perhaps his greatest contribution to the tobacco control movement. In brilliant media choreography, he forced the seven tobacco chief executives in a row to swear, under oath, that the earth was flat—that they did not believe tobacco to be addictive. In doing so, Waxman gave a human face to tobacco company villainy—mobilizing public outrage against the industry.

And then, by the mid-1990s, David Kessler vaulted to national prominence as tobacco control's strategic "inside" leader—the leader who found himself in the critical government role to initiate fundamental change and the diplomatic skill to bring a politically uneasy White House along.

In 1995 came Bill Novelli, whose strategic communications skills, harnessed to The Robert Wood Johnson Foundation's resources and Matt Myers's strategic insights, put the political spotlight on Congress's corrupt campaign-financing indenture to the tobacco lobby—loosening the industry's hold on a Congress increasingly sensitive to public revulsion.

Meanwhile, John Seffrin, the dark-suited revolutionary who, with a strong hand, transformed the Cancer Society from the toothless supplicant of the 1960s through the 1980s to a potent public interest lobbying force—from a "national" coalition with Heart and Lung with only one full-time employee to a network of federal and state lobbyists and politically canny volunteers.

Dudley Hafner and Cass Wheeler ably followed suit at the American Heart Association.

And the nearly invisible movement builders, such as Karla Sneegas, were meanwhile patiently building and sustaining functioning and effective advocacy coalitions across the country—even in the hostile political soil of the tobacco South.

Within minority communities that had largely been ignored by the tobacco control movement, there now emerged focused movement leaders like Jesse Brown, Charyn Sutton, Jeanette Noltenius, and Rod Lew.

And there was Matt Myers, "the leading movement strategist," as Kessler called him, and the "inside" lobbyist—the movement's most connected and trusted advocate in Congress and with the White House.

This movement was indeed blessed with diverse—and complementary—leadership that provided the necessary skills and roles that brought tobacco control to the brink of extraordinary success: scientific and moral authority, strategic vision, "outside-inside" strategic advocacy, kick-starting energy, strategic mass media advocacy, and the transformative shaping of once passive movement organizations into an effective grassroots political force.

So what leadership flaws in this phalanx of strong leaders led to the lost opportunities of 1997 and 1998?

In part, at least, the diverse leadership skills and roles that had proved complementary and synergistic as the movement was rising also harbored the seeds of dysfunction at the moment that a once unimaginable—if still imperfect—victory loomed into sight.

Stan Glantz, the strategist who practiced and preached the virtues of "outside advocacy," without negotiation or compromise, stayed outside so long he froze. Nothing in his experience or his temperament enabled him to consider the possibility that the political environment had so changed—thanks in part to his own skill—that negotiation and compromise might now yield enormous benefits. In California, where the voluntary health agencies were timid and cautious and dependent upon hired lobbyists too timid to annoy legislators with "unreasonable" demands, Glantz's internal movement warfare against weak compromise was exactly right. As Matt e-mailed him in the heat of battle: "It may be easier to throw bricks from the safety of the outside, but it is not more effective." But, in Washington, in the extraordinary political environment of 1997 and 1998, the lessons he drew from his California crucible served him and the movement badly.

For Julia Carol, the building and nurturing of a community-based movement had become an end in itself—a passion and a vocation that closed her mind to a top-down solution—no matter that the public health benefits of community action were approaching their apparent limits, and only Congress had the power to regulate nicotine and the carcinogens out of cigarettes and stem the addiction and the risks.

Dr. Koop, never a fine-tuned policy strategist, came to believe that his undoubted preeminence affirmed his strategic wisdom and his right to lead.

Dr. Kessler, by contrast, had been a crafty strategist at FDA but took on Koop's mantle—and grandiosity—and lost his strategic bearings.

Congressman Waxman, the model of the pragmatic and skilled legislator, including negotiating skills and the art of prudent compromise, could not accept the possibility that significant legislation could be achieved without his controlling hand; he demanded that Matt and the attorneys general continue their cases and abandon their efforts to extract FDA and other legislative concessions from the companies. Jim Tierney comments:

> Congressman Waxman was a great friend of the anti-tobacco movement, but he was dead wrong in criticizing Matt and the attorneys general for trying to make progress when he was powerless to do anything but issue press releases. He wasn't even able to call a hearing to help us. Waxman is a hero of mine and has made America a better place by knowing how and when to strike deals with the devil, but his arrogance at stating that attorneys general should continue their cases beyond a point that they thought appropriate remains shocking. It was the cases filed by the attorneys general that got the tobacco industry to agree to FDA jurisdiction, not Henry Waxman.

Ralph Nader, though not specifically a tobacco control leader, nevertheless had served a generation of public interest advocates as the visionary who taught them to raise their sights beyond the small incremental advances that conventional political wisdom decreed as the limits of the doable. During the settlement struggles, Nader had a compelling and grounded vision: the cascade of blows against the industry

that would sweep away the power of the tobacco lobby—criminal indictments from the Justice Department grand juries; new explosive
revelations from Minnesota attorney general Humphrey's promised trial
release of explosive secret documents; the Republicans' fear that toady-
ing to Big Tobacco would threaten their hold on Congress. Congress
would enact a strong tobacco control law with no concession to Big
Tobacco. Nader's vision was clear, but, this time, his horizon was
clouded by the wishful forecasts of his allies. None of these expected
blows fell.

John Seffrin's strong hand in leading the American Cancer Society's
support of the settlement faltered over the volunteers and staff advocates in the field—advocates empowered by his advocacy-building
initiatives—who demanded participation in ACS decision making and
were no longer prepared simply to follow their titular leader.

And Bill Novelli, the cool strategist who saw clearly the promise of
the settlement, did not see—because he was not "of the movement"—
the potential train-wrecking power of a few hundred grassroots activists scorned.

Perhaps the saddest lesson to be drawn from our chronicle of the
June 20 settlement is that, while the combination of the leadership roles
that graced the tobacco control movement may be essential to the success of any movement, they are not automatically complementary. Visionaries can lose touch with reality and clash with strategic pragma-
tists; unrestrained "spark plugs" can paralyze as well as energize; and
communicators can degenerate into propagandists, manipulators of
science and the truth.

These leadership conflicts, if not acknowledged and remedied, can
arrest a movement's progress, transforming a potentially dynamic and
complementary leadership into a nightmare of dysfunctional conflict,
and a downward spiral of distrust, frustration, and anger.

If anything, this chronicle teaches that internal balance and self-
knowledge are needed in all of our leaders to assure that their very
strengths don't morph into undermining weaknesses, that each leader
needs to strive to balance advocacy and detachment. Sociologist John
Lifton encapsulates these essential leadership qualities: "sufficient
detachment to bring to bear one's intellectual discipline on the subject, and sufficient moral passion to motivate and humanize the work."
Our leaders surely had admirable passion; almost uniformly, they lacked
the balancing detachment.

38

Engaged in the Work of Democracy

How did Matt Myers meet the standards I've applied to others?

Of course, my judgment is especially suspect here. After all, as I have acknowledged, my first impulse to write this book came from my own anguish and anger at what I saw as the unfairness of Matt's critics.

Still I have tried throughout this book, if not always to keep my judgments at arm's length, at least to allow Matt and the other key players to have their say in their own words. In citing published sources and direct interviews, I did not scant Matt's keenest critics. And I have sought to test my instinct to defend Matt's actions against the same standards to which I have held the others.

Did I learn much about Matt's thinking and behavior of which I had no inkling when I started researching this chronicle? Absolutely. Did what I learn change my view of Matt's motivations or the rightness of his actions? Mostly it strengthened the convictions with which I began.

I was prepared, for example, to accept the criticism that Matt's outsize ego, his exaggerated confidence in his own judgment and abilities—his "supreme" confidence, as one critic put it—led him to consult only himself in participating in the negotiations, to go it largely alone.

I was wrong. To be sure, it took uncommon confidence to stay with the negotiations when he was under assault from colleagues whose judgment he had earlier relied upon. And it is also true, as Nancy Kaufman wryly observed: "Oh, sure, Matt has a big ego too. Let's be honest here. Matt loved being the guy at the table, and all the surrounding hoopla—you know, NBC coming out to interview him, and all that. There's a part of Matt that loves being the center of attention, loves being quoted by the press, and he too, wants to be the head Mullah. I think that's somewhat why he resisted several of us saying, 'Don't go in there alone; this is a huge mistake.' "

Yes, Matt went in there alone—but it was not without almost desperately seeking others, especially David Kessler, to join him at the negotiating table. We know now how determinedly Matt and Bill Novelli regularly briefed and took counsel from the steering committee of public health CEOs, including, until he withdrew, the American Lung Association's John Garrison. Matt had, almost daily, briefed either David Kessler or Mitch Zeller; had sought guidance from FDA on critical drafting issues; had briefed Dr. Koop at great length shortly after the negotiations leaked; and had unsuccessfully urged Dick Scruggs and his colleagues at the onset of the negotiations to inform and involve Henry Waxman. As Nancy Kaufman also acknowledges: "Matt didn't see himself as omniscient, as knowing everything. You could pull Matt back. You could say, 'Here's a point; and here's a point, and there's a point.' And he'd listen, internalize, and later he would act on it. It wasn't, 'I'm in charge of making every decision and I'm the only one who knows what's good for everybody.' I didn't hear that coming out of Matt, and I did hear that coming from the other Mullahs."

Rather than egotism, the quality Matt displayed in the days that he characterized as "the worst days of my professional life" is better captured by that cliché of leadership, the courage of his convictions.

In another misapprehension, I initially assumed that Matt had been ready to trade off virtually any liability relief for the industry in exchange for the public health objectives that were uppermost on his agenda. What I discovered is that he cared as passionately as most about holding the companies accountable; that he had fought unremittingly against excessive liability concessions to the industry, from the settlement negotiations through the McCain bill negotiations; and that he fought against them harder than most of the attorneys general or the trial lawyers at the table—and suffered their enmity for his efforts.

One safeguard against my having too rosy a view of Matt came from Matt's own unrelenting criticism of himself—some of which, it must be noted, is well taken:

> Among the mistakes I made was not doing more between November 1994 and April 1997 to force a discussion more broadly in the movement about goals and priorities. I responded—wrongly—after the November 1996 meeting [seeking common ground with Glantz and others] by turning to a small cadre of trusted leaders.

After the November 1996 meeting, I feared that Stan's ferocity would so intimidate others that a discussion at large in the abstract was doomed to failure, but that the results would be different once a concrete proposal was on the table. I was wrong, and it should have been obvious. Compromise is never possible if the groundwork for it hasn't been laid. Later, we were so busy rallying the troops that we failed to help them work through the issues.

He rues his stubbornness in resisting his staff's entreaties to quit the settlement talks in their last days, as it became apparent he would lose the battle to limit the liability concessions in an effort to use his remaining leverage to force change in these provisions. He regrets his failure to emphasize the need to correct the settlement's flaws on the day it was announced. He regrets neglecting Dr. Koop's powerful need to be assured of his leadership role.

Looking back, he would have reached out more aggressively to grassroots activists during the negotiations as soon as he was free to do so, explaining to one and all the reasons for his decision to participate in the talks. He would have sought more insistently to overcome Scruggs's and Moore's resistance to informing Henry Waxman at the onset of the talks.

Matt also sees justice in the criticism leveled by Michael Eriksen, former head of the Centers for Disease Control's Office on Smoking and Health. Eriksen is generally respectful of Matt's leadership in the settlement but makes a telling point that Matt's straddling of two leadership roles, the movement builder and the independent advocate, compounded his troubles:

> Part of Matt's problem was he had promoted the Center as the hub of a new coalition, yet the Center didn't act as a coalition. It acted unilaterally and strategically capitalized on an opportunity. You either are part of a coalition, where you move forward only by consensus and spend a lot of time seeking consensus—or you act unilaterally and strategically. You can't have it both ways.
>
> I don't believe Matt could ever have forged a consensus within the movement, or if he had, it would have been far too late, and he would have missed the opportunity. But his failure to consult broadly angered many people who had been led to believe they were part of a Center-led coalition.

For his actions when the McCain bill came to the Senate floor, Matt faults himself most bitterly. He recalls that the McCain bill, as it was reported from the committee with a 19–1 vote, with its $6.5 billion annual caps on liability recovery but no other "immunity" provisions, was even stronger on "immunity" than the compromise that Kessler, Waxman, and Humphrey had secretly agreed to in September 1997— and that Kessler had even briefed the Senate Democratic caucus on. But by May 1998, it was not enough for them; they insisted upon what became the Gregg amendment, which stripped even the caps from the bill.

"David changed—or more accurately, in retrospect, always needed a reason psychologically to say no, because he could not tolerate saying yes. This is where I perhaps most failed," laments Matt, "when I did not urge that we oppose the Gregg amendment—a fatal mistake by me, perhaps out of weariness, but that is no excuse!"

Richard Lucas, a trained historian, worked as a senior research analyst during the period the events chronicled in this book took place. Lucas observes that Matt labored under a severe handicap throughout this process—one not of his own making:

> Bill Novelli was not seen by other tobacco control leaders as "of the movement." He was not Matt's "partner," though he treated Matt as such, but his boss—and the visible embodiment of the Center—still a very new organization, rich in resources but lacking in the credibility that comes from years in the tobacco control trenches. This *institutional* situation left the Center vulnerable from the outset to skepticism and even mistrust.
>
> Indeed, the Center's main source for movement credibility at the outset was that Matt was the executive vice president, and he was a known quality to many. But he was not nominally in charge, and the guy who was was a relative unknown in the tobacco world. This situation left the Center vulnerable to unfair charges of conflicts of interest, etc., from those who did not share their views. It also made it easier for Koop and Kessler to take advantage of their high standing in the movement to run roughshod over Matt's efforts to bring folks together around a strengthened settlement.

Matt acknowledges that his lawyerly exchanges with Julia Carol rightly led her to lose trust in his truthfulness. As he said to me, "Sometimes I'm a drop too clever for my own good, and while my lawyerly words are accurate and precise, fairness required me to realize that not everyone parses them as carefully as people like Julia have now learned to parse them. I'm not going to do that again."

In the end, he is not inclined to see himself as a hero, or as anything more than a journeyman public interest lobbyist. But Matt for the most part avoided the deadly ways his counterparts found to derail good legislation, as I have catalogued them:

- When he finally determined that the opportunity for serious negotiations had indeed come, he was able to shift from warrior mode to negotiator. He generally maintained a healthy balance between fighting and talking. If he stayed a little too long inside the negotiations, the very real danger of his co-option by the process was at least partly balanced by his ability, demonstrated time and again, to force change within that process.
- Unlike so many of those around him, he was not lulled by the seemingly endless string of damning industry revelations and seeming victories into an unrealistic view of what the future might hold.
- Metaphoric thinking did not cloud his vision of the industry as devil rather than amoral business. Instead, he probed constantly to understand the precise reasons why the negotiators were at the table, what they wanted and why, and what they could be forced to give up for it.
- Though his patience was tried and he was near exhaustion, he reached out, remaining open to civil and even much uncivil discourse and debate with his movement critics long after most of us would have slammed the phone down and the door shut and deleted the e-mails unread.
- He did not scorn the community activists, the grass roots—and he struggled to persuade his impatient colleague, Bill Novelli, that for all their unreasonableness, they had to be heeded and reconciled.
- He kept his focus on the public health. And he never lost sight of the prime objective: sparing lives and misery.
- Matt is among the few who actually looked back and acknowledged his errors and sought to learn from them. He comes closer than any other leader to meeting sociologist John Lifton's dual test of leadership: passion illuminated by the capacity for detachment.

Richard Lucas observes:

In the leadership roles and styles that were illuminated by the settlement and its aftermath, a useful distinction emerges between two key aspects of leadership; I'll call them (clumsily) "strategic positioning," and "movement maneuver." By these terms, I mean "choosing the right place for the movement to go" to achieve its most important goals, and "finding a way to get there," respectively.

Much of the tension surrounding the settlement revolved around the fact that key tobacco control leaders privileged one of these aspects of leadership over the other. Bill Novelli was tightly focused on strategic positioning but viewed the maneuvering of the movement around his strategic position as a simple matter of enforcing top-down authority. Julia Carol (and to a lesser extent, Glantz) viewed the process of movement maneuver itself as the fundamentally most important strategy of all. Others struck different balances between the two—often implicitly or unconsciously—in different ways.

Matt came as close as anyone could, under severe handicaps, to bringing strategic positioning and movement maneuver together. To be sure, he kept his vision of policy priorities centermost; but he recognized that he had to build broad support within the movement to achieve that vision. And he tried. He worked hard to keep the leaders of the voluntary health organizations fully informed and together; he tried endlessly to reach common ground with Kessler and Koop. He made his case to his critics in Chicago in a way that even Robin Hobart, Julia Carol's ally in undermining the settlement, acknowledged "moved folks (even those opposed to negotiations) from a frame of 'why negotiate?' to a frame of 'What are we getting/what should we get?' "

It is possible that, without the handicaps Matt labored under—the challenged legitimacy of the Center and Bill Novelli, the implacable opposition of Glantz and his allies to any realistic settlement, the conditions and demands of the negotiations that left Matt so little time and excess energy to reach out—he might well have shaped a movement consensus. What his efforts suggest is that movement leaders such as Matt can practice both strategic positioning and movement maneuver in ways that allow a movement to be both coherent and nimble in action, and to advance its goals by using the power of its solidarity to take advantage of strategic opportunities as they present themselves.

David Cohen, both practitioner and scholar of citizen advocacy, also closely observed the events chronicled here. He places Matt's work in the larger context of democratic striving: "What Matt tried to do, and did over and over again, is the work of Democracy, what Isaiah Berlin heralded as 'public work,' the highest of callings. The give and take that Matt engaged in mattered because he knew what the prize is—keeping young people from smoking and saving an incredible number of lives. That's not only honorable; it's what's needed to stop the tobacco companies from addicting young people and killing them when they come of age. It's what will give so many people a choice to live."

Conclusion
With a Little Bit of Luck

In the last chapters, I have argued that the collective leadership of the tobacco control movement, heroes all, nonetheless blew the opportunity of a lifetime. Of course, Big Tobacco's lobbying and propaganda machine, and its indentured politicians, undermined the McCain bill. But it was tobacco control's own leadership that helped deliver the killing blows.

Yet fairness mandates the acknowledgment that this same leadership came close, very close, to extracting from Congress the strongest bill possible—that this book might, instead, have celebrated the brilliant citizen lobbying campaign that led to the development of the McCain bill and its successful enactment into law. Such a campaign need have differed very little from what actually took place—at least in its public manifestations.

Let us go back in our imaginations to that November 1996 strategy session in which Matt Myers and Dick Daynard convened a cross-section of tobacco control leaders to contemplate the possibility of a proffer of compromise from the tobacco industry. Recall that Matt asked the group, "What set of public health provisions, if any, would we demand as the price for giving the industry relief from the threat of bankruptcy posed by litigation?"

Let us now imagine that instead of chilling the very discussion of compromise, the assembled group deliberated long and hard, explored mutual goals and concerns, recessed, and agreed to go home and consult quietly with their colleagues and come together again early the next year.

Then imagine that they did just that and forged a consensus that comprehensive public health policies like those in the McCain bill, but nothing less, would indeed be worth conceding to the tobacco companies predictability in their lawsuit payments—caps on their annual liability payments—but otherwise preserving all existing avenues of litigation against them.

Now imagine that the assembled group, having come to that consensus, then turns to "movement maneuver," the ways to achieve such an ambitious objective. As they assess the political environment, they painstakingly develop a delicate outside-inside strategy. The establishment leaders and groups—the Center, ACS, AHA, AMA—will play the insider role, agreeing to negotiate and extracting as much as possible in public health concessions from any negotiations that might take place.

Secretly, all the players would continue to meet to coordinate strategy. Publicly, however, those leaders and groups more attuned to aggressive modes of outside advocacy would soon distance themselves from the negotiations, demanding far more than could be achieved in any negotiated settlement. They would set up a din, constantly threatening to pursue litigation to the death of the industry and to challenge in the upcoming elections any member of Congress willing to accept less than all of their public health provisions.

To make this outside-inside strategy credible, the leaders agree that they must publicly splinter, to create the public perception that the antisettlement forces are all truly furious with the settlement negotiators. And not wink until Clinton signs a good law.

Now imagine nothing other than what actually ensued:

First, Matt Myers negotiates and is able to tell the tobacco industry negotiators that he comes to the table with the knowledge and support of major public health leaders—and the tacit assumption that their organizations will support a settlement if it meets most of Matt's demands on their behalf.

Now imagine that the leak to the *Wall Street Journal* is not a shock to Julia Carol or other key grassroots leaders in the tobacco control movement, because Matt has kept them informed and they, in turn, have abided by the conditions of confidentiality.

Matt reports to a secret meeting of the November 1996 group augmented by Drs. Koop and Kessler, and by Congressman Henry Waxman and Minnesota attorney general Skip Humphrey. Matt has made progress, but there remain unresolved issues both on the public health provisions and on the extent of liability protections that the industry insists upon. They all agree that they now need publicly to distance themselves from the negotiations—and from Matt—so that they can make effective demands that the settlement be strengthened. They also agree that it is critical during this volatile period that they hammer away at the perfidy of the industry, lest the public and Congress drop their guard against the inevitable industry chicanery.

Once again, the leaders and groups do exactly what they did: they disdainfully distance themselves from Matt. Even ACS, AHA, and AMA announce that while they support Matt being at the table, he doesn't speak for them, and they will each have to make independent judgments on the adequacy of the settlement that emerges.

As the settlement negotiations come to a close, Matt briefs the group secretly once more: we've made great public health gains, but as with any negotiations, we didn't get everything we fought for. Indeed, he's angry at the caving in of the attorneys general and the trial lawyers on key issues, especially liability relief.

Henry Waxman and Skip Humphrey suggest that the best way to create pressure for strengthening the settlement will be to utilize Kessler and Koop—who have thus far played their assigned roles perfectly by keeping a skeptical if not scornful distance from the negotiations. It's agreed that Koop and Kessler will convene a committee broadly representative of the tobacco control community to create a template for model tobacco control legislation, against which they will all measure the settlement as it emerges, and which will provide the foundation for demanding strengthening changes in the legislation needed to implement the settlement.

And, again as it happened, the Koop-Kessler Committee is formed. When the settlement is announced, the committee utters not a word of praise for it or Matt but zeroes in on the most dreadful flaws in the settlement, demanding that the White House and Congress start from scratch and write the right law.

Kessler and Koop spend the summer denouncing the settlement, while even Matt and the ACS's Seffrin highlight its shortcomings, although praising much of the settlement sufficiently to assure that the settlement initiative doesn't die prematurely. The White House hears them both, and in September, they all come together for the first time in *public* harmony, in the Oval Office ceremony at which the president announces his five principles for judging an acceptable law—principles that embody the Koop-Kessler demands.

For that brief moment, Matt and all the rest are singing from the same sheet music.

But now it gets tricky. They meet in secret again, for a very long but cordial strategy session. Matt and Bill Novelli argue that it will now be important for them and the establishment leaders to form a coalition—"We'll call it ENACT"—to lobby in support of the president's principles. "But we're going to have to leave room in our principles for allowing some form of liability relief in order to gather enough support from key congressional leaders, like McCain, who want to give us all we want on the public health side but are convinced that the industry and its allies within the Congress will kill any bill that does not provide some substantial concessions to the tobacco companies. If we oppose *any* liability relief, we'll be seen as too unrealistic to deal with, and we won't be able to develop the kind of working relationships with the senators and staff that we need to get on the inside of the drafting—and to make sure that all the public health provisions are properly drafted."

"Well, Godspeed!" say Koop and Kessler. "We certainly understand why you need to do that. But at the same time, let us lead the formation of a second coalition, which denounces you and threatens to go to the wall against anyone considering liability relief. That way, we keep our hole card—the ace of liability relief—in our hands for a while longer." They all agree, and they shake hands.

Then comes forth McCain, determined to produce a bill that the public health community will support, and that will pass. And Matt is on the inside, earning the trust of McCain and his staff, and strengthening the bill day by day. Kessler and Koop are listening to McCain and, on alternate days, praising and denouncing him, just to keep the maximum pressure on.

In the last moments of the drafting of the McCain bill, Matt's in a brutal confrontation with the attorneys general and trial lawyers, who are insisting on giving the industry far more liability relief than caps—and he's ousted from the negotiating table. At that moment, what might have been the secret strategy proves its brilliance: Matt goes to the leading Democrats on the McCain committee, who have gone along with the attorneys general and the trial lawyers, and warns them that if they support the McCain bill with its current broad liability provisions, Koop and Kessler and the Glantz and Godshall zealots will crucify them—as they have done Matt. This helps persuade Senators Kerry and Wyden to insist that McCain drop everything but liability caps—and he does.

The group meets in secret one last time. Matt thanks the assemblage warmly: "Without all of your outrageous rhetoric over the last several months, I never would have convinced Kerry and Wyden to hold out on liability. But I could look them in the eyes and say, 'You just don't want to go through all the misery I've been through, all the shit that's been heaped on me. And believe me, that's what you will get.' " That, indeed, is exactly what Matt told Kerry and Wyden!

Yet one more piece of secret strategy remains. As good as it is, the McCain bill as it was reported out of committee still has some drafting flaws. Matt says, "I think we can work with McCain, now that we've built up his trust, and with the White House, with whom we also have a good working relationship, to fix those flaws."

He turns to Koop and Kessler, telling them that, just to be safe, although McCain has every right to expect praise for what he has done, they're going to have to disappoint him by criticizing his bill as still fatally flawed.

This, you will remember, is precisely what Koop and Kessler did. And two weeks later, McCain and the White House agreed that they would fix those flaws (including raising the liability cap from $6.5 to $8 billion).

As a result, the bill that McCain actually brought to the Senate floor was as good as it gets.

And *now*, says Matt to Koop and Kessler, is the time to do what you have always said you would do, quoting Koop to himself: "We will compromise when it gets to the point where we cannot survive without compromising."

It was indeed, the near-perfect bill. And it would not have been possible without the exquisite choreography of this classic outside-inside strategy.

But then the fantasy bursts, and the reality diverges from the dream. For most of the SAVE LIVES coalition members, the struggle against any semblance of "immunity" transcended their desire for comprehensive public health legislation. As Stan Glantz and Julia Carol said at the November 1996 meeting, there were *no* concessions the industry could make on public health that would lead them to support any liability relief for the companies. Kessler, Koop, Waxman, and Kennedy each wavered over the months following the settlement in his privately expressed willingness to accept some form of liability relief. But as the McCain bill emerged, each had become so locked into his crusade against immunity—spurred on by Glantz and the other settlement foes—that he was unable to support the McCain bill when that support most counted.

It is my belief that the McCain bill would have passed the Senate by close to the 80–20 vote the tobacco lobbyists feared, had Koop and Kessler (and the Democrats who followed their lead on health policy) publicly endorsed the McCain bill as it came to the Senate floor as "not perfect, but the very best we can hope for," and joined with all the public health groups to support the bill—*without any amendments, whether to strengthen, weaken, or divert focus from the goal of protecting young people from the tobacco companies.*

To be sure, there would remain the risk that a hostile Republican leadership would have sought to pass a far narrower and weaker bill, that there would have ensued a treacherous Senate-House conference, with the White House, eager for a legislative capstone, prone to compromise.

But compromise to what? The House leadership was on the record, and consistent, in condemning *any* liability relief for the companies. The industry propaganda campaign, of course, never mentioned liability relief but attacked the fairness of the tax on working smokers. And this conference, unlike many, would have taken place in the full glare of public scrutiny—with Koop and Kessler, the Democrats, and all the public health groups united in condemning any move by the House to do Big Tobacco's bidding, and any move by the Senate leaders or Clinton to backslide.

Thus Matt—and Dick Scruggs—believed that, if the bill had reached the conference stage, the house managers would have insisted upon lowering the price somewhat to meet the tax-on-the-working-poor argument, but surely not as low as the multistate settlement that the attorneys general later agreed to. With FDA authority and the other public health provisions secure, Matt says, "I could have lived with that." So could thousands, if not millions, of will-be smokers who now won't.

Afterword

Lessons of the Tobacco Wars

Jeremy Brecher

In traditional democratic theory, the people debate the issues and elect representatives from one or another political party who then establish laws and policies that embody the people's interests.

But what if the political process itself—from the media of public discussion, to the political parties, to the means of getting elected, to the making of laws and policies—is dominated by special interests wielding overbearing wealth and power?

That was the situation faced by the tobacco control advocates described in this book. And, far from being an exception, it is increasingly becoming the rule in American politics.

Because the public interest is so poorly represented in the traditional political process, there is a growing belief that social problems need to be addressed not just by government, but in civil society. The result has been a growing role for social movements and public interest advocacy. Where once those promoting a policy agenda might have worked in a political party, supported candidates for office, and then waited for them to enact the party's platform, today much more elaborate and indirect strategies are required to affect policy in the public interest.

The negotiations for a global settlement between tobacco companies, state attorneys general, and a public health advocate illustrates how the decline of traditional means of government accountability and the rise of new forms of action in civil society can create virtually unprecedented situations. Indeed, these negotiations in some ways resembled those between undemocratic political authorities who have lost their legitimacy and subject peoples with no formal system of political representation. Perhaps that is why more than one activist saw parallels between the tobacco negotiations and the negotiations of Irish nationalists and the British government at the end of the Irish rebellion. There are similar echoes from the delegation Gandhi led to England to negotiate over India's political future. Perhaps even closer were the "roundtable" discussions held between declining autocratic regimes and rising popular movements over the future forms of political rule in Eastern Europe.

Situations like the tobacco global settlement negotiations are likely to become increasingly common. For example, for the past several years, under the auspices of the Apparel Industry Partnership unions, human rights groups and apparel corporations have been negotiating to establish a code of conduct for labor conditions in transnational corporations and a code authority to certify products produced under acceptable conditions. Initially, human rights groups not included in the negotiations attacked the process. After meetings that included both the labor and human rights negotiators, and their critics, an "outside-inside " strategy very much like the one advocated in this book emerged. Those on the inside remained in the negotiations but maintained that the companies' concessions were inadequate. Those on the outside generally did not condemn those participating but insisted that the concessions made were inadequate. Both continued to put pressure on the companies in the public arena. This "good cop, bad cop" cooperation broke down when the inside groups split and some left the negotiations; the future of this process is now in doubt. What is not in doubt is that all those involved in the process—or any similar process in the future—could have benefited from the experience of the tobacco control community to better understand what the process would be like.

All of these cases raise profound questions regarding representation. Clearly a government dominated by private corporate interests or an authoritarian political party cannot be regarded as the sole legitimate representative of its people. But what about movements? They claim to speak for unrepresented people, but they are always vulnerable to the charge of being a "self-appointed representatives" with no legitimate right to speak for anyone but themselves.

Ultimately there is no solution to this problem other than the reconstitution of genuinely representative institutions. But neither national movements nor social movements can wait for that—and besides, they are among the prime vehicles by which such democratization can be promoted. So what they must do—and generally try to do—

is to make themselves so genuinely representative of the needs and interests of their constituents and of the public in general that most people support what they do even though they have not been formally authorized to do it.

But that is not something that is easy to begin in the midst of a crisis. The tobacco industry's decision to come to the bargaining table, for example, plunged the tobacco control movement into murky and uncharted terrain. It was difficult to develop, on short notice, a new strategy appropriate to the new situation. And even if a terrific strategy, such as an outside-inside strategy, had been clearly conceived at the start, the movement would have been ill equipped to implement it.

What can be done in advance that will help prepare a movement to deal successfully with the kind of situation that arose for the tobacco control during the global settlement negotiations? How can a movement develop processes and cultures that support good strategic decisions—and make it possible to implement them?

Many movements start as responses to something bad. The move to regulate tobacco advertising, for example, responded to the emergence of Joe Camel and the Marlboro Man. While movements are motivated by underlying hopes and values, these are often left vague, a subject for rhetorical flourish, not concrete definition.

This leaves movements disarmed when they confront concrete possibilities, such as those that emerged in the tobacco global settlement negotiations. While all tobacco control advocates were concerned to distinguish meaningful change from cosmetic co-optation, there was no way to do so in the absence of a clearly formulated set of objectives.

A result was that short-term tactical needs tended to determine the way long-term objectives were defined. For example, at any given time, protagonists seemed to accept or oppose some limits on tobacco company liability based less on analysis of the actual effects of such limits than on whether they thought it tactically wise to support or oppose a settlement at that time. Movements need venues in which they can debate objectives in ways that are insulated from immediate tactical positions. And those discussions must include representation of all of those who will ultimately be needed to achieve the movement's objectives.

Of course objectives must evolve over time. What a movement needs is not a final statement of its goals for all time. Rather, it needs a process for debating and sorting out its long-range goals.

There is practical use in being able to say more than "Just say no." For example, in 1999 a group of nongovernmental organizations from around the world formed an alliance in response to the effort of governments in the Organization for Economic Cooperation and Development to negotiate a "Multilateral Agreement on Investment" (MAI). Initially, the NGOs were split on whether simply to oppose any agreement outright or instead to lobby for inclusion of environmental, labor, and other protections. But they were able to agree on a common strategy. They would put forward a common program for fixing the MAI, and if it was accepted by the governments they would agree to support it. But if their common demands were not met, they would all agree to oppose the agreement, even if some concessions were made. Their program was not accepted, whereupon they worked together to effectively bring the MAI negotiations to a halt.

Strategy is a concept with military origins; it literally means the choice of ground on which to engage the enemy. Strategy is the means for achieving a movement's long-range goals in concrete situations. While a movement's goals must develop gradually over time, its strategies need to be flexible so they can adapt to rapid change.

Like war, social conflict generally takes place in a murky zone in which the actual configuration of forces and the actual results of any particular course of action are more conjecture than certainty. If the enemy changes its strategy (for example, by seeking to enter negotiation with its opponents), a movement must be able to revise its strategy in turn or face being rapidly outflanked.

A long-range perspective on movement goals helps make such flexibility possible. The strategy known as "fight-fight, talk-talk" is based on knowing the difference between the battle and the war. Negotiations, truces, and compromises do not represent the end of struggles; rather they represent phases and aspects of struggles. Within that framework, any particular compromise can be evaluated as part of a wider movement strategy, rather than as a moral absolute which either is or is not "good enough."

To hold effective dialogue on goals and strategies, movements need to cultivate a supportive culture. This is largely a question of norms that are modeled day-to-day both by leaders and by the rank-and-file.

The right of all positions to be heard is a norm that is necessary if a movement is to incorporate all who are needed to fulfill its objectives. Conversely, the use of personal abuse as a weapon in internal movement debates is an example of behavior that should be defined as out-side of movement norms. (A prohibition on abuse must be linked to the right to be heard: abuse may be the last resort for resourceless, powerless groups, a technique they will turn to if they have no other way to make themselves heard.)

Movements also need to develop standards in advance regarding whom organizations should and should not take money from, to fore-stall both irresponsible charges and actual sellouts. (The battles over the Apparel Industry Code, like the tobacco wars, brought charges that some organizations were negotiating to "feather their own nests" by gaining funding for future activities that they themselves would be paid to conduct.)

Social movements are made up of overlapping and conflicting in-terests. Movements and their leaders have different perspectives, goals, methods, styles, and organizational forms. It is perilous to ignore or paper over these differences; if they are not acknowledged, they are likely to explode at crisis points, with catastrophic results. The divi-sion of the tobacco control advocates is a case in point.

Movements generally develop in waves. Each wave brings with it new concerns, practices, organizations, and leaders. For example, while earlier tobacco control activists focused on dangers to smokers, a later wave focused on "nonsmokers' rights." Movements need to work con-sciously to integrate new waves with ones that went before.

Because movements combine common and conflicting interests, it is helpful for them to develop a culture of negotiating those differences. The principles of negotiation may be a useful inclusion in movement training. (It may also lead to shrewder choices when the movement has to deal with the complex combination of common and conflicting interests that emerges in situations like the tobacco global settlement negotiations.)

Addressing differences sometimes needs to be a conscious objec-tive. Some organizations—sometimes described as "bridging organi-zations"—deliberately take on the role of linking different groups and helping them address their differences. Specific "trust-building initia-tives"—like those that are used in international diplomacy—are also sometimes needed.

All of this requires a vision of the movement as a whole that tran-scends particular organizations and sectors. Only with such a common vision is it possible to conduct the kind of multipronged but coordinated and mutually supportive approach that is representative of the outside-inside strategy.

When movement representatives enter into negotiations with their opponents, it puts tremendous pressures on all parties—pressures that can easily split the movement, as happened both with the tobacco settlement and the Apparel Industry Partnership. Whether this happens depends in part on the practices the movement developed before.

Movements needs to develop ways to control leaders, hold them accountable, support their strengths, and restrain their weaknesses. This obviously includes formal means like election of officials, but it also involves informal norms of accountability. With such patterns of accountability in place, it is far easier for leaders to enter into complex negotiations without the danger of acting like "lone rangers" operating on their own analysis or instincts—or the danger that they will be accused of doing so. At the least, movement participants have the right to expect and insist that movement leaders will act as a team.

Finally, there is an inevitable divergence between the experience and concerns of those at the organizational centers of movements and their grassroots, rank-and-file members. Even with the best of leaders, there is bound to be a difference between grassroots "local knowledge" and the "inside knowledge" of those at the center—and in the opinions that accompany those knowledges. Movements need a process to continuously synthesize these. If they do so in normal times, they are far more likely to be able to do so in a time of crisis.

Epilogue

As this book took shape, I began sharing drafts with several veteran advocates not involved in tobacco control, leaders of other progressive movements who had in common a track record of concrete achievement—good laws, enforced and effective over time—to match their passion. I knew, of course, that the conflict I had recorded among leaders in the tobacco control movement was not unique, but I was nonetheless startled by the extent to which these advocates identified with Matt Myers and saw his burdens and frustrations mirrored in their own.

"I want to meet Matt Myers," said Brock Evans, a lobbyist for the Sierra Clubs, the National Audubon Society, and others, with a solid track record in saving ancient forests, clean drinking water, and endangered wildlife species. "I want to share war stories and frustrations with him!" Brock had secured a series of victories throughout the years of the Clinton administration, including the banning of logging in the pristine Tongas National Wildlife Refuge in Alaska, but he feared that a Bush presidential victory over Gore would lead to reversals of all the gains, and worse. He had been struggling for a year to keep environmental leaders and activists who had been frustrated with what Clinton and Gore had *not done* for the environment from backing and voting for Ralph Nader—and assuring a Bush victory.

Vinny DeMarco has led extraordinarily successful election-oriented, nonpartisan issue campaigns for gun control measures and tobacco excise tax increases in Maryland, campaigns that now serve as the envied model for other state advocates. As this book was being finished, Vinny was skillfully building a broad, new coalition of support in Maryland for state-mandated universal health care coverage, an initiative with realistic expectations of making Maryland the first state in the nation to achieve that objective. By the close of the year 2000, Vinny had succeeded in recruiting over a thousand community-based organizations, ranging from churches to unions, even many doctors, behind the campaign's statement of principles. But, to gain the needed base of broad support, Vinny and his allies had come to understand that they could not demand a pure single-payer, government-run health care plan that would have destroyed the health insurance industry and forced many otherwise supportive citizens, such as the teachers, to abandon health care plans that were working well for them. His reward was bitter internal coalition warfare from the single-payer advocates. "I couldn't sleep," Vinny confessed, after a particularly bitter meeting in which the single-payer advocates attacked, and Vinny's supportive allies waffled.

At about the same time, just prior to the convening of the new Congress in January 2001, Matt Myers was asked to attend a meeting organized by former Massachusetts attorney general Scott Harshbarger, an early advocate and leader among the attorneys general for a strong tobacco control settlement. He had now taken up the challenge, as president of Common Cause, to build a strong base of support for the determined efforts of Senators John McCain and Russ Feingold to press for congressional action to stem the spill of independent corporate and other plutocratic campaign contributions that had so polluted our national elections. Matt reflected on this experience:

> I thought that Scott wanted me at that meeting because he believed, as I do, that to dramatize the social costs of corporate campaign abuse, issue advocacy groups like tobacco control needed to step forward to illustrate how the flood of money has diverted Congress and the White House from taking right and needed action.
>
> But I was wrong. At the meeting, to which key members of Congress and their staffs had come seeking assurance that their renewed effort would be backed by a unified army of grassroots advocates, there was an attack by the most vocal of those there on the McCain-Feingold bill, or *any* campaign-financing reform legislation short of public financing of campaigns.
>
> So I realized, without Scott ever saying so, that the main reason I was invited was to tell the story of the missed opportunity of the tobacco settlement. I flew home from that meeting with Feingold's staff person, and I thought to myself, how discouraging it must feel to launch such a major legislative campaign with an army fighting itself.

Witold Zatonski, the epidemiologist turned advocate, has almost single-handedly built a powerful tobacco control movement in Poland. He successfully launched a media and lobbying campaign that led, first, to modest but path-breaking legislation mandating strong health warnings on labels and public education on the hazards of smoking. As Zatonski looks back, he is grateful for the counsel and support he received from American and Western European tobacco control experts, but there came a moment when he decided that their counsel made no sense for Poland—at that point in the evolution of Polish public opinion and law. "They were all saying to me," he recalled, "if you do not have a total ban on cigarette advertising, your law will not be good— and you must reject it!" But Zatonski recognized, after months of confronting the hard fact of a successful tobacco-lobbying blitz of the Polish Parliament, that he could get a good bill, but not a perfect bill—not a total ban on advertising. He supported the bill and celebrated its passage.

Five years later, he and his allies had built on that modest bill to gain enactment of as close to the perfect bill as any of his Western counselors has yet achieved—including a ban on political contributions from tobacco industry sources. And he is convinced that the process—the struggle for the first bill, the tangible impact of that bill in terms of measurably reduced cigarette consumption backed by a continuing national media advocacy campaign—set the stage for the later, stronger law. That "perfect law," he firmly believes, would never have been enacted had he heeded the counsel of those who insisted that he take all or nothing.

Finally, I talked often and long with my partner at the Advocacy Institute, David Cohen, who had been a lobbyist and leader in many a public interest campaign, from the Civil Rights Act of 1964 to the shutting down of funding for the notorious MX nuclear missile in 1984— the only time a citizen movement succeeded in stopping a weapons system already scheduled to be built. He had watched and had commiserated with Matt's troubles throughout the tobacco settlement negotiations and the McCain bill's failure. From the perspective of his thirty years of public interest lobbying, he reminded me that there has almost always been conflict between those advocates he calls "apocalyptic," and those for whom he fondly claims the title "movement leaders."

For the apocalyptic advocate, David also employs a colorful Yiddish term, the "Farbrente" (best but inadequately translated as the "firebrands"), for whom less than total victory over the forces of darkness is worse than defeat. As David notes, "in the Yiddish lexicons, Farbrente is defined as 'zealous' and 'ardent,' and when used as a verb it conveys the passion to 'scorch,' to 'cremate.' "

By contrast, David observes, movement leaders channel their passion for their cause into their determination to effect significant, tangible change. This is the quality that signifies the advocacy of Vinny DeMarco, Brock Evans, and David himself. And it has fairly characterized virtually all of the leaders and advocates in the book in most of their campaigns, not just Matt, but Waxman, Kennedy, Kessler, Koop—yes, and Glantz and Carol. Even Ralph Nader, whom many now see as stiff-necked and uncompromising, worked strategically to achieve a long string of major public interest laws—though only after flogging his allies to focus their sights on the strongest laws attainable.

Indeed, uncompromising passion is often vital to long-term success in prodding a sluggish movement to elevate its horizons and pursue fundamental change rather than timorous increments—increments that can sap the energy for change, halting the momentum generated by the campaign in the first place. This was the profound contribution of Stan Glantz in California, where the health voluntaries were chronically poised to settle for far less than was ultimately achieved.

So what is the quality that separates the effective passionate advocate from the destructive Farbrente? I'm indebted to Andrew Delbanco, who gives us insights drawn from an essay on literary critic Lionel Trilling in the *New York Review of Books*, January 11, 2001. Delbanco calls attention to Trilling's focus on writers who teach us, in Trilling's words, that "the highest idealism may corrupt." So, Henry James's aspiring young anarchist in *The Princess Casamassima* learns, Trilling tells us, "something of what may lie behind abstract ideals, the envy, the impulse to revenge, and to dominance." And, in "Manners, Morals, and the Novel," Trilling argues "that the moral passions are even more willful and imperious and impatient than the self-seeking passions."

So in 1997 and 1998, in Congress, it was the smoke from the embers of such passions that blinded the advocates who could not rally to the McCain bill, when it had come so close to achieving all that they had ever demanded—or dreamed of—in a public health regime to combat the risks of tobacco use.

And it was my own passion to hold the Farbrente accountable that was the prime motivation for writing this book, and its central theme. But that acknowledgment leads to yet another frustration expressed by sympathetic readers of the manuscript: what, other than teeth gnashing, is a useful strategic response to the wreckage wrought by the

Farbrente? It is surely not, as Bill Novelli discovered to his chagrin, to scorn, ignore, and seek to isolate them.

Perhaps the answer lies in my own response as a withdrawn leader of the tobacco control movement. And that response was best captured in a memorandum written to me by my wise and intrepid research assistant Joel Papo, on the failures of leadership he had observed in chronicling—and judging—the events of the settlement as they unfolded: "Why did the occasional friendly fire among tobacco control advocates turn into a civil war so consuming that for six months activists basically ignored their real enemy, the tobacco industry? The answer to this question is not found in the honest policy disagreements over immunity protection for the tobacco industry, but in the breakdown in communication and trust allowed to fester by the inaction and indecisiveness of leaders like Mike Pertschuk."

Joel was right. For the truth is that I would and should have stood publicly with Matt and his handful of defenders were it not for my own aversion to the abuse that would have accompanied the decision to tangle with the remorseless and indefatigable Stan Glantz. I had seen what it did to Matt, and I wanted no part of it.

I hope, if and when I am faced with a similar conflict, that I will do better. And I hope that those who read this book among my colleagues in the tobacco control movement, who withdrew as I did from the discomfort—even the pain—of intramovement conflict, will also do better. I believe it would make a difference, and that the voices of the Farbrente will not again drown out the far larger chorus of those drawn to the tobacco control movement through an overriding vision of sparing massive future illness, pain, and death from tobacco.

And for those readers who are engaged in other campaigns for human rights, social or economic justice, or public health, I urge the same.

Chronology of Key Events

5/23/94 – First state legal action against the tobacco companies filed by Mississippi attorney general Mike Moore, with the support of trial lawyer Dick Scruggs.

4/7/96 – In the Sunday *New York Times Magazine*, Richard Kluger, historian of the tobacco wars, pronounces the time ripe for public health advocates to "dance with the devil" and forge a grand compromise with the tobacco companies.

11/96 – First indirect settlement talks between Moore and Scruggs and tobacco industry representatives begin.

11/18/96 – Meeting of tobacco control advocates convened by Matt Myers and Richard Daynard to explore common ground on settlement terms with the industry.

4/3/97 – Philip Morris CEO, Geoffrey Bible, and RJR CEO, Steven Goldstone, meet in Crystal City, Virginia, with state attorneys general, trial lawyers, and Matt Myers to initiate secret global settlement negotiations.

4/16/97 – Secrecy blown as the *Wall Street Journal* discloses the existence and much of the substance of the negotiations.

4/25/97 – Federal district court in Greensboro, North Carolina, upholds FDA claim to legal authority to regulate tobacco products.

5/28/97 – "Peace" meeting of tobacco control advocates convened by the American Medical Association in Chicago.

6/5/97 – First meeting of Koop-Kessler Advisory Committee, in Washington, D.C. *Waxman afraid passing - Committee disapproved*

6/20/97, 3:15 P.M.– Global settlement reached and announced.

9/17/97 – President Clinton convenes attorneys general and public health leaders in the Oval Office to announce principles to guide White House position on tobacco legislation developed by Congress.

10/1/97 – ENACT coalition formed and publishes full-page ad in *Washington Post* supporting Clinton principles.

11/25/97 – Anti-immunity coalition announced and named SAVE LIVES, NOT TOBACCO, the Coalition for Accountability.

2/98 Conrad Bill

4/1/98 – Senate Commerce Committee votes 19–1 to approve and send McCain bill to the Senate floor.

5/18–21/98 – Senate floor debate.

5/21/98 – Senate votes 61–37 to adopt Gregg amendment stripping McCain bill of liability caps.

6/17/98 – Senate defeats cloture motion 57–42 to end debate and bring the bill to a Senate vote, effectively defeating McCain's effort to pass his bill.

Acknowledgments

I have written books before this one, and I have always had the generous help of friends and colleagues. But I have never before been so indebted to so many for so much.

I begin with those key actors whose roles are central to my narrative, most of whom readily agreed to be interviewed, several, more than once. Among them, I reserve special gratitude for those who knew that I did not share their views of the events and that I might well be critical of them, but who nonetheless spoke openly: David Kessler, C. Everett Koop, Ralph Nader, Henry Waxman, Rob Weissman. Matt Myers was appropriately wary of a project that forced him to recall and relive much pain and frustration, so I am doubly indebted for his patience and forbearance, and his determination to help me get the facts right.

Julia Carol, especially, not only gave me hours of her time, as she struggled openly and eloquently with the painful conflicts engendered by the settlement, but trustfully opened the meticulous files of Americans for Nonsmokers' Rights, so that I could reconstruct from contemporaneous e-mails and other communications not only the events but the immediacy of the passions.

Supplementing my own interviews were those conducted for an internal case study by Jeffrey Finn, commissioned by the Center for Tobacco-Free Kids to examine the Center's first five years.

Two good books on the litigation and the settlement helped me flesh out the key events, Peter Pringle's *Cornered: Big Tobacco at the Bar of Justice* (New York: Henry Holt, 1998) and *The People vs. Big Tobacco* (Princeton: Bloomberg Press, 1998) by the *Bloomberg News* team—Carrick Mollenkamp, Adam Levy, Joseph Menn, and Jeffrey Rothfeder. And Richard Kluger's definitive history of the tobacco wars, *Ashes to Ashes* (New York: Knopf, 1996), supplied much detail and insight that my memory could not.

At each stage of the book's progress, there were generous and wise readers. While invariably encouraging, they also chastened me. Someone once remarked that the only upright politician is one who is pressured from all sides. My readers supplied that pressure. They constantly challenged my biases, corrected my errors, filled in my gaps, choked on excessive and unilluminating quotes.

Fellow warhorses in the tobacco control movement for many decades provided wisdom and perspective: Russ Sciandra, Ken Warner, Karla Sneegas, Mitch Zeller, Judy Wilkenfeld, Dick Daynard, Jeff Koplan, Phil Wilbur.

In the summers, in our cabins in the northwest corner of Connecticut where much of this book was written, our friends and neighbors on Yelping Hill, especially Robert Hunt and Nancy Dubler, brought the discipline of psychic distance from the turmoil of the controversies. Jeremy Brecher, friend and counselor, Connecticut neighbor, and historian, speaks for himself in his afterword. But I need also acknowledge his guidance throughout the shaping of this book.

For the rest of the year, in Washington, more good friends read, encouraged, and counseled, especially Bill Byler, poet and storyteller, and Laura Tracy, our teacher of reading and literature for the past fifteen years, both of whom provided strong guidance to the book as story, early and late.

My colleagues at the Advocacy Institute, especially my partner for more than fifteen years, David Cohen, offered the balanced judgment that only decades of public life can bring. Richard Lucas, with the combined insights of a close observer of the events and the framework of a trained historian, helped guide me from my primitive outlines to what I thought was a final manuscript. I had the sustaining support and independent judgment of my colleagues, the institute's tobacco control team leaders, Kay Arndorfer and Theresa Gardella. And, all along, team members Laura Wyshynski (with uncanny sharp eyes and clear head) and Carl Roller brought order out of the chaos of the paper mess.

Patti Pancoe and, later, Diana Strodel performed with patience and grace, transcribing with great accuracy the interviews, though these were often acoustically inept and full of arcane names and references.

As the book progressed, other friends, professional editors, unveiled for me serious flaws in the early drafts, which I took to heart and heeded: Diane Wachtel and Andre Schiffrin, of the New Press; Todd Baldwin of Island Press, and Amanda Mecke of Bantam/Broadway Books.

Jill Cutler has been my close friend and editor through three earlier books, and once again, all the way through, provided that mystical balance between encouragement and stern discipline. Every once in awhile, my attachment to a phrase or quote or what I've taken for my own wit persisted. But 99 percent of the time, I do what Jill says, and the reader is the undoubted beneficiary. Later came Michael Ames, director of the Vanderbilt University Press, whose swift embrace of the draft manuscript, equal measures of enthusiasm and firm guidance, belie the current image of the cool-handed publisher. And the final touches from copyeditor Bobbe Needham, the elegant gardener, pruning the overgrowth and tidying up the debris—with not a hint of reproach!

Then there is Joel—Joel Papo. "Research assistant" does not begin to encompass Joel's role in the forming of this book. Political scientist Michael Goldstein, Joel's teacher, matched us up in the fall of 1997, as the settlement was festering, and Joel has been my intellectual companion, challenger, exhaustive chronicler, kibitzer, critic, gopher. The reader will note, in my epilogue, a quote from Joel critical of my own failure to assume a leadership role in the internal movement struggles around the settlement. I had been preoccupied with other work during the first three or four months Joel was researching and preparing files on every aspect of the settlement. When he had completed that task, he set out, on his own initiative, to evaluate the performance of the various movement leaders at the center of the storm, and as you see, he was neither impressed nor intimidated by age or standing. He was more sympathetic with the harsh critics of the settlement than I was, and he chastened me to recognize my blind spots.

Support for this book came from The Robert Wood Johnson Foundation. By "support," I mean, in the first instance, a grant sufficient to allow me to spend the time—and get the assistance—I needed to get it as right as I was capable of. But "support" means far more here. At the foundation, Joe Marx and Nancy Kaufman first championed the grant among colleagues who were skeptical and then offered editorial guidance at every step. Steve Schroeder took the risk of supporting them and me. They, of course, neither influenced nor bear responsibility for any of the judgments (or errors) herein.

Family sustained me, reading, lightly guiding, and always encouraging: Above all, my son Mark, tobacco control veteran leader and strategist—though differing with me on many issues raised by the book;

my daughter Amy and son-in-law Chris; warm cousins Ann Whiteside and Jonathan McCurdy. And my brother, Leo, stood guard against the most tedious passages!

Throughout the three years of work on the book, my wife, Anna Sofaer, gave me far more than patience and forbearance at my pre-occupation. Her judgments about people and their behavior are clear and unsentimental; her eye for fatuousness, unfailing. But, much more, it has been her love that sustains me.

Index

Waxman, Henry, 113, 174–75, 180, 213; and "bottom-line" legislation, 170–71; importance of, to tobacco control movement, 15, 44, 83, 93, 106, 281; and Koop-Kessler Committee, 157, 158; as leader, 267, 274, 278, 283; on liability, 133, 194; and settlement talks, 103, 105–6, 146, 147, 148, 161

Weber, Vin, 202

Weissman, Rob, 249–50, 274; and industry accountability, 180, 261; on McCain bill, 217, 220, 224

Westmoreland, Timothy, 190, 204

Wheeler, M. Cass, 182, 192–93, 229, 282. *See also* American Heart Association

White House, 30, 49–50; on liability, 173–74; and Myers, 45, 66; settlement, response to, 157, 161–64; and settlement talks, 25, 34–35, 81, 140; and tobacco control lobbyists, 34–35, 165, 169, 170, 171, 172, 209. *See also* Clinton, William; Lindsay, Bruce

Wigand, Jeffrey, 43

Wilkenfeld, Judith, 84–85, 129, 163

Winston Salem, 43

Woods, Grant, 72, 137–38, 139

workplace smoking. *See under* smoking, legislation of

World Conference on Tobacco OR Health, 54

World Health Organization, 250–51

Wyden, Ron, 251, 274; and McCain bill, 205, 208, 209, 243

Yale Medical School, 82

Youth Advocate of the Year, 94

Youth Protection Law, 19

youth smoking, 45, 46, 169, 249; and addiction, 16, 46; and cigarette prices, 78, 169, 170, 213; Clinton goal for, 78, 173, 174, 176; and Congress, 76, 200; FDA regulation of, 24, 71, 75, 166, 222; in McCain bill, 207, 213, 214, 215, 219, 224; reduction of, as key, 46, 73, 98, 167, 215; rhetoric on, by tobacco industry, 25–26, 36, 46, 247; in settlement agreements, 154, 241; as target, by tobacco industry, 67, 78, 196. *See also* look-back penalties

Zatonski, Witold, 252–54, 307–8

Zeller, Mitchell, 35, 38, 163; and Scruggs-Moore settlement, 30, 31, 32; and settlement talks, 82–83, 84, 110, 128

Zieve, Allison, 49